THE ROYAL ROAD

A Popular History of Iran

Eileen Humphreys

Scorpion Publishing Ltd
London

First published in 1991 by Scorpion Publishing Ltd,
Victoria House, Buckhurst Hill, Essex, England.

ISBN 0 905906 94 2

Editor: Leonard Harrow
Typeset by MasterType, Newport, Essex, in Linotype Bembo

Printed and bound in England by Hartnolls, Bodmin

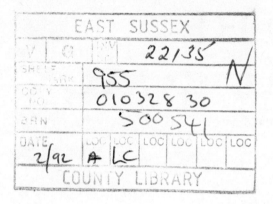

Foreword

Nowadays we speak of Iran but until relatively recently the country was almost universally known as Persia. In antiquity the province of Fars in the south west was called *Parsa* or *Persis* and the name was later applied to the nation as a whole. But the Persians have always referred to themselves as *Irani* (and to the land as *Iran*) on account of their Aryan origins and Reza Shah decreed in 1935 that the country was to be known as Iran. In the text I have conformed with his wishes from that date; otherwise I have used Persia or Iran indiscriminately.

Where there is a variation in the spelling of proper names I have usually opted for the more familiar, hence *Avicenna* instead of *Ibn Sina* and *Tamerlane* in preference to *Timur*. Through the classical period I have kept to the better known Latinised spellings: *Cleopatra* rather than *Kleopatra*. I have been grateful for help in the more problematical area of the transliteration of Arabic and Persian names into English. The omission of diacritical points and macrons makes for easier reading (and writing) but if anomalies or inconsistencies have crept in, they are mine.

Where they do not occur within the text sources for quoted material will be found among the footnotes and the Bibliography.

If there are any omissions in respect of rights for quotations or illustrations the publishers will consider claims.

EH

To Roma

Traveller along many roads
who showed me the way

Acknowledgments

I am grateful to Dr Ronald Ferrier for commenting on parts of the text, to Patrick Humphreys for reading it through to see if it made sense, to Doffla Bennett for the drawings and to Mary Reeves for the calligraphy.

My thanks are also due to Ellen Titcombe for one drawing (the Parthian horseman) and to Dr Emrys Phillips for the maps; to Marinel Fitzsimons of the Royal Society for Asian Affairs, to Mary Gueritz of the British Institute of Persian Studies, to Anne Hughes and Peggie Robertson; also members of the staff of the Departments of Western Asiatic and Oriental Antiquities and the Reading Room in the British Museum, the India Office Library and Records and the Arts Library of the University of Wales, Cardiff for their help.

Finally I should like to thank my publishers, Scorpion Publishing Limited, and my editor, Leonard Harrow, for his help in a number of ways not the least of which have included steering me through the minefields of diphthongs, dashes, apostrophes and spellings to the preferred rendering of Arabic and Persian names.

Contents

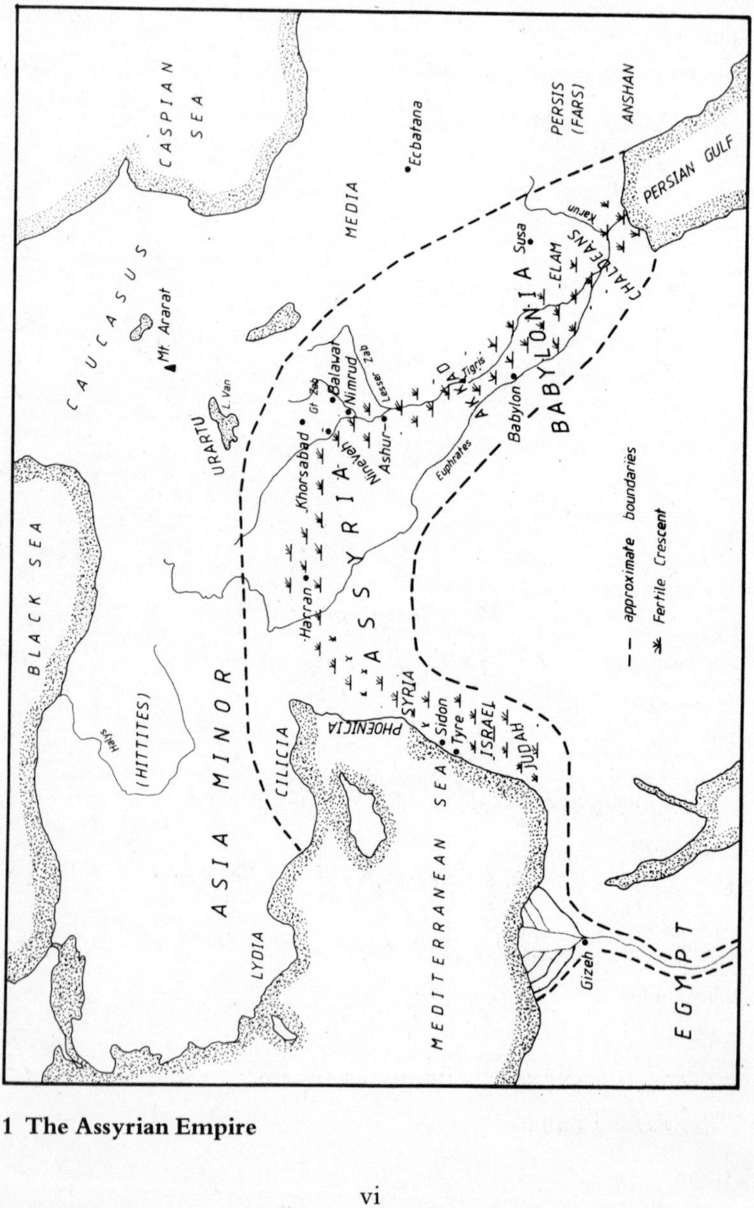

1 The Assyrian Empire

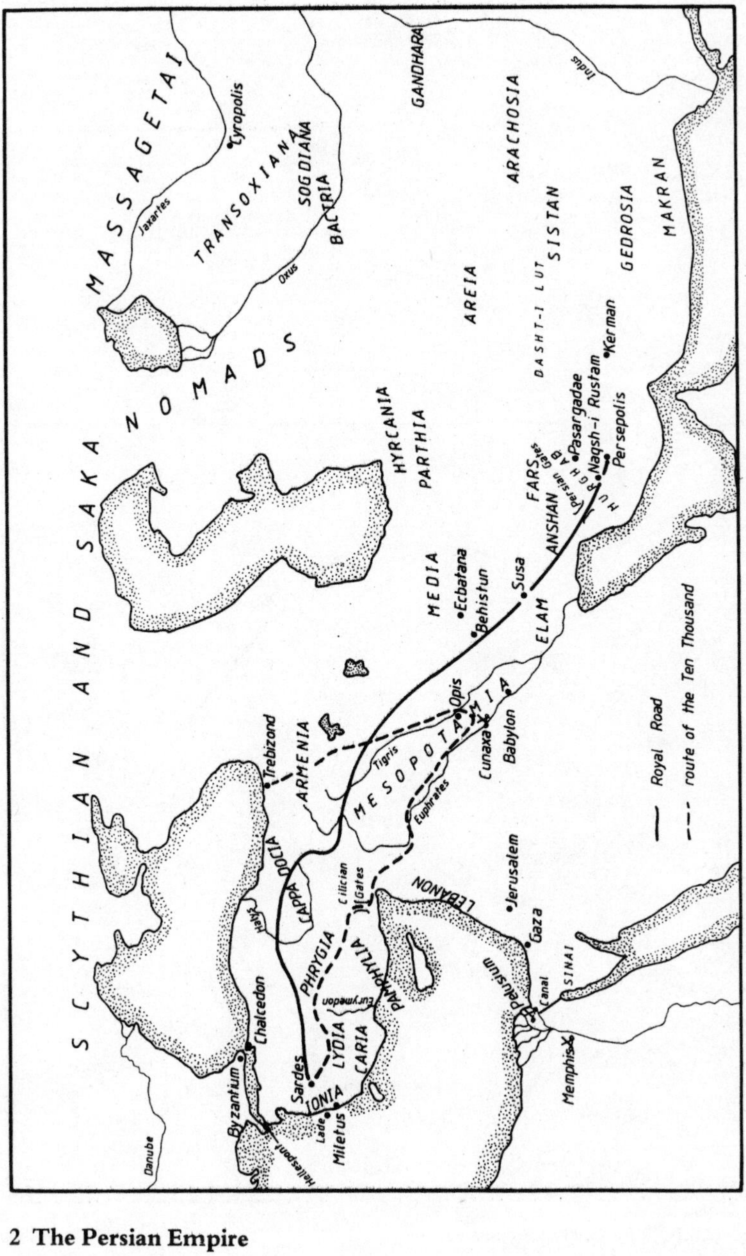

2 The Persian Empire

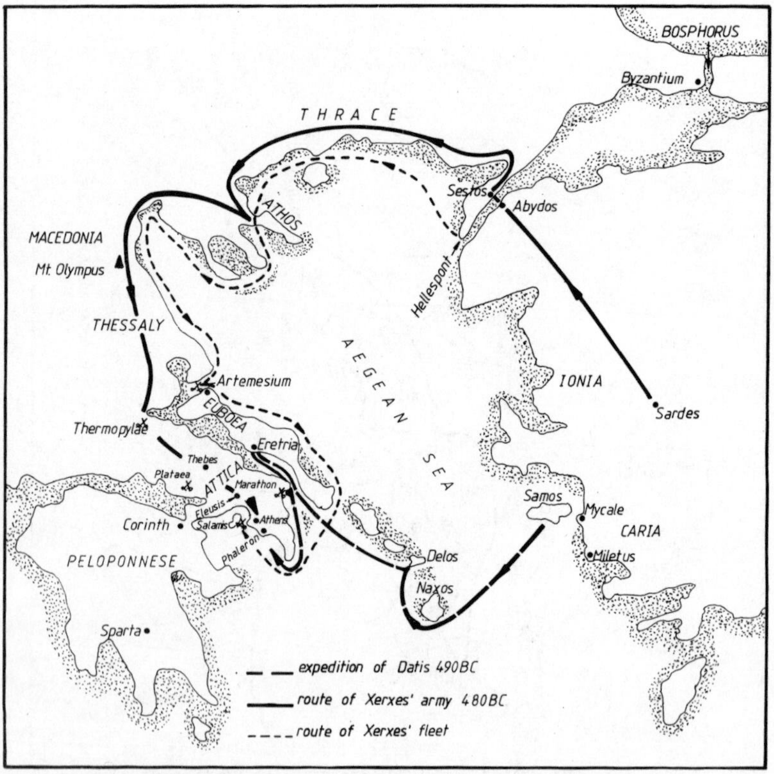

3 Persian Wars with Greece

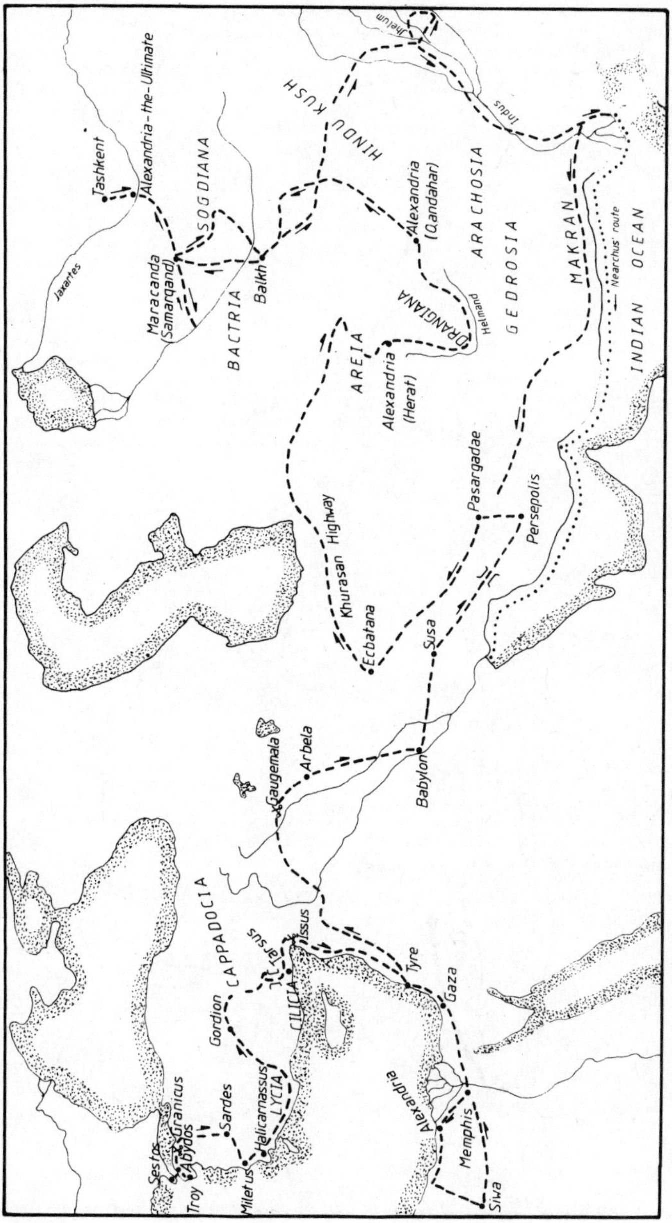

4 Alexander's route

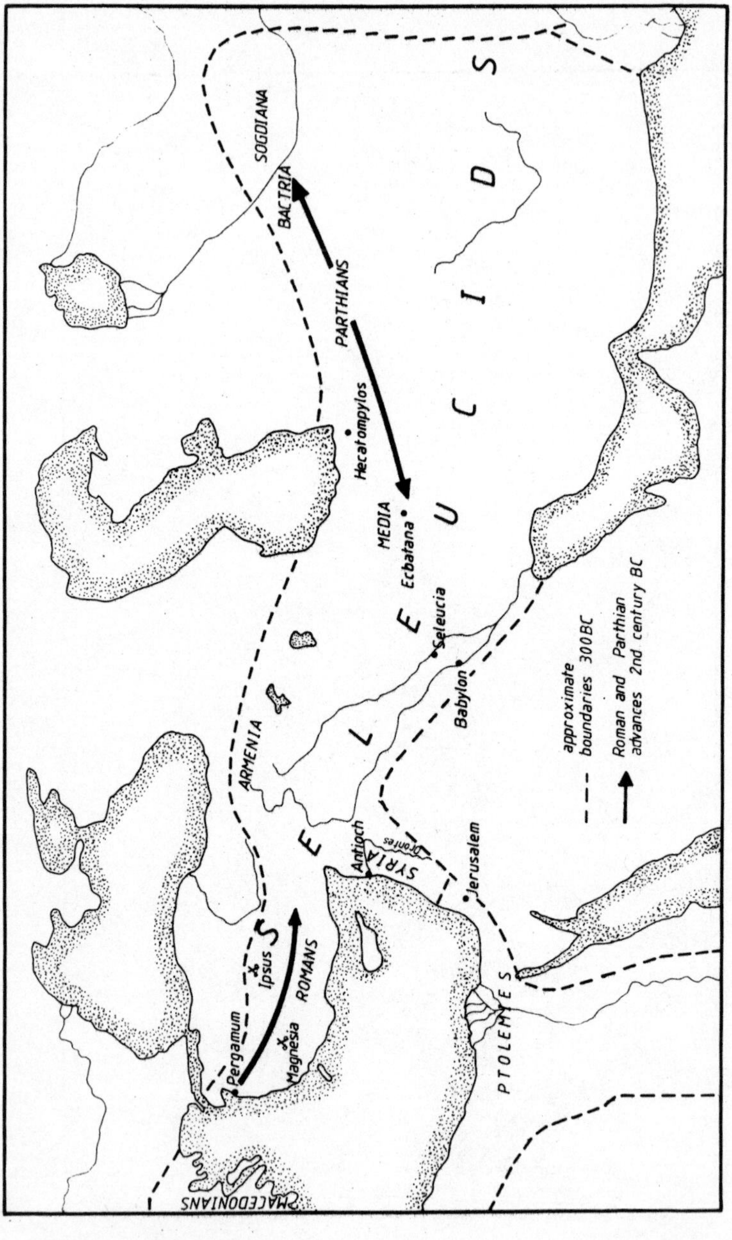

5 The Seleucid Empire

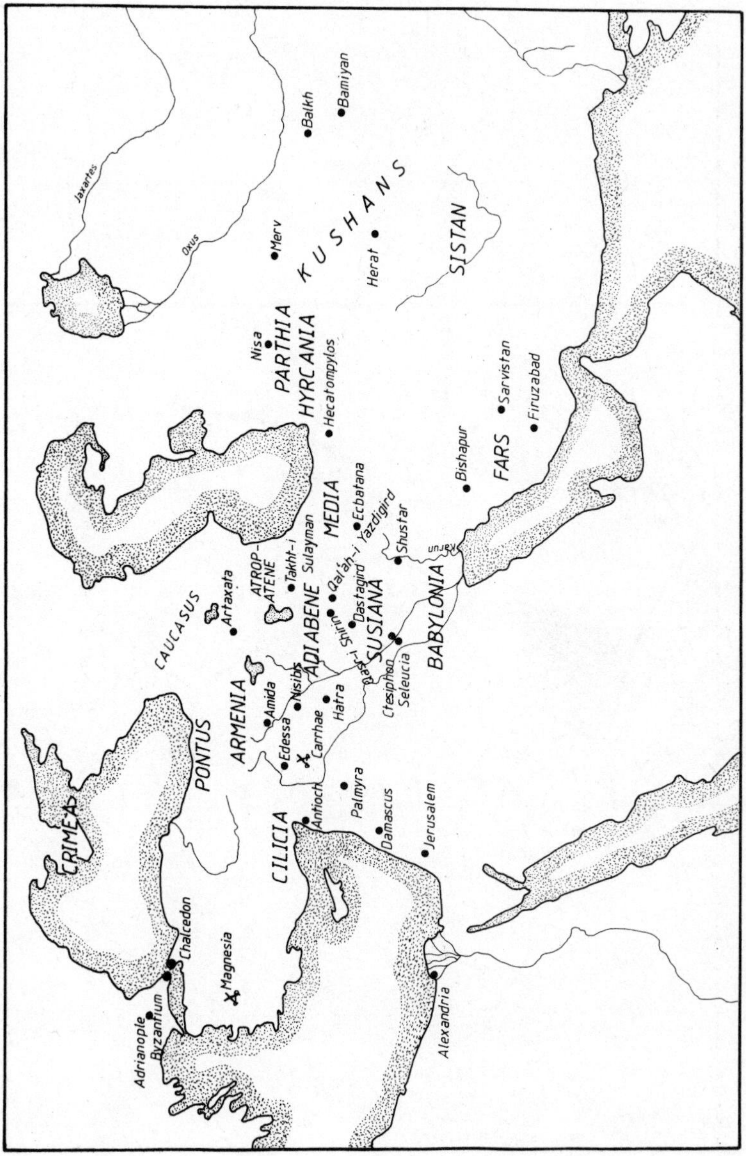

6 Western Asia in the time of the Parthians and the Sasanians

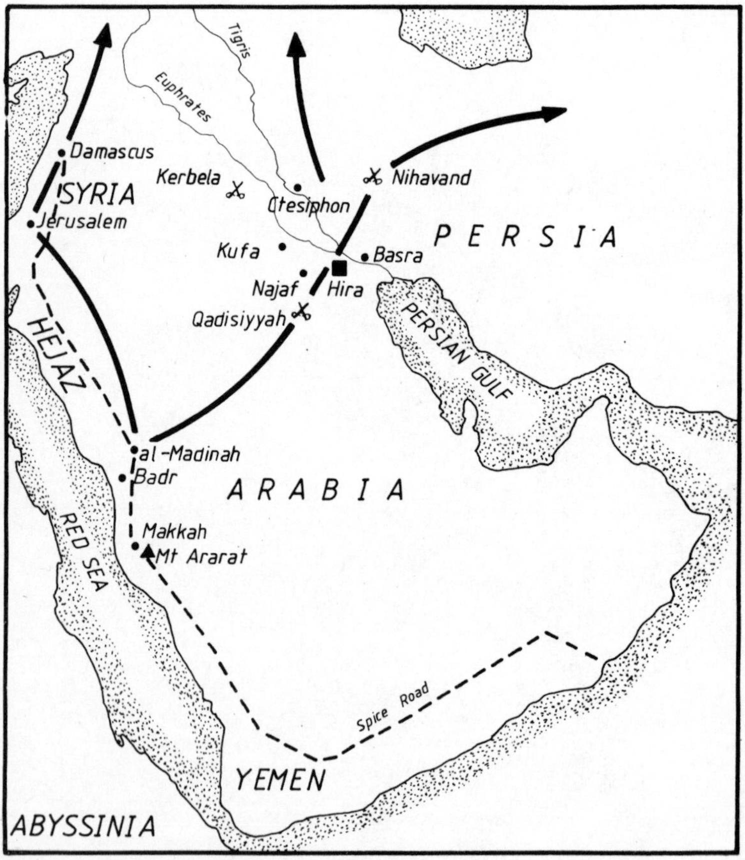

7 Arab advances under the early Caliphs

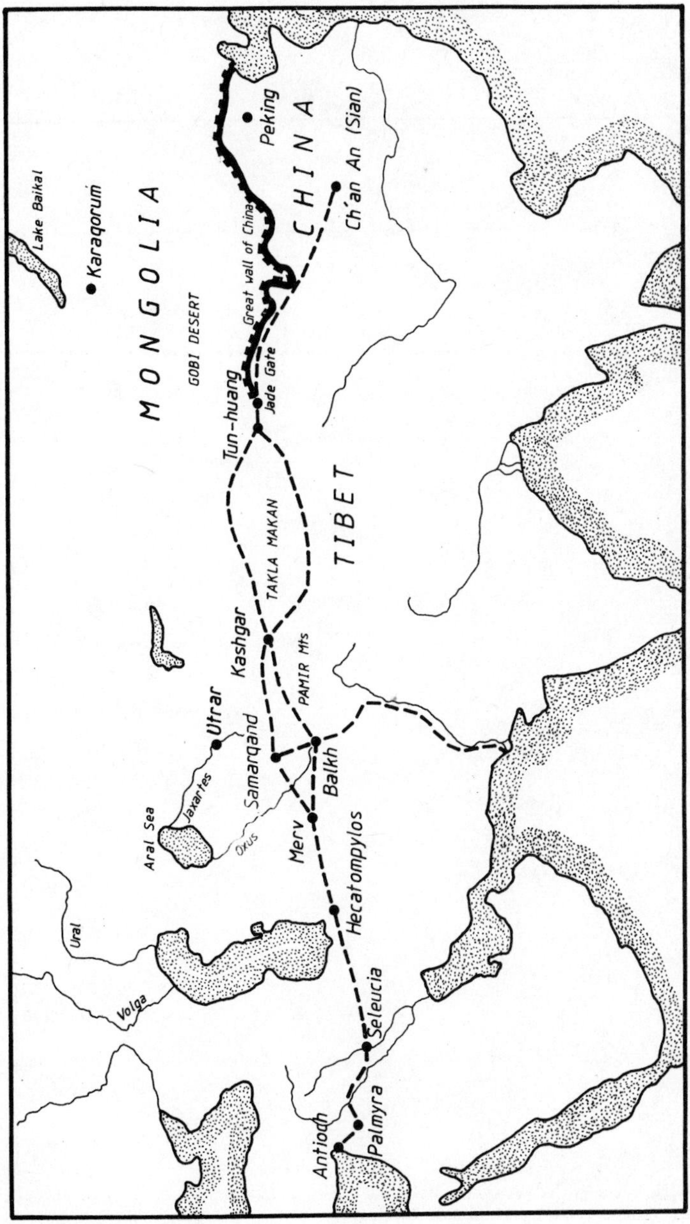

8 The Silk Road

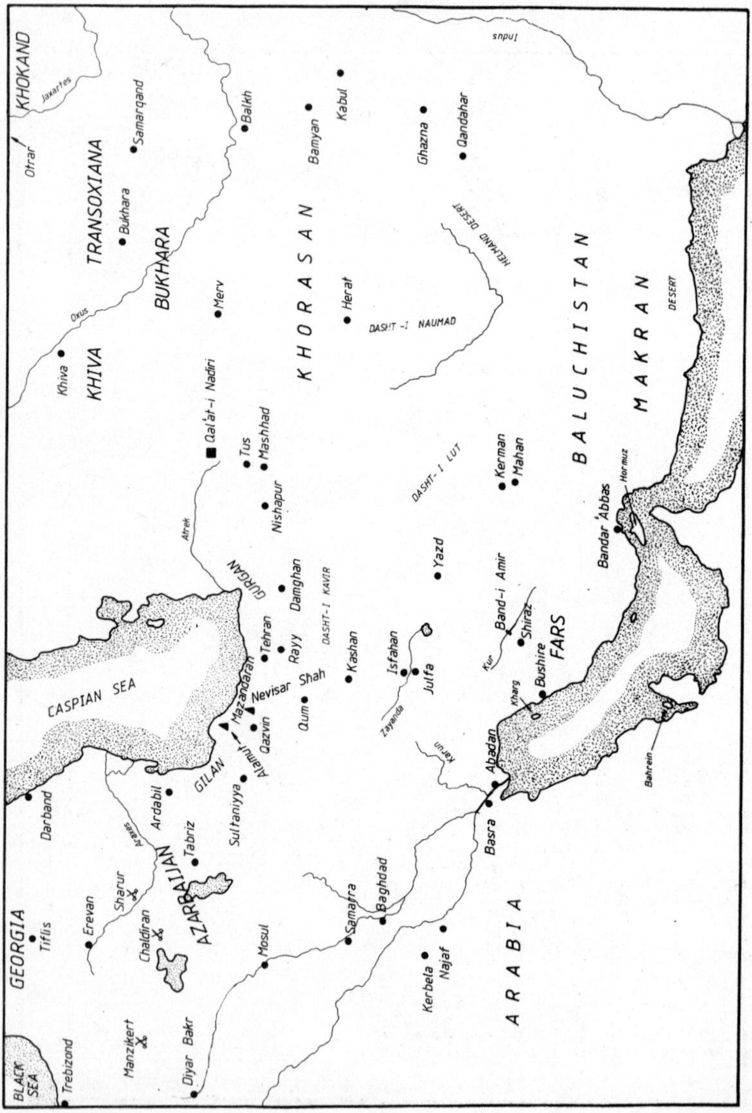

9 Western Asia in the age of Islam

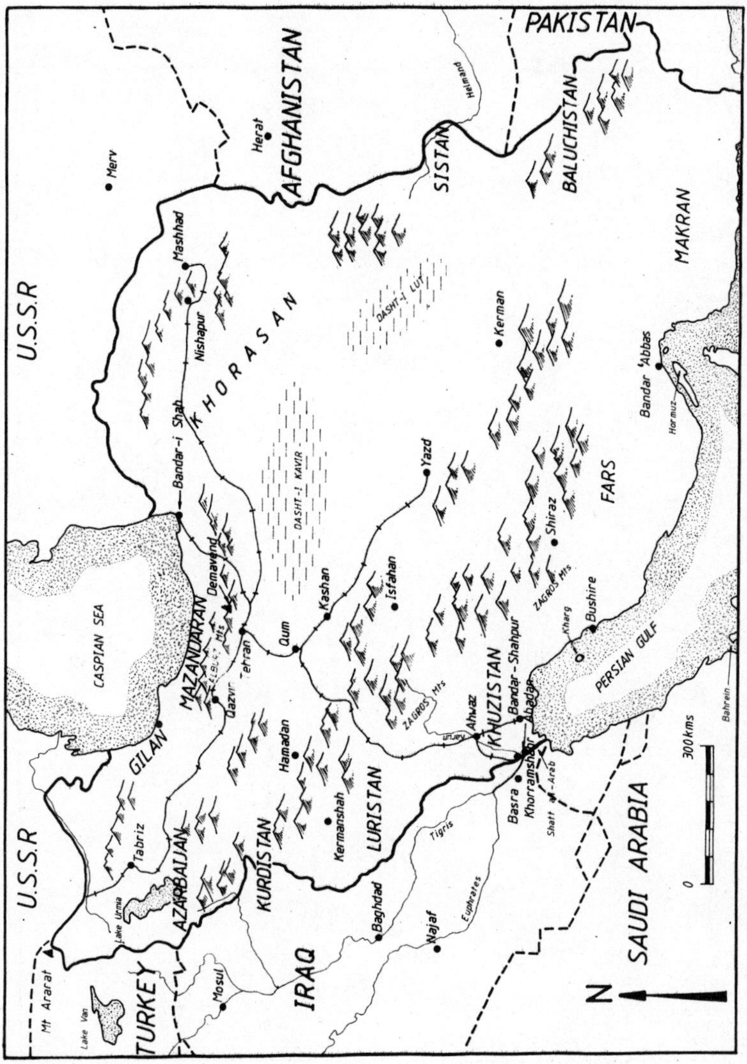

10 Iran under the Pahlavis

Introduction

This book is written for the general reader. It is a narrative history of Persia, an overview, condensed into one volume. It makes no claim to be a work of scholarship. As a popular history it might be frowned upon in academic circles. But if it encourages the reader to pursue some aspect of Persia's civilization in greater depth it will have served a purpose. It is, I hope, readable.

The material is taken from standard histories, specialist journals and primary sources, as well as the more popular works; some of the literary quotations, essential for conveying contemporary attitudes, are derived from them. Those readers who are curious to go further are referred to the select bibliography. Among the standard works such as the *Cambridge History of Iran* and the *Cambridge History of Islam* they will find more extensive bibliographies.

My attachment to Persia began early on with a childhood collection of stamps in an album arranged in continents for my geographical education. Tiring of the unprepossessing array of republican presidents of Europe that came my way, I abandoned them to their philatelic fate (and, rather reluctantly, the leopards in the jungles of French Equatorial Africa) in favour of the countries of Asia where the colourful scenic pictures, perplexing monuments and portraits of eminent personages in turbans, tarbooshes and *keffiyehs* were more to my liking. So too were the gentlemen resplendent in military uniforms, one of whom was Reza Shah. Later, when working in British missions in the Levant, my closer acquaintance with the Middle East began.

The theme of this book is that Persia in her progress down the ages retained both her identity as a nation and (until 1979) her monarchy.

Travelling back into the recesses of history we find that China and Egypt were the only major mainland countries to share such an enduring distinction.

Already in the biblical antiquity of the sixth century BC her kings ruled over an empire that stretched from Egypt and Asia Minor to the borders of India and central Asia. The main architects, Cyrus and Darius, introduced a style of government which for the Babylonians and others, who had languished under the yoke of the Assyrian and Chaldean kings, was infinitely more tolerant and enlightened. Their magnanimity is exemplified in their treatment of the exiled Jewish community, which had been held captive by the Chaldeans and forced to labour by the waters of the new city of Babylon. Cyrus allowed them to return to Jerusalem taking with them the gold and silver vessels which Nebuchadnezzar had carried off when he destroyed the city. Darius financed the rebuilding of the Temple from the Persian treasury.

Persia had reached an advanced state of civilization when much of northern Europe was still languishing beneath a blanket of primeval forest and the people of Britain were living in the late bronze age. The Britons of the time had no organized government, they relied on flint-headed arrows for their protection and food; they dwelt in small primitive communities of hut-villages and their pottery was fashioned without the aid of the wheel. In southern Persia the monumental splendours of Persepolis, with its high columned halls, audience chambers, stairways and palaces, were rising over the plain of Murghab. Persepolis was the inspiration of Darius, whose laws of the Medes and Persians feature in the books of Esther and Daniel. Two centuries later, when the armies of Alexander the Great invaded the plateau and set fire to the city, they did not succeed in destroying it, nor did it disappear as other cities have done, to lie buried and forgotten waiting to be rediscovered by the archaeologist. Persepolis in its ruined grandeur, in spite of some abuse, has withstood the passage of time. It has survived for 2,500 years to form a link in the age-long chain of Persian history.

Our ability to interpret the past is limited by the sources available and where that material is restricted or out of balance, as it may be in the remote past, the historian must make deductions as objectively as he can. But the line between prejudice and reasoning can be finely drawn. Consider that contentious subject, the burning of Persepolis. Classical writers and others have said it was an act of retribution for the firing of the Acropolis by Xerxes, that Alexander himself hurled the torch that set fire to the palaces. But my reading of his character does not accord with that view. To me Alexander was an idealist who sought to unite the countries of Europe and Asia, who chose to build cities rather than destroy them. I do not believe, that even when he was intoxicated, he would have perpetrated an act of such vandalism. But if the reader judges that I am prejudiced I plead guilty.

The imbalance of available material also means that we have to rely on accounts that may be biased. Take Herodotus, our main source for the Persian wars with Greece in the fifth century BC. He was a Greek (though born in Caria in Asia Minor); his *Histories* may have been entertaining reading for his compatriots, but they are not always reliable. Similarly with Aeschylus, though, unlike Herodotus, he was present at the battle of Salamis; his drama, *The Persians*, was written for his own people and allowance must be made for poetic licence. Nevertheless, his account carries conviction and encourages us to believe that he took part in the engagement. A dramatised version is better than none at all and it is our misfortune that there was no Persian Aeschylus, or even some lesser light, to strike a balance for the enemy and to describe the other great battles: Marathon, Thermopylae, Plataea and the final attack from the sea at Mycale.

Records continue to be fragmentary in the time of the Parthians, the semi-nomadic horsemen who ruled Persia after defeating the Seleucid successors of Alexander. For four centuries they were the dominant power in western Asia. In 40 BC they invaded Palestine and were welcomed in Jerusalem as the enemy of Rome. But rather disappointingly they receive only a passing reference in the New Testament (Acts II, 9) and no mention at all in the Old Testament.

The Parthians and the Sasanians who followed engaged in a 700 year power struggle with Rome as successive emperors sought to extend their eastern frontiers into Mesopotamia. The favoured invasion route lay through Asia Minor to the upper waters of the Euphrates. But, though the legions several times entered the capital, Ctesiphon, and sacked it, they never conquered the country. Trajan alone reached the shores of the Persian Gulf, but he too was forced to turn back and the 'Land of the Twin Rivers' remained an integral part of the Persian empire.

In the seventh century the pattern of power in western Asia underwent a dramatic change. The Arabs broke out of the desert. Carrying the black banner of the new faith before them, they swept round the Fertile Crescent (the lands bordering the Syrian desert) on to the Persian plateau and the margins of central Asia. The process of conversion began and Persia for ninety years was a province of the Muslim empire subject to the Umayyads in Damascus until the 'Abbasids assumed the caliphal role and Baghdad became the centre of the Islamic world.

In the 16th century under the Safavid kings Shi'ism became the established 'church' of Persia. This change of spiritual direction from orthodox Sunnism, more than any other development, except the conversion to Islam itself, was to have a profound effect on her future, as we have seen in our own time. In cultural terms this was a colourful period for the three major Islamic powers, Ottoman Turkey, Safavid Iran and Mughal India, and the arts flourished. But the annexation of Iraq by the Turks in 1639 signalled the territorial decline of the 'Greater Iranian world'. It continued in the 19th century when the Qajar dynasty surrendered whole regions of northern Persia to Russia.

Under the Qajars Persia's inability to adapt to the changing circumstances of the industrialised world and her deteriorating economic position provoked a constitutional crisis. And it was left to the Pahlavis, after the Great War, to improve the flagging economy and introduce reforms. But oil wealth brought its own problems and in moving towards a more secular society Mohammed Reza Shah did not carry the nation with him. In January 1979 he left the country never to return.

Iran today is nearly three times the size of France and by European standards is still a large country. The plateau is bounded down the west side by the Zagros mountains and along the north by the Alburz range, whose high peak, Mt Demavand, at over 18,000 ft is snow covered all the year. South west of the Zagros at the head of the Persian Gulf is the oil-bearing region of Khuzistan. From within the angle of the two great ranges the plateau extends eastwards through Khurasan to the Afghan and Pakistani borders. Much of it is desert: the Dasht-i Kavir, the Dasht-i Lut and the Makran are great wastes of salt and sand intersected by low mountain ranges. In contrast, on the coastal strip north of the Alburz, where the land slopes down to the Caspian Sea below mean sea level, the climate is tropical, the hills are forested, rainfall is plentiful and the atmosphere humid.

The western end of the plateau is an upland wilderness relieved by the occasional oasis or desert town. Here the air is clear, the outline of the distant hills is distinct and the sky is velvet blue. In spring the grazing is good, sheep and goats wander as they must have done long ago when the Persians and the Medes first moved in from the steppe. This is the eternal landscape of Persia. Later in the year the land turns arid brown and the flocks search among the camel thorn, their hunger unsatisfied. Most of the nomad population live on the slopes of the Zagros mountains and in the hot weather they move their flocks to the pastures above.

Iran is poorly supplied with rivers as most of them run dry before they reach the coast. Crop cultivation and the continuance of life itself have long depended on the *qanat* system of irrigation. These underground canals have carried melting snows from the mountains to the desert fringes since the time of Darius and may have been in operation in pre-history.

As in antiquity so in the Islamic age, neither the mountain ranges nor the deserts to east and west inhibited the invaders. They came from all directions: Arabs from the south, Ottomans from the west Afghans from the east. But the most frequented approach was through the plains that border the Caspian Sea. Nomads from central Asia and beyond crossed the Jaxartes and Oxus rivers into Khurasan or skirted the Caucasus into Azarbaijan.

In 1258 the Mongols brought the 'Abbasid dynasty to an end by killing the caliph and sacking Baghdad. Judged by the death and destruction which Genghis Khan, Tamerlane and others left in their trail over the better part of two centuries, these were disastrous years. Yet despite the upheavals (and possibly in part because of them) which conquest wrought, Persia's cultural legacy from medieval times was a brilliant one. The Saljuq Turks, Mongols and Timurids who overran the country set up their own dynasties. But each ended by merging with the indigenous population and even the Mongols eventually identified with the civilization they had intended to overthrow.

In the 10th and 11th centuries, as 'Abbasid power was declining, a number of minor kingdoms grew up. Some of their rulers were great patrons of the arts. The most enlightened were the Samanids in Bukhara: their territory stretched across the Oxus into Khurasan. Further south were the Ghaznavids, whose king so conspicuously failed to honour the merits of Firdawsi's *Shahnama*, which was destined to become Persia's national epic.

These minor kingdoms were overtaken by a wave of Saljuq Turks from central Asia which engulfed the country. They were converts to the faith and their period of power coincided with a resurgence in that form of mystical belief known as Sufism. This concept, which had a particular appeal to Persians, centres round the need for man's soul to return to union with God and the theologian, Abu Hamid al-Ghazali, who lived at this time, incorporated this philosophy in his writings. It drew a popular response, especially from the *madrasas* (theological colleges) and was echoed over the next four hundred years by a talented line of poets, among them Jalal al-Din Rumi:

> List to the reed, that now with gentle strains
> Of separation from its home complains
>
> from the *Masnavi*, tr. E H Palmer

Helped no doubt by the expertise of Persian architects and craftsmen, the Saljuqs were soon adorning the face of Persia with their monuments bringing into play their special facility in the use of brickwork and stucco. They built beacon lighthouses to guide the traveller and encourage the pilgrims and tomb towers to bury the dead. They erected new mosques and remodelled others; the Jami' in Isfahan, with its famous tomb chambers, ranks as one of the great mosques of the world.

The Mongols too, once their Il-Khanid descendants had embraced Islam, contributed to the architectural scene and they commissioned the famous vizier, Rashid al-Din, to write up their history. This, the *Jami' al-Tawarikh*, and the *Shahnama*, became favourite subjects for illustration. The painter's art was applied to tiles, lustre ware and other ceramics, even to walls, as well as manuscripts and books. It reached its apogee in the schools of Shiraz and Herat, where Bihzad, the great miniaturist, was head of the academy. From their capital at Herat, Shah Rukh and his Timurids successors took an interest in the task of restoration and building. At Yazd the majestic facade of the Jami' mosque with its towering twin minarets rose from a portal of blue-green mosaic tiles and in the holy city of Mashhad Gawhar Shad, wife of Shah Rukh, erected the mosque that bears her name.

In the Islamic age the panoply of oriental monarchy exhibited by the Saljuqs, the Timurids, the Safavids and the early Qajars, each in their way made a contribution to Persian culture, just as the great dynasties of antiquity had in their day. But in the nineteenth century the androgynous jewelled finery favoured by Fath 'Ali Shah, the glittering thrones on which he posed cushioned and cross-legged for his court painters, were discarded by his Qajar successors. They chose to present themselves in the more sombre garb of the military. Their braided uniforms, decorated with epaulettes, sashes and medals, displayed all the insignia of a European field-marshal. Only the headgear – a peaked hat bearing the aigrette held in place by some huge diamond – was characteristically Persian.

Few of the uniformed shahs led their armies into battle; they were symptomatic of a declining dynasty and a country that was politically and economically bankrupt. For the inspiration of the Islamic age we should perhaps look further back and return to the legacies handed down by the Saljuqs and the Timurids, to the astronomers and the mathematicians, the philosophers, the writers and artists who lived in and survived the traumas of medieval Persia. It is at such intervals in the passage of time, when intellectual and religious belief and the creative ability to express it come together – whether it is articulated through the sciences, in paintings, literature, music or architecture – that the supreme achievements of man's endeavour are realised.

Ex oriente lux

Eileen Humphreys
Abergavenny
Gwent
January 1991

PART I
THE AGE OF ANTIQUITY
834 BC-651 AD

CHAPTER 1
The Unmade Road

ASSYRIAN WARPATHS
834 BC–c. 700 BC

By the 834th year before Christ, King Shalmaneser III of Assyria, then in the third decade of his reign, had moved into his new fortress palace at Nimrud-Calah. The Assyrians were compulsive builders—every self-respecting king at this time liked to out-do his predecessor by erecting a larger residence for himself—and Shalmaneser was no exception. Having over 200 apartments, a throne room, halls and courts, barracks, parade grounds, arsenals, magazines and store rooms for the spoils of war, the new complex was twice the size of the palace built by his father, Ashurnasirpal II, in the citadel on the hill above. The area enclosed within its walls covered twelve acres and had taken thirteen years or more to build.

This parade of royal wealth and power, as well as gratifying the vanity of oriental monarchy, was designed to impress foreign emissaries and tribute bearers. Perhaps it was also calculated to strengthen the king's authority over the toiling masses, particularly the disruptive elements in an unwilling workforce: the captives from conquered territories set to dig canals or haul monster blocks of quarried stone and those who laboured on the site itself. The more abject their servitude—so the reasoning seemed to run – the more secure was the position of the king.

When Shalmaneser moved down the hill he did not abandon the old home altogether, nor for another 2,700 years did the human-headed lions and bulls he left guarding its portals, nor did Ninurta, God of Hunting, who 'allowed the dykes to flow'. Touching down on the ziggurat in the upper palace grounds he kept watch over the waters of the Tigris coursing through the plains below on their way

Fig. i. Human headed winged bull; seen from this angle it has five legs, seen from the front or side it has four legs. From Khursabad, now in the British Museum

down from the great city of Nineveh to the cult centre of Ashur, residence of the god of that name. Ashur was the supreme national deity: his temple was the powerhouse that drove the Assyrian war machine. From him (by reading the entrails of sacrificial animals) his high priest—the king—received his marching orders; to him he reported his victories:

> To Ashur, father of the gods, the great lord, who dwells in his great temple Ehursaggal-kurkurra, may it be very very well!
>
> H W F Saggs, *The Greatness that was Babylon*, London, 1962, p. 370.

So ran the salutation from one king who submitted his report in writing.

Back in the second millennium the Assyrian kings had been subordinate to the Babylonian rulers. Now the tables had turned and under Ashurnasirpal and Shalmaneser they were entering the world lists as the great warrior race of antiquity. They owed something to the introduction of iron; on the land metal tools had contributed to increased productivity and freed men for other tasks; in the army, with its nucleus of highly trained regulars, the superiority of iron weapons and the invention of the siege engine had helped to make the Assyrian host the most formidable force ever to engage in battle.

Intimidation was another weapon in the kings' armoury. Visiting vassals and foreign envoys, as they were conducted through the new palace precincts, would have had ample opportunity to view the royal collection of coloured sculptures and wall paintings: the sieges and assaults, lines of captives, tortures, decapitations, mass deportations, the taking of spoil. And he would have been a brazen emissary who, by the time he reached the throne room, had not modified his message, should it be unfriendly. He had been warned that magnanimity had no place in the creed of Ashur or his lieutenants on earth:

> I filled with their corpses the ravines and summits of the mountains. I cut off their heads and crowned with them the walls of their cities; I brought away slaves, booty, treasure innumerable.
>
> W G de Burgh, *The Legacy of the Ancient World*, London, 1947, p. 23.

This inscription by an early prince was one of many that were written across their monuments. Judging by such testimonies and by the proliferation of obelisks, statues in the round, stelae, low reliefs and wall paintings that lined the walls of their palaces or were displayed around the country, a front-line Assyrian king was almost as anxious to proclaim his victories to his contemporaries and his successors as he was to achieve them. For the message was plain. Whether his armies were seen to be attacking the enemy or whether he was taking part in a hunt, the king always triumphed. We see him standing in his chariot as prisoners and the spoils of war are paraded before him; we see him killing the king of beasts with his own hands or aiming his bow as the lion prepares to spring at him.

The meaning of the formal ritual scenes, namely that earthly and divine power are fused in the person of the king, is more subtly conveyed. A formidable figure, he stands, sometimes larger than life, on equal terms with other divinities. He wears the familiar long robe and flower-pot hat. His dark curled beard outlines a face that is impassive, yet his whole demeanour is at once both commanding and respectful as he raises his hand towards the winged disc of the supreme god, Ashur.

But even Assyrian kings had their informal moments. Between campaigns, having attended to the affairs of state, they planned their palaces and designed their pleasure parks. Ashurbanipal, the last of the great kings, invites us to witness a domestic interlude as he and his queen sit drinking in their garden to the sound of music. And the king, as he reclines on his couch, has the gratification of watching the head of his erstwhile enemy, the defeated king of Elam, swinging in a tree above.

By the ninth century BC the great days of Sumer and Akkad and the early Babylonians had passed into history but their legacies had contributed materially to the progress of civilization. They included a form of writing, from which cuneiform had evolved, and the code of laws devised by the famous Babylonian statesman, Hammurabi.

In Anatolia (Asia Minor) the Hittite kingdom had collapsed and the power of Egypt too was on the wane. Eighteen dynasties had come and gone since the last great pyramid builder had been carried to his burial chamber at Gizeh. With Egypt relegated, the focus of world events had shifted northwards to the Fertile Crescent, to that grassland bay whose shores had absorbed over two millennia successive waves of Semites from the Arabian deserts. Aramaeans (Syrians), Babylonians, Akkadians and the Hebrew tribes were among the settlers who had abandoned nomadism for a more sedentary life. The Assyrians were descended from the Akkadians. Their homeland lay in the centre astride the upper waters of the Euphrates and Tigris, which flowed across the plains down through the land of their forefathers into Babylonia and the ancient kingdom of Elam on the shores of the Persian Gulf. The bay's western end curved through Syria to Phoenicia and Philistia on the coast and the small inland Hebrew kingdoms of Israel and Judah.

Under Ashurnasirpal the Assyrian armies had penetrated to the Phoenician coast and the day was not far distant when they would sweep south through western Asia and, as the jaws of their empire closed round the eastern Mediterranean, Egypt too would be engulfed. Her rich river civilization was the ultimate prize but it did not fall to Shalmaneser. He was preoccupied consolidating and extending his father's gains further north. Not for twenty-four years was he in a position to break new ground there and when he did he turned east.

Had he attempted to invade Egypt, the Israelite kingdom of Jehu which lay along the route, could not have denied his armies passage.

The country was in turmoil as Elijah and Elisha, the prophets of the unseen Hebrew god, Yahweh (Jehovah), were in dispute with the worshippers of the idol Bel. But so long as the Syrian armies stood between them, Israel was safe from attack from the Assyrian host and for the time being Shalmaneser was content to take the tribute which Jehu found it politic to offer.

In Babylon too Shalmaneser stayed his hand. Here, after helping his vassal king suppress a revolt, he paid a courtesy call on the capital and offered his respects to the god, Marduk, the powerful head of the Babylonian pantheon. Further south, among the marshlands of the Euphrates he harried the Chaldeans, the latest wave of Semites to wash up on the shores of the Crescent, and took their tribute.

Shalmaneser concentrated much of his fire on the Syrians, to whom he devoted several campaigning seasons, on the Cilicians in the north-west and the rich trading cities of Tyre and Sidon. But his most formidable enemies, whom he fought throughout his thirty-four year reign, were the Urartians. They were a hardy, spirited upland people with their own characteristic art and culture. From their homeground round the shores of Lake Van and the plains of Mt Ararat they threatened the important trade route that ran westwards from Khorsabad towards the deposits of rich minerals and precious metals in Asia Minor and the iron mines of Cilicia. In one of his campaigns Shalmaneser describes an encounter with the forces of their king, Aramu:

> I drew near to Sugunia, the stronghold of Aramu the Urartian; I invested the town and captured it; I killed many of their warriors and carried off plunder; I made a pile of heads over against their city; fourteen settlements in its territory I gave to the flames. Then I departed from Sugunia and went down to the Sea of Nairi [Lake Van], where I washed my weapons in the sea and offered a sacrifice to my gods.
>
> B B Piotrovsky, *Urartu*, tr. James Hogarth, London, 1969, p. 46.

Supplemented with illustrations in bronze repoussé, the text was displayed on the huge gates of his palace at Balawat[1] near Nineveh. Two years later Shalmaneser was again at war with Aramu and, though he claimed he had slain 3,400 warriors and 'dyed the mountain like wool with their blood', their king lived to fight another day. That Shalmaneser went to such lengths to tell the tale is testimony to the power of the Urartians. Neither he nor his successors ever quite succeeded in destroying them. As a nation they lasted little more than two centuries, but long enough to witness the downfall of their erstwhile enemy.

Year after year Shalmaneser would march out from Nimrud to confront the enemy with 'the terrifying splendour of Ashur'. More often than not he would return triumphant, laden with gifts for the God of Battles. His master's appetite for blood and treasure was insatiable.

On one of his last expeditions Shalmaneser followed the course of the Lower Zab up through the mountains to the east. In the foothills of the Zagros he encountered among others the people of Parsua, nomadic Persians who were wandering slowly south, and, on the plains beyond, the Medes. All the tribes who lay in his path were required to pay tribute. On his return home Shalmaneser wrote an account of his campaign and the 'gifts' he had received on a black obelisk which stood up on the hill in the old citadel at Nimrud:

> I crossed over the Lower Zab ... I received the gifts of 27 kings of the land of Parsua. From Parsua I departed. To the lands of Messi (?) and of the Medes, the lands of Araziash and Harhar I descended.
>
> D D Luckenbill, *Ancient Records of Assyria and Babylonia*, Chicago, 1926, I, p. 206.

This inscription brought the Medes and Persians into the annals of recorded history. It was written in the twenty-fourth year of Shalmaneser's reign, some 834 years before Christ.

NOMAD TRACKS ACROSS THE PLATEAU

Over nearly two millennia, while successive civilizations along the Fertile Crescent had flowered and decayed, the steppeland peoples of central Asia, like the beduin in the Arabian deserts, had remained in a state of nomadism. They had no organized government, no townships, no writing. Many of these Indo-Europeans, or Aryans as they came to be called, left the steppes and fanned out in migratory waves. Some crossed into Europe, some reached India. The Hittites, who settled in Asia Minor around 2,000 BC, were among the more progressive. They formed a kingdom, adopted cuneiform writing, mined deposits of iron ore and for a time ruled an empire that extended to the Fertile Crescent.

Later, perhaps from 1300 onwards, other Aryan tribes speaking an Iranian dialect began to infiltrate onto the Iranian plateau via the grasslands, east of the Caspian Sea and perhaps through the Caucasus as well. These were the Persians and the Medes. Skirting the central desert and the Urartu kingdom in the area of Lake Van, they wandered with their flocks over the north and west of Iran towards the lowlands in the south, where they came into contact with the Elamites.

During the eighth century the Medes emerged as the dominant group on the plateau. They settled in the north-west in small fortified townships; any indigenous people had by then probably integrated with them. By the first quarter of the seventh century they had established themselves as an independent kingdom. The Persians—in halting passages and by differing routes but generally following the line of the Zagros—had begun to settle around the Elamite city-state of Anshan in the region of Persis (Fars) bordering the north-east shores of the Persian Gulf. After 646, when the Assyrian King, Ashurbanipal, is said to have destroyed the Elamite kingdom, they spread across the Karun river and occupied Susa. Some immigrants remained nomadic, sheltering in the valleys in the winter and moving back to their upland habitats for the summer grazing,[2] the siting of their tents being governed as always in Iran by the availability of water.

The Iranians were primarily pastoralists. They bred cattle, asses, mules, sheep, goats and, on the Nisaean plains of Media, horses, which became world famous and were taken by the Assyrians for their chariots and cavalry. In a land that was vulnerable to raids from Scythian nomads in the north and Assyrians in the west (among others), stock rearing was a wiser choice of occupation than arable farming, for, given sufficient warning, animals could be moved to the greater safety of the hills. Lapis lazuli imported from the east, bronze products from the mountain regions of Luristan and any metals that could be found were other forms of tribute demanded by the Assyrians.

Towards the close of the eighth century in the time of the Assyrian king, Sargon II (721-705), the mists of Median history begin to part and figures become dimly discernible. One Daiaukku (the Deioces of Herodotus)[3], a man of uncertain origin, is said to have rallied the local tribes round him and to have established his headquarters at

Ecbatana where he built a fortress. Ecbatana, which means place of assembly, lies buried under the modern town of Hamadan.

Daiaukku was deported by Sargon in 715 but some forty years later Khshathrita, perhaps his son (Herodotus' Phraortes), succeeded in uniting the Medes and forming an independent kingdom. He was killed fighting the Assyrians or their Scythian allies from the steppes. Once he was out of the way, pillaging expeditions by these horsemen became more persistent and during the third quarter of the seventh century they appear to have roamed almost at will across western Iran.

Under Sargon and Sennacherib (721-681) Assyria approached the zenith of her power. Sennacherib's new capital at Nineveh was planned on an appropriately massive scale. Covering 1800 acres, its unique feature was the water supply that serviced the city and its parks; a labyrinth of canals and an aqueduct made from two million blocks of stone went into its construction. The Urartians, who had given Shalmaneser so much trouble, had ceased to be a threat, Syria, Israel and Judah were subjugated, Babylon was sacked and the Chaldeans were brought under the direct control of Nineveh. The way was clear for an attack on Egypt and in 671 it fell to Esarhaddon, who was proclaimed king of Upper and Lower Egypt and Ethiopia. His son Ashurbanipal (668-627), the last of the great rulers, made abortive attempts to hold the country down but he had to withdraw after sustaining heavy losses. Meanwhile the Elamites had rebelled. They were a people with a highly developed artistic heritage, whose civilization could be traced back over 2,000 years. Of all the nations that were savaged by the Assyrian armies their fate was the worst. The ancient capital city of Susa was sacked, the land devastated, the temples and groves of their gods destroyed, their people deported or killed, the king and his princes spared only to drag Ashurbanipal's triumphal chariot through the streets of Nineveh.

In the early part of Ashurbanipal's reign the Assyrian empire had appeared to be as impregnable as ever. The Medes were the strongest surviving opposition but their chances of defeating the imperialist armies must have seemed slight. They had no adequately trained forces and no leader worthy of the name. They were little more than a loosely knit federation of scattered communities who were too weak to drive off the Scythians.

Yet the empire was beginning to crack. In seeking to subject Egypt the Assyrians had over-reached themselves and drained away their reserves. There were signs too that all was not well among the councils of the ruling clique at Nineveh. Succession quarrels, dissension among the military, disturbances amongst his own people and ill health continued to trouble the aging Ashurbanipal's last years. And he bemoaned his fate:

> The rules for making offerings to the dead and libations to the ghosts of the kings my ancestors, which had not been practised, I reintroduced. I did well unto god and man, to dead and living. Why have sickness, ill-health, misery and misfortune befallen me? I cannot away with the strife in my country and the dissensions in my family. Disturbing scandals oppress me alway. Misery of mind and of flesh bow me down; with cries of woe I bring my days to an end.
>
> *Cambridge Ancient History*, III, 1925, p. 127.

The end was nearer than he could have imagined. Within twenty-five years of his death the Assyrian state had passed into oblivion. Nor could he have foreseen that the annihilation of Elam, in which he had taken such vindictive delight, would influence the course of history, that from the ruins of the sacked city of Susa, where only 'the screech owl cried in the square', an empire would rise greater in extent than any over which the kings of Assyria had exercised dominion during the twelve centuries of their history.

Notes

1 Now in the British Museum

2 This mode of life with its timeless quality that has persisted through the centuries has preserved the tribal loyalties and traditions of the hill peoples. The Qashqa'i are one of several groups who continue to leave their mountain grazing in the Zagros to winter in the warmer lowland pastures to the south.

3 Herodotus, the Greek historian, who lived in the fifth century, is the main source for this period. His histories are written in a chatty entertaining style but are not always reliable.

CHAPTER 2

The Road Begins c. 700 BC–330 BC

THE FALL OF NINEVEH

Not much is known about Cyaxeres, king of Media, who brought about the destruction of the Assyrian empire. He lived in the last quarter of the seventh century; he may have been the son of the ill-fated Khshathrita; he probably brought the Persians under his sovereignty and he must have rid the plateau of the marauding Scythian horsemen. According to Herodotus the method of their disposal was simple: Cyaxeres invited their chiefs to some revels and when they were in their cups the Medes fell on them and slew them. Most of the rank and file were sufficiently demoralised by the loss of their leaders to withdraw to the plains north-west of the Black Sea from which they had originally come.

Cyaxeres' next step the same source tells us was to marshal his forces and train them. He must have studied his enemies' methods for he modelled his army on Assyrian lines with separate units for spearmen, bowmen and cavalry. The Scythians too had useful skills to offer for he employed some who had remained behind as instructors in archery.

Ashurbanipal had died in 627, a year or two before Cyaxeres won the Median throne. The mounting troubles in his country, which the old king complained of, had escalated into widespread risings among the peasants, revolts in the cities, and civil war between the nominated heir and one of his brothers from which the usurper, Sin-shar-ishkun, emerged victorious. Divided loyalties in military circles exacerbated by the hostilities had weakened the imperial armies and the Hebrew prophets in a catalogue of colourful utterances confidently predicted the downfall of the Assyrian empire. Its capital city was their special target. To Nahum, Nineveh was 'the bloody city . . . full of lies and robbery' while Zephaniah proclaimed:

> The Lord . . . will stretch out his hand against the
> north
> And destroy Assyria;
> And will make Nineveh a desolation,
> And dry like a wilderness.
> And flocks shall lie down in the midst of her,
> All the beasts of the nations:
> Both the cormorant and the bittern
> Shall lodge in the upper lintels of it;
> Their voice shall sing in the windows;
> Desolation shall be in the thresholds'.
>
> Zephaniah, II: 11-14

Meanwhile at the eastern extremity of the Fertile Crescent rebellion had welled up into full scale war. A neo-Babylonian (formerly Chaldean) army under its self-proclaimed king, Nabopolassar, was advancing up the Tigris and closing in on Assyria itself. In 615 they were pounding at the defences of Ashur. The attack failed but help was at hand, for the following year the Medes marched down through the Zagros and stormed the city. Cyaxeres and Nabopolassar met in the ruins and formed an alliance. Their treaty was sealed by the betrothal of the Babylonian crown prince, Nebuchadnezzar, and a Median princess.

By June 612 the allied armies had arrived before the walls of Nineveh itself. Roughly the shape of a flat-iron in plan, the fortress city that confronted them was protected down the east side by a moat and, on the west, by the river Tigris. Across the waters rose the ramparts—high crenellated walls supported by bastion towers—and beyond them the inner walls, seven-and-a-half miles long, were topped by a two-lane chariot way.

By any standards Nineveh was a formidable proposition. Yet after thirteen weeks, a relatively short period in siege terms, the allies had breached the walls and were storming the city. How did they do it? Tradition relates that they undermined the defences by diverting the Khosr river, which flowed through the centre into the Tigris, and causing a flood.

The allies' revenge was terrible; retribution knew no limits and the carnage was so complete that Nineveh, as the Old Testament

Fig. ii.
Plan of Nineveh

— outer walls
--- moat
1 palace of Sennacherib
2 palace of Esarhaddon
3 palace of Ashurbanipal

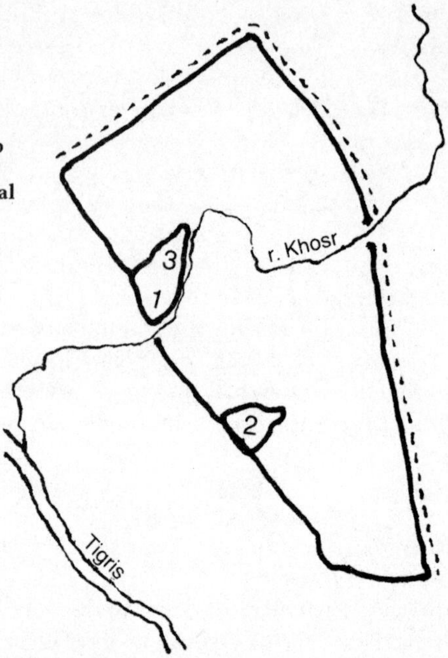

prophets had foretold, was never rebuilt:

> Thy shepherds slumber, O king of Assyria;
> Thy nobles shall dwell in the dust!
> Thy people is scattered upon the mountains,
> And no man gathereth them.
> There is no healing of thy bruise;
> Thy wound is grievous.
>
> Nahum, III: 18, 19

Sin-shar-ishkun was killed—probably in the flames that engulfed his palace—but one section of the army succeeded in breaking out. It fled westwards to Harran where it held out for a time. But once Nineveh had fallen the state of Assyria ceased to have any reality. And the Medes armed with all the spoil they could carry returned home in triumph.

The empire was partitioned. The Medes took Elam and some of

the northern fringes of the Fertile Crescent leaving the Babylonians with the greater part of Assyria and a free hand in the west.

Cyaxeres in his last years invaded the now declining kingdom of Urartu, a move which brought him into conflict with Alyattes, King of Lydia in Asia Minor. Happily their war was brought to an abrupt end at the battle of the eclipse 'when the day was darkened' by the total disappearance of the sun. Both sides, fearful of its portents, declared a truce and hastily agreed to draw the frontier line along the Halys river.

Cyaxeres died in 584. The fall of Nineveh had brought an era to an end but the new outline map of western Asia, which he and his allies had drawn, would soon be seen as a stop-gap arrangement. Even his own kingdom of Media was to lose its independence.

THE PERSIAN EMPIRE

The United Kingdom

Following the collapse of the Assyrian empire, the states of Egypt, Lydia, Babylon and Media emerged as the four dominant powers in the eastern Mediterranean and western Asia. Yet within a century of the fall of Nineveh all of them had surrendered their sovereignty and become part of the empire of the Achaemenid Persians. The kingdom of Media was the first to go: the tables were turned when Cyrus, a Persian prince, won control of the plateau. Lydia, Babylon and Egypt followed as Cyrus and his immediate successors made themselves masters of the western civilized world.

An empire comprised of peoples of such disparate races, creeds and cultures could not be contained by government on the authoritarian Assyrian model, and the early Achaemenids, in permitting a degree of autonomy among their subject peoples and respecting their modes of life, introduced a style of rule hitherto unknown in the orient. They did not, like the Assyrians, habitually deport populations (indeed Cyrus allowed the Jewish exiles to return to their homeland); they did not repudiate foreign gods (in Egypt Cambyses honoured them). Rather, as relative newcomers to the civilized world, they benefited from their contacts with more sophisticated societies. Later in their history, when the Iranian plateau itself was overrun, this ability to synthesize the cultures of others with their own was to serve the Persians well.

The success of the three main architects of the Achaemenid

empire, Cyrus, Cambyses and Darius, was due primarily to their ability to effect the transition from independence to subjugation with the minimum upheaval that conquest necessarily brings in its train, and also to the highly efficient system of government which they evolved.

Back in 584, after the death of Cyaxeres, the Median crown had passed to his son, Astyages. Meanwhile Cyrus, whose ancestor Achaemenes gave the coming dynasty its name, had inherited the kingdom of Anshan, a pocket-sized vassal state—once part of Elam—in the south. Having brought the Persian tribes in the area firmly under his control, Cyrus challenged the suzerainty of Astyages by refusing tribute. Astyages was forced to act and marched against him. But, according to Nabonidus, King of Babylon, his army mutinied and delivered him up to Cyrus.

By the year 550 Cyrus at the age of forty was installed at Ecbatana ruling over the kingdoms of Media and Persia and about to embark on a career of conquest which took him from Sardes in Asia Minor and the lands of the Fertile Crescent in the west, across Asia to present-day Afghanistan, to Transoxiana, possibly even to the Jaxartes river, far away on the borders of the barbarian steppe-lands in the north-east. Armenia, the land of the Urartu in the north, had come as part of the Median kingdom, Hyrcania and Parthia submitted, and during the next three decades Bactria and Sogdiana, Sistan, Gedrosia, Arachosia, Makran, Kerman and perhaps the remote mountainous area of Gandhara adjoining the unknown Indian world beyond—all were incorporated into the empire of the Medes and Persians.

Cyrus' success in battle came not only through his generalship, which was brilliant, but also by careful preparation and in Babylon, when her turn came, by exploiting discontent in the enemy camp. Yet once victory was achieved he was magnanimous. He spared old Astyages. True, he was his grandfather but he was not the only ruler whom he reprieved.

The autonomy Cyrus accorded to Media amounted to a form of partnership. His aim at this stage was to consolidate his position and to instil some feeling of national consciousness among the various ranks of the armies. He brought the two forces together by launching an attack on Lydia, whose king, Croesus, had extended his frontiers beyond the Halys river into Cappadocia in breach of the treaty made with Cyaxeres some forty years before. It was a hazardous undertaking to leave the new country and engage a strong enemy, whose mountain kingdom was 1,400 miles away. But if the risks were high the rewards of success would be exceedingly great. Croesus was famed for his wealth and whoever ruled in his place would have access to the flourishing Ionian city ports from which trade could be drawn eastwards.

In the spring of 547 Cyrus marched across northern Mesopotamia,[1] up through the Cilician Gates on to the Anatolian plateau, where he had an indecisive encounter with Lydian forces. As winter set in Croesus, confident that the campaigning season was over, returned to his capital at Sardes and disbanded his army. When Cyrus' men suddenly appeared before the walls only a cavalry remnant was there to give battle. Harpagus, the Median commander, brought the baggage camels into the front line and the Lydian horses, terrified by their strange smell, bolted, throwing their riders and leaving them to fight on foot. They were forced to retreat and fourteen days later (allegedly after a Lydian, who had dropped his helmet in the moat, was seen descending to retrieve it) the walls were scaled and Cyrus entered Sardes.

Rather than submit Croesus staged a public suicide:

> Croesus was not minded to await the further woe of grievous slavery. He caused a pyre to be built in front of his courtyard with walls of bronze; he mounted thereon . . . and, lifting up his hands to the high heaven, he cried aloud:- 'O thou Spirit of surpassing might, where is the gratitude of the gods? . . . The house of Alyattes is falling; [and what recompense for countless gifts is shown from Delphi?] . . . 'tis sweetest to die'. So spake he, and bade a softly-stepping attendant kindle the wooden pile.
>
> R C Jebb (ed. and tr.), *Bacchylides—the Poems and Fragments*, Cambridge, 1905, p. 259.

Then, according to the Greek poet Bacchylides, Zeus sent a rain cloud to extinguish the flames. More likely Cyrus had given orders for Croesus' life to be spared. It is said that he was admitted to the King's counsels and lived the rest of his life at the Persian court.[2]

Harpagus was entrusted with subjugating the Ionian ports. These trading posts, whose affluent and cultured immigrant communities from the Greek mainland had brought prosperity to Lydia and filled the coffers of Croesus with treasure, had been accorded the status of city state. The Ionians, mindful of their links with the mother

Fig. iii. Croesus on the funeral pyre

country and jealous of their semi-independent status, would not lightly submit to an oriental invader whom they regarded as barbarian. Nor did they. Miletus alone opened her gates. Their one chance of repelling the enemy lay in forming a united front but the Greek spirit of independence was not conducive to this, nor were the settlements, strung out as they were along a rugged coastline, prepared for defence against landward attack. One by one they were forced to submit.

Cyrus meanwhile returned home. In his Anshan days he had started work on a palace at Pasargadae. A doorway inscription, which must have been erected about that time read 'I am Cyrus the King, the Achaemenid'. Maybe as he rode eastwards he planned some embellishments, perhaps it was then he visualised a new inscription such as the one that reads: 'Cyrus the Great King, the Achaemenid'.

Persia's 'palsied hand', that 800-mile desolation of salt and sand, spreads across the central Iranian plateau down to the Makran coastline and the borders of India. But in the north, east of the

Caspian Sea, the high land undulates into the plains of the river Oxus and the steppes of central Asia. Here, following in the wake of the Iranians themselves, invaders throughout history have thrust their way on to the plateau and here, perhaps during the interim period (546-539) before he set out for Babylon, Cyrus marched all the way to north Transoxiana, drove a horde of Scythian (Saka) nomads back into the steppes and founded the frontier fortress of Cyropolis (Kurkath) on the Jaxartes river.

Seventy years had passed since Cyaxeres and Nabopolassar had joined forces against the Assyrians. In the interim, King

Fig. iv. The god Marduk with his dragon (after John Oates, *Babylon*, Thames & Hudson, London, 1986)

Nebuchadnezzar had overrun Syria and Palestine and with captive labour from Jerusalem had rebuilt the city of Babylon. Forty thousand Jews languishing by its waters had been put to work on the city walls and building sites erecting temples, ceremonial archways, a processional route and a palace set in terraced gardens leading down to the Euphrates. These—the famous hanging gardens—it was said had been designed for the benefit of the queen (the Median princess betrothed by Cyaxeres) who longed for the hills of her homeland.

During the 550s Nabonidus reigned in Babylon. He was something of an enigma, a scholar and a recluse who was preoccupied with the need for religious reform. He had upset the priests by denigrating the pantheon of old Babylonian deities—among them the god Marduk—and was calling for the removal of their images from the temples.

Cyrus must have exploited this source of discontent as the battle for Babylonia was fought, not so much in the field as behind the enemy lines in the city itself by his *agents provocateurs*. They encouraged the pro-Marduk lobby—the priests and their functionaries in the temples—to oppose the removal of the controversial images and to make it known that he supported their gods. No doubt his men gave undertakings to the Jewish community, for when Daniel was summoned to the banquet attended by the crown prince, Belshazzar, to interpret the writing on the wall, he confidently predicted:

> God hath numbered thy kingdom, and finished it . . . Thou art weighed in the balances, and art found wanting . . . Thy kingdom is divided, and given to the Medes and Persians.
>
> Daniel, V: 26-28

By October 539, after a brief engagement at Opis on the Tigris, the Persians advanced on the capital. Nabonidus fled, his armies scattered and the Persians entered the city. So well had Cyrus' agents prepared the ground that the invaders were welcomed as liberators. Cyrus staged his own entry a few days later:

> I . . . entered (Babylon) peacefully, with rejoicings and festal shouts.
>
> Percy M Sykes, *A History of Persia*, London, 1930, I, p. 151.

He kept on the crest of this welcoming wave by adopting the role of protector and by acknowledging the different local deities: he restored the displaced images to their temples, he 'took the hand of Marduk', he received homage from the vassal states of Syria and Palestine and he kept faith with the Jews:

> Cyrus the king made a decree concerning the house of God at Jerusalem, 'Let the house he builded . . . also let the golden and silver vessels of the house of God, which Nebuchadnezzar took forth out of the temple which is at Jerusalem, and brought unto Babylon, be restored.'
>
> Ezra, VI: 3, 5

Cyrus himself did not remain in Babylon. Leaving his son, Cambyses, in charge he returned home. In his last years he must have spent time supervising the building operations at Pasargadae. Situated where the rolling plain of Murghab narrows into an upland valley, the entrance through a battlemented gatehouse guarded by a pair of winged bulls gave on to a processional way which led to two black and white limestone palaces set in gardens intersected with streams. The palace of audience, rectangular in plan, had a lofty colonnaded hall whose white pillars rising from contrasting square black plinths were surmounted with black double-headed bulls, lions and horses. The second palace, thought to be a private residence, had probably not been completed at the time of his death. Beyond, on a low hill, stood the citadel and some way off in the sacred precinct the remains of what might have been a fire altar lends credence to the theory that Cyrus was a Zoroastrian.

In 530 Cyrus died at the hands of the Massagetai, a nomadic warlike tribe that had crossed the Jaxartes river into Sogdiana. His body was brought home to Pasargadae and laid to rest in a tomb which survives and which bore the inscription:

> O man, I am Cyrus, who acquired the empire for the Persians and was King of Asia; grudge me not, therefore, my monument.
>
> *The Geography of Strabo*, tr. H L Jones, London, 1966, 15.III.7.

Cyrus was a great commander, a humane ruler and an astute statesman. His unification of the plateau kingdoms and his conquest

Fig. v. Tomb of Cyrus the Great at Pasargadae

of Lydia were in themselves great achievements. But beyond that, the 'liberation' of the Babylonians, which he so skilfully engineered, and the acquisition of their empire in the west, altered the pattern of political and racial power in the countries of western Asia. Within a century they had exchanged Assyrian militarism and dictatorship for the more persuasive style of Achaemenid rule. And along the Fertile Crescent the Semitic power of the ancient river civilizations was ebbing back into the sands to give place to twelve centuries of Aryan domination.

To an advanced people like the Babylonians, who had experienced conquest in the savage manner of both the Assyrians and the Chaldeans (who were not much better), the experience of Persian rule had been encouraging. Here was a ruler who had presented himself as their deliverer, as the protector of their gods and their way of life, who in return had demanded little more than their loyalty and reasonable tribute. The Persians called him father; in the world of antiquity he was arguably the greatest of the Great Kings.

Through the long lines of Persian monarchs runs a recurring thread of distrust between fathers and sons and between brothers, which has placed the life of many a prince in jeopardy. In his lifetime Cyrus had separated his two sons by appointing Cambyses, the elder, as viceroy of Babylonia and sending his younger son, Bardiya, to govern the eastern provinces. After his father's death, when Cambyses succeeded, doubts as to his brother's loyalty must have assailed him and Bardiya was secretly murdered.

An expedition to Egypt had been planned by Cyrus and, having put his house in order, Cambyses in 526 was ready to march. From Gaza, helped by the beduin whose camels carried water and supplies, his armies safely crossed the Sinai desert, Egypt's outer defence, and reached the Nile delta. For the Egyptians the attack was not unexpected and the Pharaoh, Psamtek III, had negotiated naval support from some of the Greek islanders. But at the last moment they defected to the Persians taking with them details of the Egyptian defence positions. A battle at Pelusium on the delta was followed by another for Memphis, one of the principal cities. When that too fell all resistance ceased, Psamtek was taken prisoner and Cambyses declared himself King of Upper and Lower Egypt.

Cambyses' plans for further conquests along the Mediterranean coast foundered in the western desert when 50,000 of his men, as they neared the oasis of Siwa, perished in the region known as the Sea of Sand. He himself led a more successful expedition up the Nile to the borders of Ethiopia.

Cambyses stayed in Egypt for three years. He respected local customs, he honoured the native gods and, until he was found to be intriguing against him, he permitted Psamtek to live in his palace.

Such magnanimity hardly tallies with the tyrannical character accorded him by Herodotus. Cambyses was, however, hated by the priesthood, whose power he curbed and whose revenues he curtailed and when Herodotus visited Egypt nearly a century later their atrocity stories had apparently lost nothing in the telling.

In 522 came news of a palace coup in Media—an impostor posing as Bardiya had proclaimed himself king. Cambyses had stayed too long. He started on the journey home but did not live to challenge the usurper. Somewhere in Syria he died, perhaps by his own hand in a state of depression. He left no heir.

On the plain of Murghab not far from the burial place of later Achaemenids at Naqsh-i Rustam, stands an unfinished tomb. It is similar in design to that of Cyrus and it may well be the last resting place of Cambyses.

The Empire at its zenith

Victory in Egypt brought the entire eastern Mediterranean into the power of the Medes and Persians. The pyramid of their empire had been capped and gilded with this last glittering conquest. There would be further embellishments and some dismantling, but the main structure endured as long as the Achaemenid dynasty itself. But, had a lesser man than Darius emerged victorious in the struggle for power after the death of Cambyses in 522, it is doubtful if the empire, or even part of it, would have survived for long.

Legend relates that a group of seven princes agreed that the one whose horse neighed first after sunrise would win the throne and a ruse employed by his groom ensured that Darius was the winner. The official account of his accession was inscribed by Darius on the cliff-face at Behistun (on the road from Kermanshah to Hamadan). It is illustrated in relief and shows the king trampling the body of Bardiya's impostor underfoot:

> There was a man, a Magian, Gaumata by name . . . He lied to the people thus: 'I am Bardiya, the son of Cyrus, brother of Cambyses' . . . Persis and Media and the other lands went over to him. He seized the kingdom . . . The people feared him . . .
>
> There was no one who dared say anything about Gaumata . . . I prayed to Ahura Mazda . . . then I with a few men slew that Gaumata . . . I took the kingdom from him. By the grace of Ahura Mazda I became king.
>
> R N Frye, *The Heritage of Persia*, London, 1976, p. 96.

Nevertheless his position was insecure: rebellion was rife, the provinces were reverting to their separate kingdoms and there were disturbances in the homeland. Fortunately for Darius he was respected in military circles (he had served as spear bearer to Cambyses) and the army stayed loyal.

He stemmed a rising in Babylon, he or his governor quelled a revolt in Egypt, he suppressed rebellions as far apart as Armenia and

Arachosia, in Media and in Persis (Fars) itself. In Jerusalem he kept the peace by permitting the Jews to rebuild the temple which Nebuchadnezzar had destroyed. Only Lydia it seems remained quiet. Thus within two years, by the effective deployment of his forces and by a judicious mixture of punishment and diplomacy order was restored. The score, he recounts at Behistun, was nineteen battles fought and nine pretenders killed.

Having shown himself to be a competent commander, Darius demonstrated his abilities as a ruler. Clearly, Cyrus had meted out too much autonomy and some reorganization was necessary. Darius divided the provinces into twenty administrative areas or satrapies and placed them under strong central control. The notion that the 'Seven Princes of Persia and Media, which saw the king's face, and which sat the first in the kingdom' mentioned in the Book of Esther (I.14), were a council of ministers, who met to assist the king, has been discounted. The king, it seems, ruled directly through functionaries like the chief minister who was commander-in-chief of the army.

Darius constructed a network of roads to link the distant outposts with the new capital at Susa. Among them was the royal road which ran from Sardes in the far west to Susa and continued through the Persian Gates to Persepolis on the Murghab plain.[3] Staging posts with messengers and horses at the ready relayed the royal mail on its 1700 mile journey from the capital to Sardes—it was said—in seven days.

In administering the law Darius endeavoured to set standards. The Book of Daniel refers to 'the law of the Medes and Persians, which altereth not' (VI.8) but it is unlikely that he went as far as formulating a code as Hammurabi had done. He was concerned to see that justice was done and his inscriptions preach the need to tell the truth:

> Darius the king thus says . . . 'What is right I love. The man who decides for the Lie I hate . . . And whoever injures, according to what he has injured I punish'.
>
> A T Olmstead, *History of the Persian Empire*, London, 1970, p. 125.

He was in his late twenties when he won the throne and he reigned for thirty-six years. He extended his eastern frontier towards the banks of the river Indus and the goldmines of Gandhara; the river itself was navigated by Scylax, who crossed the Indian Ocean and after a voyage of thirty months reached Egypt. Engineers dug a canal from the Red Sea to the Nile, a feat which Darius commemorated in five inscribed red granite stelae along the banks:

> I am a Persian . . . I commanded this canal to be dug from the river, Nile by name, which flows in Egypt, to the sea which goes from Parsa.
>
> Olmstead, *op. cit.*, p. 146

Darius' motive in mounting a large-scale expedition against the Scythian tribes of eastern Europe in 512 is conjectural. These mounted nomads, who Herodotus graphically claimed, drank the blood of their enemies, made human skin into clothes and skulls into drinking vessels, inhabited the Stygian limbo world of the Eurasian steppes. Why did he want to annexe it? Was he seeking Dacian gold? This seems unlikely as he had other sources. Was he aiming to protect his northern frontiers by attacking the Scythians in the rear? Or, as seems more probable, was he intending to create a Scythian-free zone north of the Danube to give his armies a safe foothold from which to launch future operations in Europe?

After crossing the Bosphorus on a bridge of boats he marched through eastern Thrace, which submitted, to the Danube, where his sailors had built a bridge above the delta. Once across, the Scythian horsemen lured him on to the interior ravaging the country as they went. Refusing a set battle, they resorted very successfully to guerilla tactics. After two months Darius had not returned. Fortunately the guards at the bridge stayed on at their posts and eventually he managed to make his way back. But he abandoned the wounded to their fate.

He returned to Sardes leaving part of his army under Megabazos to subdue western Thrace. The Scythian expedition had been a fiasco but if Darius harboured plans for an invasion of Europe he had succeeded in establishing a bridgehead. And, as it transpired, he had only to wait on events for an excuse to come his way.

In 507 Athens was under attack from her rival, Sparta, and in desperation she sent representatives to ask the satrap of Sardes for protection. The satrap agreed to help on condition that she acknowledged Persian suzerainty and surrendered all her territories. The ambassadors reluctantly accepted the terms but by the time they had returned to Athens the crisis had passed and the agreement was repudiated. Such a *volte-face* must have hardened Darius' attitude and deepened his resolve to teach the fickle Athenians a lesson.

In 499 the Ionians rebelled and overthrew their local 'tyrants'. Athens and Eretria sent ships and reinforcements and the Greeks momentarily occupied Sardes. But the Athenians, faced yet again with disturbances at home, withdrew. Even so the Persians were unable to quell the rising. For five years it flared up intermittently along the coast from Chalcedon to Caria before the Ionians were decisively defeated at sea off the island of Lade. The ringleader city, Miletus, was stormed, the male population was killed or deported to the marshlands above the Persian Gulf, the women were enslaved and a heavy tribute was levied on all the rebel states. Darius determined now, if not before, to subjugate Athens as well as her Ionian allies.

The first expedition was frustrated. After the loss of half their supply ships in a storm off Athos, it was decided to make a direct attack from the sea. The summer of 490 saw a 600-galley armada under the command of Datis, the Mede, cross the Aegean from Samos to the island of Euboea. The capital city, Eretria, was burnt and the people enslaved in reprisal for their part in the Ionian revolt. But this diversion served to warn the Athenians of what was to come.

Datis now sailed towards the mainland and a few days later he landed his army on the beach of Marathon Bay, twenty-four miles north-east of Athens. Miltiades had gathered 10,000 men at the south end of the bay and was anxiously awaiting reinforcements from the Spartans (now their allies). But they refused to march till the full moon had passed. Warned by some Ionians, who stole across the lines, that there would be another landing at Phaleron Bay, Miltiades decided, though outnumbered by two or three to one, to attack.

At first light the hoplites (heavy-armed infantry) went into action by charging the enemy flanks at the run and driving them inwards on their centre. Taken by surprise the Persians were thrown into disarray and fled for the ships with the Greeks in pursuit. Later the Greeks re-formed, marched to Athens and by evening were bivouacked south of the city above Phaleron Bay. When the Persian galleys rowed in and saw the hoplites waiting for them they turned and made for the open sea.

In the battle of Marathon[4] the Greeks had shown the world for the first time that the massed armies of the Persian king were not invincible. Moreover—and this to them was a source of even greater pride—they had defeated them without the assistance of their questionable ally. 'At Marathon we stood out against the Persians and faced them single-handed', Thucydides, the Athenian statesman, and his fellow citizens were to remind the Spartans on several occasions.

Back in the palace at Susa some 2,000 miles away Darius viewed the defeat simply as a setback. The eyes of the aging king were fixed on a more distant shore than the beach at Marathon as he prepared himself for his final journey. He died four years later in 486.

Within a generation of the formation of the united kingdom the early Achaemenids had extended the nation state of Persia into an empire which reached across western Asia to the continents of Africa and Europe. History is a catalogue of meteoric conquests that crumble overnight. That the Persian empire endured under a succession of weaker monarchs after the death of Darius is a tribute to Cyrus, a benevolent ruler, and to Darius, the consolidator of the territories won by his predecessors. He restored order among the subject peoples, administered justice, introduced a system of taxation, encouraged trade and improved communications. As a devout Zoroastrian he led the intelligentsia towards monotheistic belief. Darius imprinted the mark of his greatness on the Persian Empire by advancing that indefinable quality of human endeavour which we call civilization.

High up in the cliff at Naqsh-i Rustam overlooking the Murghab plain he had prepared his tomb. In the fire temple below the priests guarded the sacred flame lighting him on his journey to eternity, to the lights without beginning in the solar kingdom of Ahuramazda.

And the traveller setting out on the long road to Susa, the royal road, which Darius himself had travelled and which passes below his tomb, must have marvelled at the greatness of the king who had gone before him and prayed, as he knelt before the sacred flame, for his continued protection.

Darius had written his own epitaph:

> A great god is Ahuramazda, who created this earth, who created yonder sky, who created man, who created happiness for man, who made Darius king, one king of many, one lord of many.
>
> I am Darius the Great King, King of Kings, King of countries containing all kinds of men, King in this great earth far and wide, son of Hystaspes, an Achaemenian, a Persian, son of a Persian, an Aryan, having Aryan lineage ...
>
> Much was ill-done, that I made good . . . The

> following I brought about by the favour of Ahuramazda . . . that the stronger does not smite nor destroy the weak ...
>
> Me may Ahuramazda together with the gods protect, and my royal house, and what has been inscribed by me'.
>
> R Ghirshman, *Iran from the earliest Times to the Islamic Conquest*, Harmondsworth, 1954, p. 153-4.

Darius was succeeded by his son Xerxes. During his reign events took an unfortunate turn which were in part his own making. Xerxes was a weak man and when trouble came he over re-acted. He meted out savage punishment on the Egyptians and on the Babylonians when they rose in revolt a year later: Nebuchadnezzar's fortifications were razed to the ground, temples were torn down and the gold statue of Marduk carried off. Rather more serious in the wider context was Xerxes' disposition to be swayed by the blandishments of those around him. According to Herodotus, he was not anxious to extend his dominions and it was his cousin, Mardonius, who persuaded him against his better judgment to invade Greece and avenge Marathon.

The humiliating defeats that were subsequently sustained by the Persian forces at the hands of a bunch of small city states tipped the scales of power towards the west and the spectre of retribution, after hovering over the Persian empire for a century and a half, became a startling reality. Alexander's armies swept across Asia into the Persian heartland and brought the Achaemenid dynasty and its empire to an inglorious end.

For Attica, in that gap in the clouds between the Persian expedition and the rise of Macedonia which followed the Peloponnesian war, the sun shone briefly. The immortal splendours of Periclean Athens that rose from the ashes of the city, which the armies of Xerxes had destroyed, were financed from funds raised to counter Persian aggression.

Xerxes' joint land and sea operation against Greece was carefully prepared over three years. Engineers dug a canal through the Athos isthmus and food supplies were deposited along the first part of the route.

The fighting forces were summoned from all parts of the realm and in the spring of 480 Xerxes set out from Sardes for the Hellespont. In the customary Achaemenid style he took part of his household with him: women members of his family and their servants, clothiers, smiths, cupbearers, valets, pages, kitchen staff, grooms—their numbers ran into hundreds. His luggage included furniture for his tent, gold and silver vessels for his table, water from Susa carried in mule carts, provisions from the royal larder and cattle on the hoof.

At Abydos he reviewed his fleet and his armies from a white marble throne on a hill above the shore. The size of the expedition is debatable. Greek sources are exaggerated and the claim of Herodotus that it ran into millions is a logistic impossibility. 250,000 to 300,000 including cavalry and non-combatants on land and a fleet of 800 triremes (war galleys), each with a complement of 200, is a more realistic estimate.

A sea crossing of the Hellespont for such a massive army was not feasible. A bridge was constructed but it collapsed in a storm and the engineers responsible were executed. Another team successfully yoked 'the sea's neck in a bridge of boats' and Xerxes, having commanded the waves to be scourged into submission with 300 lashes, the bridge held and the army got safely across. The invasion had begun.

With the armada keeping level, the armies steamrollered southwards past Mount Olympus—Macedonians and Thessalonians fell back before them—till they were in the heart of Hellas and closing on the gates of Athens itself.

In the pass of Thermopylae a vanguard force under the Spartan King Leonidas had sent the main army of 6,000 back to fight another day. Spurning retreat for themselves, he and each of his band of 300 fought to the death.[5] To the Persians the taking of the pass was a preliminary battle won. But to the allies the action served as a rallying call and the spirit that now pervaded their armies was exemplified by the Spartan soldier who, hearing that the Persians showered so many arrows that they hid the sun, exclaimed: 'This is pleasant news . . . for if the Persians hide the sun, we shall have our battle in the shade.' (Herodotus).[6] At sea, following an indecisive encounter off Artemesium, the Greek galleys withdrew southwards to Eleusis Bay behind the island of Salamis, evacuating the people of Athens en route and leaving only a small defence force to die heroically on the steps of Athena's temple. As the flames shot up from the Acropolis they illuminated the empty city below: the invaders had scored a hollow victory—the Athenians lived on, their forces still intact.

Xerxes now held a council of war. Should they advance on the Peloponnese and fight on land or should they risk a battle at sea?

Artemisia, Queen of Caria, knowing the Greeks were short of supplies, urged a blockade of the enemy fleet. But it was already September and Xerxes was in a hurry. He accepted the majority view and ordered the fleet, now in Phaleron Bay, to weigh anchor. Next day, as the armada came into sight round the headlands, the Hellenes saw the extent of their peril.

According to Aeschylus, who was present at the battle of Salamis and may have taken part in it, the king was persuaded by a message from the enemy statesman, Themistocles, that the Athenian fleet would make for the open sea under cover of night. The turn events took is described by the poet in his play *The Persians*, when a messenger from Xerxes brings news of the battle to the queen mother in the palace of Susa:

> . . . when Xerxes heard this, with no thought
> Of the man's guile, or of the jealousy of gods,
> He sent this word to all his captains: 'When the sun
> No longer flames to warm the earth, and darkness holds
> The court of heaven, range the main body of our fleet
> Threefold, to guard the outlets and the choppy straits.'
>
> . . . All night long the captains kept
> Their whole force cruising to and fro across the strait.
> Now night was fading; still the Hellenes showed no sign
> Of trying to sail out unnoticed; till at last
> Over the earth shone the white horses of the day

The sun shone too on weary oarsmen now ordered to attack under the unrelenting eye of the king seated on his throne above the narrows:

> At once ship into ship battered its brazen beak.
> A Hellene ship charged first, and chopped off the whole stern
> Of a Phoenician galley. Then charge followed charge
> On every side. At first by its huge impetus

Our fleet withstood them. But soon, in that narrow space,
Our ships were jammed in hundreds; none could help another.
They rammed each other with their prows of bronze; and some
Were stripped of every oar. Meanwhile the enemy
Came round us in a ring and charged. Our vessels heeled
Over; the sea was hidden, carpeted with wrecks
And dead men; all the shores and reefs were full of dead.

Then every ship we had broke rank and rowed for life.
The Hellenes seized fragments of wrecks and broken oars
And hacked and stabbed at our men swimming in the sea
As fishermen kill tunnies or some netted haul.
The whole sea was one din of shrieks and dying groans,
Till night and darkness hid the scene.

(tr. Philip Vellacott, Harmondsworth, 1961, pp. 133-134)

The Athenians, more skilfully captained and better disciplined, were the victors but they did not exploit their triumph. They failed to give chase to the departing Persians nor did they venture up the coast to cut the Hellespont lifeline and the fruits of their victory ebbed away on the outgoing tide.

As to the Spartans, though the Persian columns were withdrawing, they were unwilling to give chase while the enemy was so near home. This time an eclipse of the sun gave them a suitably unfavourable omen.

Pan-hellenic prejudice inclines to accuse the Persian King of cowardice for returning home at this point, of making an ignominious and hasty retreat. But his armies remained in good order, Attica was still in his power and his own life was in no danger. What he did fear was that news of the defeat would encourage the Ionians to revolt and this prompted him to return to Sardes.

As Xerxes travelled north he moved out of active involvement in state affairs. Once back in Persia he never again left his three capitals. Pre-occupied with palace building and the pleasures of the harem, he let the reins of power slip into the hands of eunuchs. Intrigue invested the court and culminated in his assassination fifteen years later by the captain of the guard.

Mardonius meanwhile was left in command of a picked force of 90,000, which included some of the élite 'Immortals'. He evacuated Athens and withdrew to Thessaly for the winter. His efforts to drive a wedge between the Hellenes and their wavering ally by sending an envoy to Athens offering reparations and an alliance with Persia were rejected. Despite their plight the Hellenes stood by the Spartans and sent the famous reply:

> Tell Mardonius . . . that so long as the sun keeps his present course in the sky, we Athenians will never make peace with Xerxes.
>
> (Herodotus, *op. cit.*, VIII, 143)

In the spring the two sides prepared for battle. Mardonius took up his position by his supply base at Thebes and waited. The Athenians and the Spartans (who had been persuaded to join in only at the last minute) advanced cautiously towards the Persian lines. The allied force was under the command of Pausanias, regent for the son of Leonidas. After days of manoeuvring battle commenced near the small town of Plataea. By evening the Persians had the advantage and the Greeks were retreating in some disorder. Next morning at dawn Mardonius on the Persian left entered the lists at the head of the Immortals and it was here that the battle was decided. The Spartan archers opposite had lost contact with the neighbouring Athenian contingent and Mardonius ordered the Immortals to attack. They advanced closing in behind a barricade of wicker shields. So long as the sacrificial offerings were unfavourable the Spartans had to stand their ground, all the while taking a hail of arrows. When the omens changed and the Persians had closed up, Pausanias gave the order and they charged the barricades pressing in on the enemy. The issue was still in the balance when Mardonius, a conspicuous target on a white horse, was killed. His death tipped the scales, his men lost heart and fled for their stockaded camp. The Spartans, joined now by the Athenians, followed. The camp was stormed, few prisoners were taken and most of the Immortals, flower of the Persian army, were slain. Not all the Persian forces had been deployed and Artabazus, who had assumed command, deemed it wiser to withdraw from the field altogether and march for home.

The Persian fleet meanwhile had arrived off the coast of Ionia. Part of it had been disbanded once the king had arrived safely back on Asian soil and only a small section of the original fleet remained. Rather than face the Greeks at sea, the Persians had beached their ships on the shores of Cape Mycale and joined up with the local garrison. It was probably just a few days after the battle of Plataea that the allies sought them out. As they leapt ashore, the Ionians (unwilling conscripts in the Persian army) deserted and came over to help the attackers. Between them they fired the Persian ships.

Mycale, though the allies did not realise it at the time, was the decisive battle of the war: the allies had won command of the sea and the islands were safe from attack. Although some of the Asian cities had yet to gain their independence it was only a matter of time before they might too be free.

After the battle the Spartans returned home but the Athenians sailed for the Hellespont. They stormed the fortress at Sestos, though they failed to arrest Artabazus' retreating army, which marched on and crossed at the Bosphorus. However, the huge hemp cables, that had formed the roadway over the bridge of boats and were hanging limply across the narrows, were a welcome trophy. The ship accorded the honour of towing them home was commanded by the expedition's leader, Xanthippus, father of the young Pericles.

Athens became the leading power in the Aegean and under her chairmanship a defensive alliance of the islands and city states was formed into the Delian League. Ten years after Plataea the League went over to the offensive and on the banks of the river Eurymedon in Pamphylia, Cimon, the son of Miltiades, won the last of them their freedom.

The Persian side had suffered the greater number of casualties. Perhaps 25,000 never crossed back in to Asia. But if in the short term their losses were serious they were not catastrophic. The bid for eastern Europe had failed and news of the defeat would bring about some weakening at the seams. As yet the empire remained intact. Thanks largely to the legacy of Darius, the administrative network with its greater emphasis on centralised control proved strong enough to carry a degenerating dynasty through another century.

In 449 the two sides came to the negotiating table and signed the Peace of Callias. The terms were never published but there can be little doubt that written into some face-saving formula was an undertaking by King Artaxerxes I that the Greek cities of Asia would be left to their own devices.

The state of Persia under the Achaemenids

Early on in the Achaemenid period the future pattern of society in the home provinces began to take shape. While some tribes continued to move up into the hills for summer pasture, others had settled. Iran in the rural areas was evolving into a feudal society of landowners and labourers. The chiefs appropriated the land and the tribesmen or peasants worked it for them. Community life centred on the village, which was walled or protected in some way against attack.

The duties of the Empire's twenty satraps, some of whom might have been heads of the principal tribes, were to maintain order, administer the law and collect taxes. A garrison commander posted in each location was also responsible to the king and roving inspectors with their own militia, the 'king's eyes' and the 'king's ears', formed an additional safeguard.

Taxes were paid partly in gold or silver and partly in kind: Cilicia, for example, had to raise '500 talents of silver, together with 360 white horses . . . Babylon and Assyria—1,000 talents of silver and 500 eunuch boys' while the Ethiopians brought 'gifts' of gold, ebony and ivory. Fars alone was exempt from taxation: as the home of the Immortals her tribute came in the form of manpower. (Herodotus, III, 90, 92, 97).

In Babylon bankers (descendants of the Jewish exiles) opened their doors. Among the services they offered were loans for the purchase of land, property and livestock on which their clients paid interest at the rate of 20 percent. Coins, which had first been minted in Lydia under Croesus, were brought into wider circulation by Darius and merchants, whose caravans travelled into Egypt, Greece, India and elsewhere, exchanged the gold 'daric' and the silver shekel for glass and beads from Egypt, textiles from Greece, spices from India and so on.

Improved methods of written communication were coming into general use. New writing materials—parchment and papyrus—were replacing the clumsy clay tablets; the laborious wedge-shaped cuneiform characters were being superseded by the alphabetic script of the Aramaeans. These enterprising Semitic people had been trading round the Fertile Crescent in Assyrian times and their language was becoming the *lingua franca* of business and diplomacy.

When the king sent a despatch to a distant satrap he would dictate it in Old Persian to a secretary for translation into Aramaic and the recipient's scribe would translate the letter into his own language. Fortunately for the historian royal proclamations were inscribed in more durable rock. The famous Behistun relief commemorated Darius' victories in three languages: Old Persian, Elamite and Akkadian (neo-Babylonian).

These advances in trading methods and communication served to improve the country's economy. But to the man working on the land, whether he was growing crops or raising cattle, the constant problem then—as it has been throughout Iran's history—was to ensure an adequate supply of water. By the time of the Achaemenids a method had been devised of directing the melting snows from the mountains into underground channels which could reach to the margins of the desert. This system known as *qanat* irrigation was of inestimable benefit to the people on the Iranian plateau.

The faith of Zoroaster

Legend relates that the Iranian prophet was born somewhere in eastern Iran. He lived about 1300 BC and could have been a contemporary of Moses. Though he is a dim figure, his message sounded down through the centuries into the Christian era. In the 400 years preceding the Islamic invasions of the 650s Zoroastrianism was the state religion of Iran.

Fig. vi. The god Ahuramazda

Ahuramazda (the Wise Lord), he taught, is the supreme God, the Creator of all. The world is divided by good and by evil (which is associated with the spirit, Ahriman), by Truth and the Lie, and man himself is free to choose his destiny. After death 'at the last turning point of existence' the soul crosses the bridge of separation where the righteous ascend to a solar paradise, to 'the lights without beginning' and the evil go to their doom. Nevertheless the God of Righteousness and Truth is supreme and his will must ultimately prevail.

Truth itself is symbolised by fire and the sacred flame burns eternally in the temple. All the elements: earth, air, water, and fire, must be kept pure. In later times to prevent defilement of the earth, the dead were carried up to 'towers of silence' where their flesh was consumed by vultures.[7]

The principal scriptures of the prophet were memorised by his followers and it was not until the fifth century AD, or thereabouts, that they were incorporated in the Avesta, an amalgam of writings by different authors. Prayers, liturgies, rituals, purifications and spells proliferate but parts of the work are attributed to the prophet himself. As for instance when he recalls a vision which transported him back to the creation:

> Then, Mazdah, did I realize that thou wast holy when I saw thee in the beginning, at the birth of existence, when thou didst ordain a [just] requital for deeds and words, an evil lot for evil [done] and a good one for a good [deed]: by thy virtue [shall all this come to pass] at the last turning-point of creation.
>
> R C Zaehner, *The Dawn and Twilight of Zoroastrianism*, London, 1961, p. 44

He saw himself as 'God's friend' and recounts his communings with the Creator with an endearing familiarity:

> . . . tell me truly, Ahura:
> How should prayer be made to one like you?
> As to a friend, Mazdah, teach thou me.
>
> Olmstead, *op. cit.*, p. 99

While at other times his supplications have a psalm-like quality:

This do I ask Thee, Oh Lord, tell me truly;
Who is the creator, the first father of Righteousness?
Who laid down the path of the sun and stars?
Who is it through whom the moon now waxes now wanes?
All this and more do I wish to know, Oh Wise One.

This do I ask thee, Oh Lord, tell me truly;
Who holds the earth below and the sky as well
from falling? Who [created] the waters and the plants?
Who harnesses the [two] coursers to wind and clouds?
Who, oh Wise One, is the creator of Good Mind?

Frye, *op. cit.*, p. 35: Yasna 43.5; 44.1, 3-4.

Hitherto the people of the plateau had followed their own ethnic faiths. Mithra, the sun god, and Anahita, goddess of fertility, were among the deities they worshipped. Given that the concept of a supreme being who watched over all mankind was a difficult one for the common folk to grasp, it is not surprising that Zoroaster complained 'Nor are the peasants to me pleasing' and that he turned to the upper echelons of society, to the tribal chiefs and kings of his time, in search of converts.

Centuries passed and the tide began to turn when the Magi,[8] an ancient priestly cast of Median origin, adroitly merged the new faith with their cult of the old gods. They accepted the omnipotence of Ahuramazda and incorporated him along with Mithra and Anahita into their pantheon. Among the Achaemenids it is not certain that Cyrus was a believer. Darius certainly was and so were his successors, though they sometimes deferred to the pagan divinities in their inscriptions. By their time the prophet's message had travelled beyond the plateau, it had reached the borders of India and was known to the Jewish exiles in Babylon as well as their kinsmen in Judah.

The paganisms practised in Pharaonic Egypt, in Ancient Greece and Rome and by the Bel worshippers among the Jews were all destined sooner or later to fade into the limbo of mythology. But of Zoroaster it has been said that he 'crossed at one step a decisive stage in the history of human thought' and there are still houses in south Persia today where youths don the mystic girdle and repeat after their elders the ethic first enjoined over 3,000 years ago:

> *Humata, Hukhta, Hvarshta*—Good thoughts, Good words, Good deeds.
>
> Sykes, *op.cit.*, I, p. 114

Ceremonial and the royal household

Darius and his son Xerxes were the main Achaemenid builders. Susa, the ancient capital of Elam, became under Darius the administrative capital and there his operations began:

> This is the . . . palace which at Susa I built. From afar its ornamentation was brought . . .
>
> Olmstead, *op. cit.*, p. 168

Cedar from Lebanon, marble from Caria, yaka timber from India, ivory from Ethiopia, and so on. Then in his native Persia not far from Pasargadae he and his immediate successors built that most famous of Achaemenid monuments. On an immense 32 acre stone platform, large enough to accommodate a dozen football pitches, a series of audience chambers, columned halls and palaces were linked by gateways, squares, stairways and terraces.

This was Persepolis but what was its purpose? The magnificence of the vast complex and the splendour of the ceremonial portrayed in the sculptures suggest that it was designed to venerate the king and to promote the image of God's representative on earth. Persepolis was:

> the ritual and dynastic centre of the empire where, enthroned in state, the king presided over the parades of dignitaries rendering honour, the army pledging service, and the subjects offering homage.
>
> R W Ferrier, 'Persepolis', *JRSAA*, February 1972, p. 23.

On the great day of the New Year Festival (possibly at the vernal equinox), we may conjecture, the dignitaries climbed the stairs to the platform, the more eminent—the Seven Princes—passed through the Gate of All Lands on horseback. Susians, Persians and Medes stood guard as they filed across the square and ascended the

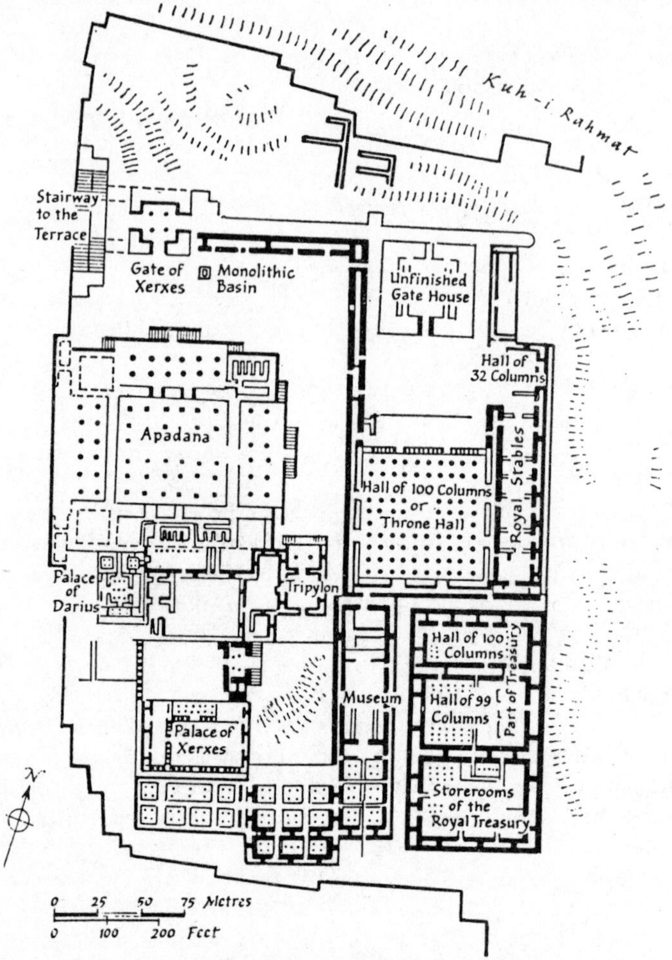

Fig. vii. Plan of Persepolis (University of Chicago Press)

double stairways leading to the Great Audience Hall (Apadana). There they were received in audience and there from a portico the king watched the March of Nations, slow processions of delegations paying homage and bearing gifts: horses from the Saka, a lioness and her cubs from Elam, gold from India, camels from Bactria—the line was endless. Later, after a banquet for 15,000 guests the king would be carried into the hundred-columned throne hall, where the 10,000 Immortals would pass in review before him.

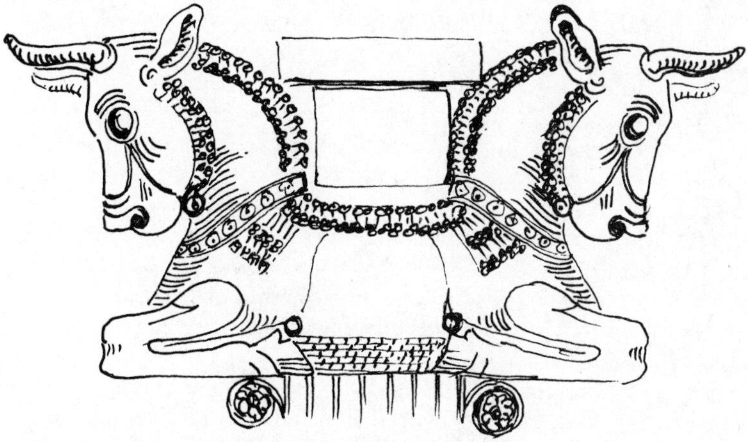

Fig. viii. Detail of a capital at Persepolis

The king commuted between three palaces. After wintering in Susa, the court might move to Persepolis in March for the New Year celebrations and spend the summer in the mountains at Ecbatana. Though the road was apparently partly paved between Susa and Persepolis and Susa and Ecbatana, it is unlikely that all three sites were visited annually or that the New Year celebrations when held were always on the grand scale. Add to the king's own household the members of the court, the Immortals, servants, the camp followers and the baggage trains and each journey can be seen as a major undertaking. Whether they were at peace or war the Achaemenids never travelled light.

The last of the New Year processions has long since moved on but they still pass symbolically along the walls of the audience halls and up the stairways, a 2,500 year old testimony to the might of the Achaemenid dynasty.

How did the king himself live? From Darius onwards the pattern is established. In the Persepolis reliefs he is seen giving audience to the commander of the royal bodyguard with whom the business of the day is being conducted. Two soldiers attend the officer as he bows on arrival in *proskynesis*, a form of homage made by kissing the finger tips. Behind the king's throne stands the crown prince, Xerxes, who shares the royal platform, and behind him is a eunuch, an officer and two Immortals. In one doorway Darius walks with two attendants: one holds a parasol over his head, the other carries a fly whisk and a towel and in another the king is seen in his paradise or hunting park stabbing a wild beast. In Xerxes' palace the areas set aside for more intimate pleasures are indicated by the columned hall of the harem and the doorway reliefs of youths with censer, pail, napkin and perfume bottle. When the king walks (which is seldom) the throne and the protecting parasol accompany him and a purple carpet, on which only the royal feet may tread, is spread before.

He usually dines alone, his concubines providing music and song. At state banquets he watches his guests unseen from behind a curtain. Ahuramazda's vice-regent on earth must be remote and unapproachable but a favoured few may be called in for a cup of wine in his presence afterwards.

The royal princes in their first five years were seen only by their mother 'to spare the father distress if the child should die in the early stages of its upbringing.' According to Herodotus (I, 136), once free of the harem the boys were taught to ride, to shoot and to speak the truth.

The king was restricted in his choice of wives to the families of the Seven Princes, which included his own family (Cambyses married his two sisters). Among the queens, the mother of the crown prince usually wielded some influence (not always to the good) so did the queen mother, as Parysatis, a malevolent woman who lived later in the dynasty conspicuously demonstrated. But the king was not restricted in the number of his concubines. Darius and some of his successors are said to have had 360—one for each night of the year. Incarcerated in the harem they lived in permanent seclusion. According to one source just 300 of them had to be available to assist the king through the night hours with song and music. Evidently they worked on a rota system. Noble women did not appear in public nor do they feature in the sculptures and when the court was on the move, they travelled in closed carriages.

Some of the palace eunuchs, as well as serving in the harem, played a part in state affairs and were sent on diplomatic missions. As their power increased so did their capacity to do harm. It was a eunuch who connived at the murder of Xerxes and his assassination was only a foretaste of what was to come later on. Gibbon described them as 'that pernicious vermin of the east.'

The King's Armies

The expansionist policies of the Achaemenids called for enormous armies. Every able-bodied man was liable for military service and when Xerxes set off on his Greek expedition: 'there was not a nation in all Asia that he did not take with him' (Herodotus, VII, 22).

They were a heterogeneous assortment. Herodotus describes the forty-six contingents. Most of the infantry, which included Medes, Persians, Hyrcanians and Bactrians, were equipped with spears, bows and arrows; the Indians' arrows were iron tipped, those of the Ethiopians were stone headed. The Scythians carried daggers and battle axes, the Colchians short spears and swords, the Thracians were armed with javelins and daggers. The Indian soldiers were clad only in cotton; the Thracians had fox-skin headdresses. The cavalry generally were armed like the infantry but the Sagartians from the Gulf coast carried leather lassos. The Arabs were mounted on riding camels. Soldiers who travelled with the fleet wielded boarding spears, heavy axes and riphooks.

On the march the king rode in the centre. Immediately in front eight Nisaean horses drew the sacred chariot of Ahuramazda, its charioteer walking behind held the reins 'for no mortal man may mount into that chariot's seat' (Herodotus, VII, 40). The royal bodyguard, the Ten Thousand Immortals from Fars, marched before and behind. Their numbers were constant for if one fell he was instantly replaced. They mounted the silver pomegranate on their spears, save the élite Thousand whose pomegranates were in gold. Back at Persepolis they still stand in petrified rank immutable, impassive but watchful, guarding the passages and stairways to the royal presence.

The Tide Turns

Cyrus and Darius formed the head and shoulders of the dynastic lion and Xerxes the body. It survived another thirteen decades of lesser kings to die after a final flick of the tail. The inadequacies of the Achaemenids themselves, their failure to maintain the administration and to keep the imperial armies up to strength led to a loosening of control at the centre and the downfall of the Persian empire.

But for the first forty years after Xerxes' death his son, Artaxerxes I, held the throne (465-424). He was the exception. Unlike his successors he was a peace-loving man, who endeavoured through a long reign to maintain the status quo. But he had to contend with a revolt in Egypt in 459 which was supported by Athens, then at her Periclean zenith and the pinnacle of her maritime power. She sent a fleet to aid the Egyptians. Hostilities dragged on for six years until the Persians succeeded in marooning the Greek ships in the Nile delta by draining their anchorages. Most of the crews surrendered and the revolt died out.

Under Artaxerxes the war begun by Xerxes was brought to an end. After the battle of Eurymedon the Peace of Callias was negotiated (see p. 42) and the king conceded that the Ionian cities should be granted autonomy.

During the turning of the tide revolts in Egypt broke out with monotonous regularity and in Asia Minor repercussions from the war with Greece were overtaken by new developments, among them a Spartan invasion. On the diplomatic front Persia became enmeshed in a complicated web of relationships with Athens and Sparta as the Asia Minor satraps, who were skilled in the arts of political manoeuvre, negotiated first with one side then with the other on the king's behalf.

At the centre palace revolutions, in which women members of the royal family and eunuchs played a part, were sure signs of a deteriorating dynasty. All but two of the last seven kings died a violent death and only three held on to their thrones for more than a decade: Darius II presided over a court that was beset with intrigue, Artaxerxes II, the best of the three, was weak and easily led and Artaxerxes III, though he arrested the decline, was devious, debased and cruel.

Artaxerxes I's death in 424 was followed by the year of the four emperors. Two of his sons were crowned in turn before a third climbed to power over their dead bodies. Darius II was ably complemented by his wife and half-sister, the infamous Parysatis, who played the part of consort to her husband's Macbeth. Their complicity in the dark deeds that brought them the throne set the tone for a reign which was as notable for some underhand dealings in the conduct of foreign affairs as it was for dissimulation and corruption at home. There were risings in Media, in Sardes and (as always) in Egypt and many dissidents who were pardoned found themselves consigned to an agonizing death in the ashes. Among them was Pissouthenes, satrap of the province of Sardes. When he fell out with the king, though assured that his life would be spared, he was escorted to Susa and thrown into the embers.

When Athens and Sparta became locked in the long drawn-out Peloponnesian War (it lasted on and off from 432 to 404) a skilfully conducted series of negotiations enabled the king to prolong hostilities by a judicious distribution of gold first to Athens then to Sparta. Eventually, after some twenty years, his master of intrigue, the formidable Tissaphernes, satrap of Sardes, acting as go-between assisted the outcome by paymastering the Spartan fleet to victory.

If few are acquainted with King Artaxerxes II (405-359), many schoolboys will have heard of his younger brother, Cyrus, whose death led to the expedition of Xenophon. Among the nefarious aims harboured by Parysatis was her desire to see her second son inherit the throne. Cyrus was a personable ambitious man, who might have made a better ruler. His attempt to assassinate his brother at the time of his coronation failed but his scheming mother persuaded the king to restore Cyrus to his post of commander of the forces in Asia Minor. Here he was well placed to raise a private army and by 401 he had mustered some 13,000 mercenaries, most of them Greek. They marched unchallenged across the sub-continent and down the banks of the Euphrates before they encountered Artaxerxes' army at Cunaxa. In the battle that followed Cyrus sighted the royal standard and rode towards it. He wounded his brother but was himself struck down and killed.

All at once the battle ceased to have any meaning, the fighting petered out and the expedition found itself leaderless, lost and stranded in a hostile country two thousand miles from home. The story of the return of the Ten Thousand is told by Xenophon in his *Anabasis*. Harried by the Persians, they followed the river upstream into the highlands, where they suffered attacks from hostile tribesmen and endured the rigours of an Armenian winter. Some five months later, as they climbed to the head of a pass, cries were heard coming from the front of the column:

> Xenophon mounted his horse and, taking . . . the cavalry with him, rode forward . . . they heard the soldiers shouting out "The sea! The sea!" and passing the word down the column . . . they all began to run . . . and when they had all got to the top, the soldiers, with tears in their eyes, embraced each other.
>
> Xenophon, *The Persian Expedition*,
> tr. Rex Warner, Harmondsworth, 1949, p. 211

Nine days later they reached the safety of the Greek port of Trebizond.

So Artaxerxes II kept his throne but under his rule the Achaemenid dynasty reached its lowest ebb. On the periphery, at the outset of his reign, Egypt had revolted and won her independence. Nearer home, as we have seen, an invading army of Greek mercenaries had been allowed to escape. At the centre the queen mother, only temporarily disgraced for her treason, was soon back in the palace at Susa and taking revenge: those who had wounded or killed her son were sent to their deaths but Parysatis could not at this stage touch her arch-enemy, Tissaphernes. The king was indebted to him for warnings about Cyrus and for keeping him on his throne.

Artaxerxes became increasingly dependent on his mother for advice on the conduct of affairs. Within the palace she appeared to reign supreme. The gossip of the harem, the increasing numbers of concubines, the scores of sons and daughters—all were potential sources of conspiracy. But Parysatis, aided by her eunuch informers, did not scruple to kill off the miscreants.[9] Inevitably the weakening power of the king, the suspicion, intrigue and fear that issued from the royal apartments, lurked along the corridors and clung round the columns of the audience halls, filtered through to the satraps and the wider world beyond.

The Spartans, victors of the Peloponnesian war, were well aware of the situation at the centre and in 396 their king, Agesilaus, invaded Asia Minor. Neither the army of Tissaphernes nor those of the neighbouring satraps succeeded in ejecting him and it was Athens (in return for a gift from Persian coffers) that stirred up trouble for him at home and brought about his recall. 'The king', Agesilaus commented rather bitterly in reference to the bowmen stamped on the gold coins, 'was driving him out of Asia with ten thousand archers.'[10] No doubt Parysatis played a part in the plot by which Tissaphernes was seized and executed for his failure.

The complicated interplay of relations between Sparta, Athens and Persia continued but for Artaxerxes there was one positive achievement. With the Spartans safely out of Asia Minor, the Athenians compromised and both parties too exhausted to join in another war, he was able to reassert his authority over the Ionians and annul the Peace of Callias. Their ties with the mother country were in any case becoming more tenuous and they must have recognized that their prosperity would be more assured and their political future better safeguarded if they conformed to geographical realities. In the final outcome Artaxerxes II succeeded where Xerxes had failed. Athens and Sparta finally renounced their claim to the city states and the 'King's Peace', as the Peace of Antalcidas was called, endured.

The agreement was only a temporary halt in the downward turn of the empire's internal affairs. General lawlessness, peasant revolts against oppressive taxation, plots among the satraps themselves and abortive attempts to reconquer Egypt had played their part. Humiliation and grief further darkened the king's declining years. Discontent among the satraps in the west caused them to unite against him. The revolt came to nothing but within the palace walls treachery reared its head more blatantly when Parysatis poisoned the queen and one by one the royal princes died or disappeared until only Ochus remained.

As Artaxerxes III he reigned for twenty-one years (c. 359-338). He has been variously described as savage, unscrupulous and bloodthirsty. Eunuchs and others, who had assisted his passage to the throne, continued their work until the family slate was wiped clean. The surviving sons of some 360 concubines and perhaps some of the women were killed.

Artaxerxes determined to restore the central control, to bring the satraps to heel and to reconquer Egypt. He gathered together a huge army. The first attack on Egypt failed but in 343 his forces under the command of Bagoas, the chief eunuch, regained the Lower Nile. This show of strength had its effect on the western satraps who hastily reaffirmed their allegiance.

On the face of it then, the old order had been restored. But in reality the patchwork quilt of the satrapies had only been lightly cobbled together. Darius' carefully organized administration, which was the basis of unity, had disappeared. Achaemenid rule had nearly run its course and the days of the empire were numbered.

Nor was it only in the orient that the pattern of power was changing. The city states of the Greek mainland, whose rivalries Persia had so successfully exploited, were yielding pride of place to the rising star of Macedonia in the north. But Artaxerxes did not live to face the armies of Alexander. He and his sons were murdered—poisoned by Bagoas. Being a eunuch he could not win the throne but he had a taste for king-making. One son of Artaxerxes, Arses, was spared to take the crown but when he showed signs of independence he too was despatched. As no immediate member of the royal family was left alive, Bagoas next selected a cousin. Darius Codomannus was the last of the Achaemenid kings. He ensured his own survival by forcing Bagoas to drink his own draught. But he too was destined to suffer a violent and humiliating death. Darius III was one who deserved a better fate.

Under the umbrella of Achaemenid rule most of the peoples in the Persian Empire enjoyed two centuries of freedom from invasion. Cyrus had secured the north-east frontier and the communities in that most vulnerable region experienced what proved to be an unprecedentedly long era of peace. Though continuing friction overlaid the more prosperous outlying regions of Egypt and Asia Minor, trading activities in all probability were hardly impaired. The peasantry there, as elsewhere, laboured on and rose against their overlords only when exploitation neared the limits of human tolerance. In the more arid areas—on the plateau and in the eastern marches—they may even have received government assistance, as Darius I is thought to have sanctioned grants for irrigation schemes.

The culture of the Iranians was rooted in soil which had been fertilised in previous millennia by the ancient civilizations of the Middle East, when they had roamed the grasslands of central Asia. Architecture became the supreme outward expression of their culture and the Egyptians and Babylonians were among the artists and craftsmen who contributed in some measure to it. A new Achaemenid style—eloquent in both scale and design—had been devised that symbolised the power and grandeur of the imperial monarchy. The adoption of Aramaic speech and writing helped to oil the wheels of the administration and to facilitate trade, but there were as yet no noteworthy Iranian contributions to literature or science.

Despite the shortcomings of the later kings, the Persians were respected, even by the Greeks, for their code of honour. Darius as a Zoroastrian associated his belief with abhorrence of the lie. But he did not seek to impose his faith on others, nor did Cyrus attempt to oppose the customs or beliefs of the peoples he conquered. The greatest of the Great Kings, as well as wielding the most power, were the most humane and the most tolerant.

Notes

1 The name given by the Emperor Trajan to Assyria and Babylonia, meaning the land 'between the rivers'.

2 Bacchylides was born about 510, 35 years or so after the event. Herodotus, who was born some 30 years later, makes Cyrus condemn Croesus to death. This is unlikely: the near contemporary red amphora in the Louvre shows Croesus himself giving the order to light the pyre; also if, as is quite likely, Cyrus was a Zoroastrian, he would not have allowed the air to be polluted by a human sacrifice (see p. 45).

3 Traces of this last lap have been found but here as elsewhere the exact route is uncertain.

4 Some scholars consider that the Parthenon frieze in the British Museum represents a procession of the heroes of the battle.

5 When you go home,
Tell them of us, and say,
For your tomorrow
We gave our today.
(epitaph to Leonidas. tr. by the late J. M. Edmonds,
The Times, May 1976)

6 Herodotus, *The Histories*, tr. A de Sélincourt, Harmondsworth, 1954, VII, 227.

7 This custom is continued by the Parsees in India today; they are descended from Zoroastrians who fled the Islamic persecutions in 916.

8 Their descendants featured in the story of the Christian Epiphany.

9 Punishments for palace intrigues under Darius II and Artaxerxes II seem to have been particularly unpleasant: one woman was hacked to death, others were buried alive.

10 Plutarch, *Lives*, tr. B Perrin, London, 1917, xv.

CHAPTER 3

Greek Dominion 330 BC-250 BC

THE RISE OF MACEDONIA

The 4th century BC witnessed a radical change in the balance of power in the Balkan peninsula, when Athens and other city-states came under the hegemony of Macedonia. This rough mountain country in the north was ruled by Philip II. As a youth in Thebes he had been schooled in the profession of arms and he had disciplined his tribesmen into an efficient fighting force. The skills he exercised in the field were matched by an adroitness in diplomacy, so much so that within twenty years he brought the greater part of Greece under his leadership.

When Philip fell victim to an assassin in 336 the city-states attempted to break away. But his son, Alexander, managed to assert his authority. Order was restored and the states were formed into a Hellenic League. At a peace conference in Corinth he was elected to lead an expedition against Persia.

Across the Hellespont and 2,000 miles to the east the centralised rule of the early Achaemenids had bequeathed the notion of national identity, which nomad hordes from central Asia ravaging with fire and sword over the coming centuries would never fully dispel. But the fire now flaming in the western skies was of a different colour. The European conqueror evolved a vision of international unity. He sought not to subjugate, but to create a partnership between east and west, a world state under his own rule. Such was the concept of Alexander of Macedon.

The invasion had been projected several times since Xerxes' armies had swept down the eastern seaboard and destroyed the city of Athens. But 150 years had passed since the last Persian had left Greek soil. What was Alexander's purpose in eliciting the confederacy's support for such a venture? Was it retribution? Was it liberation of the Ionians? Was it the declared mission of the house of Macedon? Or were these window dressings to screen a lust for conquest, the pursuit of power, the challenge of the unknown?

Certainly he was carrying out his father's wishes in setting out to destroy the Achaemenids. But Alexander was also an idealist, a romantic, steeped in the writings of Homer, who longed for glory. Demosthenes, the Athenian orator, had denounced him as 'a mere boy', when at the age of twenty he had inherited Philip's crown. Yet within two years he had brought the city-states to heel and shown himself a worthy successor. Eleven years remained for him to display his military genius, to formulate his unique vision of political unity between east and west and to leave the firm imprint of Greek civilization on western Asia.

ALEXANDER THE GREAT AND HIS HEIRS IN WESTERN ASIA

The march begins

Alexander crossed the Hellespont, as Xerxes had done, between Sestos and Abydos, in the spring of 334. The army, something under 40,000 strong—perhaps a third of it Macedonian—was ferried by the fleet. There was no sign of the enemy. He was the first to leap ashore and he crossed the plain of Troy to pay homage at the tomb of his supposed ancestor, Achilles, slayer of Hector and the bravest of all Greeks. Then, assuming his hero's mantle, the young Achilles rejoined his men and marched inland.

Fifty miles on they were confronted by the forces of the western satraps, who had taken up their stand across the river Granicus. In numbers they were fairly evenly matched. Parmenio, the cautious second in command, who counselled waiting till morning before attempting a crossing was rebuffed by his chief: 'I should be ashamed, having crossed the Hellespont, to be detained by a miserable stream like the Granicus.'[1] Alexander had already sized up the situation. It was nevertheless a close fight in which he nearly lost his life but the enemy fled from the field and the army marched on Sardes whose gates were opened to them.

In the Ionian city-states of the south, significantly, the 'liberators' were not always welcomed. Miletus resisted and so did the heavily defended port of Halicarnassus, Darius' western headquarters, to which Memnon, a Greek-born commander in the king's service, retired. He defied siege towers, battering rams and catapults. And when he was finally forced to withdraw to the inner redoubt he fired the city.

Meanwhile Alexander was having difficulty maintaining the fleet. He could not finance it from his own resources and Athens (now that he was out of the way) was proffering only token assistance. He decided to disband it, to risk his Hellespont lifeline and to blockade the enemy fleet from land by capturing the bases along the south littoral and the Phoenician coast.

It was already autumn. The main army under Parmenio returned to Sardes to take the royal road through the central plateau, trundling the heavy siege equipment with it, while Alexander led a light force eastwards through Lycia to block the enemy anchorages. This done he turned inland to await Parmenio and reinforcements from home.

This rendezvous was at Gordion in Phrygia. Here according to legend the man who could untie the knot of bark attached to the wagon of the ancient King Gordius would become lord of Asia. To Alexander the theatrical appeal of the challenge was irresistible but try as he might he could not unravel it with his hands and, as he had an audience, he could not be seen to fail, so he cut the Gordion knot with his sword.

With his forces augmented he marched on into Cappadocia and returned to the coast down through the Cilician Gates to Tarsus. Having broken through the satrapal barrier in the west he had ranged almost at will over Asia Minor as Xenophon and Agesilaus had done before him. He had yet to meet the armies of the Great King.

At the onset of the invasion Darius had given orders that Alexander was to be captured and taken to Sardes. Neither he (nor his commanders) had studied the tactics of the enemy. Putting his faith in numbers, in his own generalship and his scythed chariots (a new weapon), he had rounded up an enormous heterogeneous force as Xerxes had done to support the professionals (the Immortals), the cavalry and a contingent of Greek mercenaries. They made their processional way north with the royal family along with the other non-combatants, the furniture and fittings of the mobile palace, the sacred chariot of Ahuramazda, and waited on events.

Alexander relied on a smaller co-ordinated army: the cavalry who attacked on the wings, the heavily armoured hoplites or the phalanx, who moved in close formation with shields linked, the light infantry and the missile shooters. The cavalry and some of the infantry wielded the *sarissa*, an eighteen-foot pike; others carried spears.

The first major battle took place near Issus in the armpit of Asia. Darius, who had selected the site, directed operations from his chariot in the centre. In the heat of the engagement he panicked; he turned and galloped from the field and, as news of his flight spread through to the wings, his men scattered.

Alexander did not give chase. He supped that night at the king's table. Next morning, with his close friend, Hephaestion, he visited the royal family and promised them protection. Darius, once he had reached safety beyond the Euphrates, wrote to Alexander and offered him an alliance if he would return his wife and children. He was firmly rebuked:

> I am Lord of all Asia, and therefore you should come to me ... to ... receive your mother and wife and children ... And for the future, whenever you send, send to me as the Great King of Asia, and do not write as to an equal ... But if you dispute the kingdom, then wait and fight for it again and do not flee; for I shall march against you wherever you may be.
>
> Bury and Meiggs, *loc. cit.*.

The march continued down the coast. Tyre resisted in a seven-month siege. Gaza too held out but, by the winter of 332, Alexander was sailing up the Nile to be received by an obsequious Persian satrap at Memphis. Freed at last from Persian domination, the Egyptian people welcomed the new king who paid homage to their deities and venerated the Apis bull.

The Egyptians believed that the Pharaohs were sons of the ram-headed Ammon. As king of the gods he was identified by the Greeks with Zeus. Alexander, anxious to establish his own divinity and hoping perhaps for confirmation that he was the son of Ammon, visited the god's sanctuary. With a few followers he made the hazardous journey into the western desert to Siwa, 'the Egyptian Delphi' and, as he enigmatically related later 'he heard what pleased him.'

Of all the cities Alexander founded none was a more inspired choice than the port which carries his name. Situated to the west of the Nile delta, Alexandria was designed to serve both as a naval base (in place of Tyre and Sidon) and as a port from which grain could be shipped to Greece. Leaving a strong Hellenic-Egyptian administration behind him, he retraced his steps to Tyre and crossed the Syrian desert to the Euphrates. When in 331 Darius' next offer—a share of his kingdom, his daughter in marriage and a huge ransom—was rejected, he mustered his armies again and took his stand on the plain of Gaugamela to the north of Arbela (modern Erbil). Again Darius was defeated, again he escaped. But this time his armies were routed beyond recall, there could be no retaliation. Darius had become a fugitive in his own country.

For Alexander now the way to the Persian homeland lay open. His aim was to receive the submission of the royal cities and to establish himself as king.

Babylon welcomed him as it had welcomed Cyrus 200 years before. Susa too surrendered. In the palace there, as he ascended the gold throne of the Achaemenids, the Greeks wept for joy, a Persian eunuch cried. The palace coffers yielded bullion—enough to finance a lifetime of campaigns—while among the art treasures the most exciting discovery was the statuary taken by Xerxes of the lovers Harmodius and Aristogeiton, slayers of Hipparchus, which Alexander returned to Athens.

Turning east along the royal road to Persepolis the columns were attacked by hill tribes from the Zagros in the region of the Persian Gates. But once they descended into the plain beyond there was no resistance. Persepolis 'the richest of all cities under the sun' lay open to them.

Historians speculate on the burning of Persepolis. Was it retribution for the firing of the Acropolis? Was it intended to symbolise the destruction of Achaemenid Persia? Was it the planned finale to all-night revels? None of these reasons was in keeping with Alexander's character nor was it likely that a man said to have built more towns than any other would subscribe to such vandalism. Suffice it to say that the beam supports and roof timbers above, the panellings and carvings within—all would have been tinder dry on that sunbaked plain and, once the guards had fled, they only wanted a spark to set the terrace ablaze.

Alexander stayed four months (the site was fired just before he left). Then, turning his back on the devastation he marched north into Media in search of Darius. At Ecbatana he turned east along the Khurasan highway. Hearing that his quarry had been taken prisoner by Bessus, satrap of Bactria, he hurried on by forced marches with a few men. He found Darius abandoned in a wagon but by the time he reached him he was dead. Saddened suddenly at the sight before him Alexander took off his cloak and spread it over the body.

Deserted at his utmost Need
By those his former Bounty fed:
On the bare Earth expos'd He lyes
With not a Friend to close his Eyes.
John Dryden, *Alexander's Feast*

And so it was that somewhere between the Alburz mountains and the desert that in 330 two centuries of Achaemenid rule came to an end and Darius Codomannus paid the account of his predecessors.

The Vision of Unity—the Furthest Shore

The main task was done, the Achaemenid house destroyed, the important western homeland conquered. Alexander had set up a military and civil administration. He could return home with honour.

But Alexander had no intention of turning back. For him the expedition would continue but with an added dimension. His purpose now (if not before) was to bring all Asia into one kingdom. He would travel to its furthest shore and combine conquest with exploration.

... we shall go
Always a little further: it may be
Beyond that last blue mountain barred with snow
Across that angry or that glimmering sea'
J E Flecker, *The Golden Journey to Samarkand*

And such was the magnetism of his personality and the loyalty he commanded that his men followed.

For three years he campaigned in the river valleys and mountain fastnesses of Areia, Drangiana and Arachosia (Afghanistan) wintering first at Herat, then at Qandahar,[2] where he founded Alexandrias and settled the wounded. In the north he crossed the sterile plains of Bactria to Sogdiana (Bukhara) where Bessus, who had assumed the title of King, was tracked down and killed. Near Alexandria-the-Ultimate (later Khojend, then Leninabad) along the river Jaxartes he attacked the Scythian and the Massagetae nomads and sent them fleeing for the steppes. Maracanda (Samarqand) was a city of unhappy memory for Alexander, not for the fighting, which was troublesome but for the feast at the festival of Dionysus.

He quarrelled with his friend, Cleitus, and in his cups he slew him—an act which brought on an agony of remorse for Cleitus had saved his life at Granicus.

Ever since Gaugamela those about Alexander had noticed a change in his demeanour. In battle he fought as always alongside his men with a courage that amounted to recklessness. But as lord of Asia he had exchanged the homely cloak of the king of Macedonia for the sumptuous robes and lofty manner of the oriental despot. Those who came before him—Macedonians included—were expected to bow in *proskynesis*.[3]

> Assumes the God,
> Affects to Nod,
> And seems to shake the Spheres.
>
> John Dryden, *Alexander's Feast*

Whether Alexander really believed that he was the son of Ammon-Zeus is doubtful. But the ceremonial would have impressed those amongst his followers who did. Less understandable to the common soldiery was his attitude towards the 'barbarians'. The brother of Darius and other Asiatics mingled now with the court that circled his tent and, moreover, he had married the daughter of a rebel Bactrian chief, Roxane. Seven years of campaigning had left their mark. He indulged in increasing bouts of drunkenness, his wounds pained him and he was prone to emotional and violent outbursts (as with Cleitus).

The further Alexander penetrated into Asia the more firmly he believed it was his mission to unite east and west until he came to see himself as the Great King presiding over an empire in which all its people would live in harmony:

> I came into Asia, not in order to overthrow nations and make a desert of a half part of the world, but in order that those whom I had subdued in war might not regret my victory.
>
> Quintus Curtius, *History of Alexander the Great of Macedon*, tr. R C Rolfe, London, 1946, VIII, viii, 10

And, when resentment surfaced some three years later, he told his men:

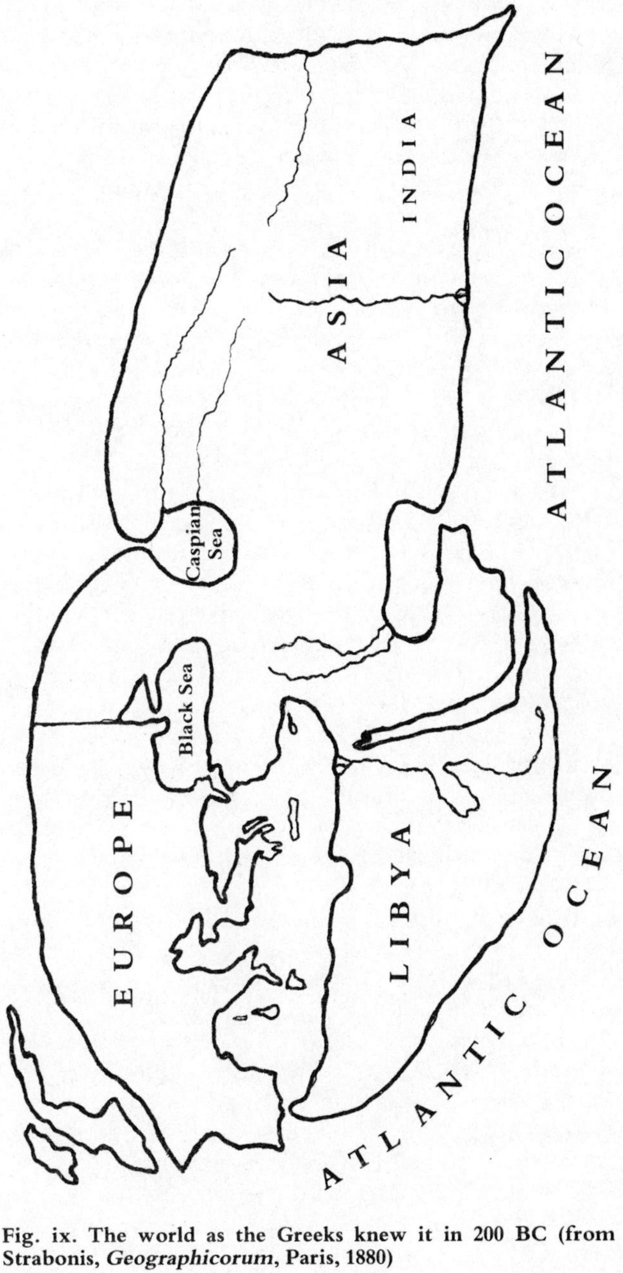

Fig. ix. The world as the Greeks knew it in 200 BC (from Strabonis, *Geographicorum*, Paris, 1880)

> Asia and Europe now belong to one and the same kingdom ... It is neither unbecoming for the Persians to simulate the manners of the Macedonians, nor for the Macedonians to copy those of the Persians. Those ought to have the same rights who are to live under the same sovereign.
>
> Quintus Curtius, *op. cit.*, X, iii, 13, 14.

The Greeks believed that the world was rimmed by sea, that the Caspian Sea reached round a Scythian shore into the southern ocean, that the world's end lay along an Indian strand bounded by an eternity of water (they knew nothing of China where the Great Wall would soon be built). To stand on that distant shore, to watch the waters of the limitless ocean, to view the last horizon of his realm—this now was Alexander's quest.

And despite mumbling disaffections the men followed. They crossed the Hindu Kush. There was fierce fighting in the foothills and drenching monsoon on the plains; they crossed the Indus, then another river and another of its swollen satellites. At the fourth river, exhausted by the elements, bedraggled and weary of battle, their capacity to follow finally deserted them. In eight years they had come 12,000 miles, many of their comrades had died or been wounded and left along the route; they wanted to return to their homeland. Darkening discontent and mutinous mutterings were finally articulated into an adamant refusal to go further.

Alexander was furious; he withdrew to his tent and brooded. Were they not near their journey's end? One more desert? One more major river, the Ganges? But all ranks had spoken as with one voice; there were no ring-leaders he could pick off. He had finally been defeated by his own men.

After two days Alexander emerged from his meditations and capitulated. And, having made his decision, with true generosity of spirit, he showed no rancour. The expedition turned its back on the east and followed the course of the Jhelum River. Along its banks the city of Sangala put up a strong defence. And it was there, as he rashly threw himself into the fray, that Alexander suffered his most serious injury. As he lay in a barge wounded in the chest and near to death the men, now in an agony of apprehension for their king, formed a shield along the shores till his vessel reached camp. There he rested till he had regained strength and the journey to the coast could be resumed. And with the help of river transports they eventually reached the Indus delta without meeting serious opposition.

The armies split for the long trek back to Susa. Craterus was to cross central Persia, Alexander—nearly recovered—would follow the coastline through Gedrosia (Baluchistan) and Nearchus, who was building a fleet, would take the heavy siege equipment across the uncharted Indian Ocean.

The Makran desert, the great divide between India and Persia, with its rocky wastes, its soft sand and searing daytime heat, inflicted more casualties on Alexander's army than any battle as he and his men floundered night by night through the dunes in search of the next waterhole. He took the bulk of the army with him but over half died in the dunes.

Months later the three arms were reunited when, having weathered a monsoon and negotiated the straits of Hormuz, Nearchus sailed up the Gulf and on to rejoin Craterus and the survivors of Makran at Susa.

In the final stages of his journey Alexander received reports on the state of the empire. Few of the satraps had expected him to return and the punishments inflicted on those found to be guilty of disloyalty or misconduct were harsh; a number were executed.

In the eighteen months of life that remained to him, Alexander worked to achieve racial equality and a united kingdom. He had settled mixed communities in his new towns. Now, in an effort to advance social integration further, he encouraged intermarriage. He took a second wife, Statira, daughter of Darius, so as to 'abolish all distinction between vanquished and victor'. Officers and men who followed suit received generous allowances and on one occasion, when there were 10,000 brides, the wedding celebrations at Susa lasted five days.

Even so in some areas integration was difficult to achieve. In the ranks orientals had been tolerated where they were needed to fill gaps. But Alexander's scheme to replace unfit officers with Asiatic cadets was resisted. The prospect of having Persians in the cavalry or standing with the Macedonians in the king's personal bodyguard aroused intense jealousy and the veterans who in India had pleaded to return home now mutinied over their discharge. But this time Alexander had his way and before the veterans departed there was a reconciliation.

Back in Babylon, his intended capital, though desolated by the death of his beloved Hephaestion, Alexander was planning an expedition round Arabia with Nearchus, when he succumbed to a fever. He died after a few days in the palace of Nebuchadnezzar on 10 June 323.

> He lived ... thirty-two years and eight months ... He had great personal beauty, invincible power of endurance, and a keen intellect; he was brave and adventurous, strict in the observance of his religious duties, and hungry for fame. Most temperate in the pleasures of the body, his passion was for glory only, and in that he was insatiable.
>
> Arrian, *The Campaigns of Alexander*, tr. A de Sélincourt, Harmondsworth, 1958, VII.28.

He was also a military genius. Seen in the wider context of world history, of his many qualities, his concept of fusion between east and west, of an alliance between victor and vanquished sets him apart. He was the pole-star outshining the lesser constellations bound by the narrow confines of city-state or satrapy. But when he died the light faded as quickly as night follows day for the reality of the vision was in the mind of Alexander alone.

The Seleucids

Inherent in man's nature is a desire to equip his progeny for the future so that they may emulate and even enhance his name. And if the man be one of a line of monarchs and the succession in doubt, he should surely name his heir to safeguard his inheritance.

No monarch in antiquity had more to bequeath than Alexander either in wealth or dominion. Yet, though his was a high-risk life and he was nine times wounded, he failed to face the inevitability of death. Asked as he lay dying to whom he bequeathed his kingdom, he is said to have replied, 'to the strongest'. From this and other tales that emerged of his last days only one thing is certain: he named no successor. His greatest failure was one of omission.

The empire soon splintered into anarchy as his generals turned on each other to carve out territories for themselves. While their leader's body was lying in the palace at Babylon they met in council and appointed Perdiccas, to whom Alexander had given his ring, as regent until Roxane's (presumed) son came of age. Ptolemy, whose plans were already laid, adroitly suggested that to protect the new régime they should split up and fan out their armies and he quickly moved on Egypt where he founded a dynasty. Most of the 'Successors' (the *Diadochi*) met violent ends but Ptolemy died in his bed.

The Macedonian rank and file also had a voice. They insisted that the dead king's half-brother should take the throne during the regency. Though a half-wit, Philip Arrhidaeus in their eyes had one overriding claim—he was untainted with oriental blood.

Meanwhile the royal family, like victims of the Borgias, vanished one by one. Roxane lured Statira to Babylon and poisoned her, Alexander's mother killed the defective Philip before she too was despatched. The murders of Roxane and the young Alexander followed.

The generals then were left in charge. Antipater, who at the start of the Persian expedition had been left behind as regent, inherited Macedonia and Greece and Antigonus took most of Asia Minor. Perdiccas was murdered in 321 by his own officers and Seleucus, who had connived at his death, laid claim to the satrapy of Babylonia where in 312, following Macedonian precedent, he set himself up as king.

Seleucus had commanded the Macedonian cavalry and had a good following in the army. He was also the most competent of the *Diadochi*. Nevertheless it took him twenty years (321-301) to win back western Asia and shake off other contenders, great and small. He campaigned over the old ground to the east; in India he traded territory for a supply of war elephants, which in Phrygia ten years later brought him a good return. They played an important part at the battle of Ipsus (301) in which Antigonus was defeated and killed leaving the way open to Syria and Asia Minor. Thus by 280, when Seleucus encountered his assassin, he had recovered most of Alexander's Asian territories and had fully justified the title of Nicator ('Conqueror').

The next four generations of Seleucids engaged in almost incessant warfare with the Ptolemies in Egypt and the *Diadochi* in Asia Minor. Preoccupied with trying to fend off their rivals in the west, they neglected their possessions beyond the Zagros. In Bactria, Seleucus had established some Greek city-states to house colonists but these were small islands in an Iranian sea; the central government maintained little contact with them; it took their loyalty too much for granted and the defection of the satrap Diodotus came as a serious shock. Even more disastrous, though it was not realised at the time, was the incursion of Parthian nomads east of the Caspian, who ultimately brought about the downfall of the Seleucid dynasty.

In 223, when the young Antiochus III ('the Great') gained the throne, the decline in Seleucid fortunes in the east was arrested, though only temporarily. Antiochus made a truce with Egypt, he put down revolts by the satraps in Media and Fars and he led his armies into furthest Iran. Crossing Media and the northern desert he occupied Hecatompylos and drove the Parthians back through the Alburz mountains to the Hyrcanian plain. But they were stubborn fighters and yielded ground so slowly that he was obliged to negotiate terms. Their Arsacid king agreed to acknowledge Seleucid supremacy but he declined to evacuate Hyrcania. The Parthians had come to stay.

In Bactria the Greek population, isolated from their homeland in the west and neglected by their Seleucid rulers, had ousted Diodotus and formed a Greco-Bactrian kingdom under Euthydemus. Antiochus blockaded their capital at Balkh and, after a year-long siege, Euthydemus sued for peace. 'What', he is said to have asked through an envoy who interceded with the king, 'is my offence?' Had he not defeated the rebel satrap? Antiochus conceded the point. Euthydemus was reinstated under his overlordship and a treaty was sealed by a marriage between the two families.

Crossing the Hindu Kush into the Punjab, Antiochus was bought off by the Mauryan emperor with gifts of elephants. In 198, after he had made further conquests in Syria and Asia Minor, he returned home on the flood-tide of success.

The turn into the second century found the balance of world power changing. Rome had entered the arena. Having crippled Carthage in two Punic wars she had won control of the central Mediterranean and forced Hannibal to flee.

If Antiochus had been content to stay his hand at this stage the Roman frontiers might have been contained in Europe. But he embarked on a foolhardy and ill-prepared expedition to Greece in a bid for the Macedonian throne. A Roman army sent to aid Philip V drove him out and defeated him on Asian territory at Magnesia in 189. He was killed two years later in Luristan.

Antiochus had over-reached himself. He had lost Asia Minor and in the process had brought his dynasty to a new and fateful low. He had shut the eastern gates for the time being on the Parthian menace but had opened them up in the west and let the Roman legions through.

Towards Hellenization

Wars were a recurring feature of the Seleucid scene but, while their kings marched and countermarched along the highways to India, Asia Minor, Syria and Egypt, changes more profound than the spectacular overlay of siege and battle were spreading in their wake.

Back in the Greek homeland the population had been expanding and the Hellenes had sought land in the new eastern territories. Some settled in Asia Minor, some round the Fertile Crescent. Others, following the trade routes to India and to China which now appeared on the world map, reached Sogdiana and Bactria, where several thousand of Alexander's veterans had been settled.

Seleucus Nicator built cities to accommodate the colonists. Temples, agoras, theatres, gymnasia and hippodromes, the outward manifestations of Hellenism, as it was later called, spread across Alexander's empire. And, just as the British Raj was to leave its mark on the Indian sub-continent, so the Greeks imprinted some of their art, drama and sport, their law and language, on Persia. The indigenous population generally lived amicably side by side with the settlers: the Greeks in their cities, the Iranians in the towns and villages, with each community respecting the other's religion. Though oriental blood flowed in the veins of the kings (Seleucus had taken a Sogdian wife) intermarriage at this stage was generally confined in Persian circles to the upper classes. It was not until the Parthians came that Hellenization made its mark more widely on society. Nevertheless, however slowly, under the Seleucids Alexander's concept of fusion was beginning to make some progress.

In the west Seleucus abandoned Babylon and the sluggish waters of the Euphrates for a new capital, Seleucia-on-Tigris. Maybe he planned an inland port or perhaps he wished to leave Marduk and his fellow deities to their own devices, for only the priests were allowed to stay in the old city. Later, among the orchards and olive groves of the Orontes valley, he built Antioch. With its elegant monuments, its colonnaded streets, its Daphne pleasure park and its royal library, his last capital came to rival Egypt's Alexandria in beauty, luxury and as a seat of learning.

Following the city-state tradition, the Greek colonists, while continuing to pay tax to the central administration, organized their own local government, as the Ionians had done in Asia Minor. Gifts of land were granted by the king to loyal 'citizen-allies' in return for military service. The country was divided into satrapies, as it had been in the time of the Achaemenids and Alexander. Each satrap had his own militia and he was responsible for the maintenance of law and order within the province.

The peaceful progress of Hellenization was arrested in the west when Antiochus IV Epiphanes, a fundamentalist philhellene, sought to impose religious conformity by invading Jerusalem and setting up an altar to Zeus in the temple. Instead he set the Jews' spiritual world alight. Under Judas Maccabaeus they drove his armies from the holy city and emerged from the conflict with their faith strengthened to await the coming of their saviour. The Hebrews had triumphed for a time but the cultural heritage of the Greeks had come to stay. And it was in the Judaean crucible, where Hebraism blended with Hellenism at the start of a new millennium that the Christian message was delivered.

Meanwhile the last Seleucids were becoming trapped between the pestle and mortar of Parthia and Rome. East of the Zagros their military and political power was on the wane but the cultural influence of Hellas lived on in many of the Greek townships. Alexander and his heirs in western Asia had laid a flight of steps that led from the old world through three centuries of human progress into the coming Christian era.

Notes

1 J B Bury and Russell Meigss, *A History of Greece to the Death of Alexander the Great*, London, 1975, p. 452.

2 The identification of the Alexandria in Arachosia with Qandahar is not fully established but there was a Hellenistic city at Qandahar in the third century BC.

3 See p. 50. Alexander never succeeded in enforcing it on the Greeks and Macedonians and eventually they were not required to conform.

CHAPTER 4

The Roman Challenge 250 BC-224 AD

CONFLICT WITH THE WEST

The Arsacids (the Parthian rulers) have been called the forgotten dynasty for their kings galloped out of the steppes into the western Asia arena only to disappear through their own dust clouds back into the recesses of history. Yet they ruled for nearly 400 years—longer than the Achaemenids and the Seleucids before them, almost as long as the Sasanians who followed. At their peak they defeated the Roman legions, they swept through Syria to the sea, they placed a king on the throne of David.

Why forgotten? As a semi-nomad tribe from the steppe lands east of the Caspian Sea they were probably despised; they had little to commend them to the more advanced indigenous populations whom they subjugated. Moving their headquarters from one site to another they ranged across the Persian plateau leaving few records of their passing. They inscribed no grandiose cliff-face monuments to commemorate their victories over the Romans, remarkable though they were, or to proclaim the valorous deeds of their ruling house; they built no ceremonial terraces; they left no identifiable royal tombs. Rock-reliefs, some intriguing statuary and figurines, a collection of ceremonial drinking horns and jewellery record their passing. Enough to tantalise. Much of their art and architecture was an amalgam of borrowed styles. Not till later was it expressed in a more innovative form that was essentially Parthian. But when it came it was in refreshing contrast to the overbearing grandeur of some of the Assyrian, to the oriental formality of the Achaemenid, or the stultifying degeneracy of the Hellenistic.

The Parthians inhabited a dimly perceived twilight world that was overshadowed by the better publicised and more spectacular ages which they linked. Though the paucity of artifacts so far discovered has hobbled the historian, the Parthians excite curiosity while remaining something of an enigma.

In their day the Parthians were renowned for their prowess in the field. Their armies drove the Seleucids out of Persia, they fended off the northern hordes and they carved out an empire which was attacked by the Roman legions time and time again as successive emperors sought to win supremacy in the east. And when after four centuries the Parthians had fought their last battle, their king had been killed, their armies finally dispersed, it was not the Romans who had defeated them but the enemy behind the lines.

THE PARTHIANS

Exit the Seleucids—Roman eagles in the sky

Their story starts with Arsaces, founder of the Arsacid house, and his brother, Tiridates, successive leaders of the Parni tribe, who won control of the province of Parthia around 250 BC and ousted the Seleucid satrap. Tiridates carried the incursion into Hyrcania. But his son, Artabanus, tested the waters too far and his advance through the Alburz mountains brought Antiochus III hurrying eastwards (see p. 70) and he was forced to surrender territory. But it was a case of *reculer pour mieux sauter.* The final defeat of Antiochus at Magnesia, the hellenizing follies of Antiochus IV and the succession disputes that followed his death, all combined to weaken further the Seleucid hold on Persia. By about 140 the eastern edifice of their empire had crumbled: Parthian tribesmen had overrun the plateau, a small breakaway state had exploded into a major power and Mithradates (c. 171-138), the true founder of the Parthian empire, ruled from the Hindu Kush to the Tigris plain. A valiant warrior and humane ruler, his phenomenal success in the field was crowned in the closing years of his long and eventful reign when Demetrius II, seeking to salvage something from the wreckage in the east, attacked the invaders but was himself caught and taken prisoner. Mithradates, after parading him round the country, treated him well. He sent him to Hyrcania and married him to his daughter. But if he hoped a family alliance would lead to political union he had miscalculated.

The Seleucids retained an unquenchable fighting spirit to the end. While sliding into decline they bobbed up here and there like a scatter of corks on the imperial pond. Their last major offensive came about 130, ten years after Demetrius' abortive attack, when his brother, Antiochus VII Sidetes, led a large Syrian army across the desert towards the Zagros mountains. His declared purpose was the reconquest of the east and the rescue of Demetrius still languishing in furthest Hyrcania, where Phraates II was now king. Many rallied to Sidetes' standard and by the autumn his forces had won through to the Median capital. Comfortably quartered through the winter months in and around Ecbatana with a retinue of camp-followers, when the spring came the Syrians were slow to resume the march. But the civilian population, exasperated by the demands of the soldiery, had by then turned against them. Phraates' agents exploited their hostility by promising support and when the Medes revolted the Parthians launched their counter-attack. The enemy was defeated, Antiochus was killed, his son taken prisoner.

Never again did the Seleucids attempt to regain their possessions in the east. Instead they fell to fighting among themselves till they were overtaken by the rising power of Armenia in the north.

For Phraates by the year 129 the way through Media to the rich lowlands of Babylonia lay open. But he did not live to enjoy the fruits of his victory. Many thousands of mounted nomads were on the move along the Chinese border. In a series of prolonged migratory waves, as one tribe took possession of the lands of another, they overflowed southwards, pressing across the Jaxartes and the Oxus into Iran. First came the Saka (Scythians) from the steppes of southern Russia. For perhaps a decade they were on the move. Phraates died fighting them and so did his successor. But in Mithradates II (the Great) the time of need produced the man. He staunched the nomad flow. Some of the hordes he pushed back, some he headed off eastwards towards India, others he apparently induced to settle in the south where they formed the vassal state of Sistan (Sakastan).

Media and the lands to the west of the central Iranian deserts were spared but Mithradates was too late to save Bactria. She had lain directly in the invaders' path and her Hellenic cities, which had flowered through two centuries, were burnt and pillaged beyond recall.

The Saka were followed by the Kushans, a group of tribes (also known from Chinese annals as the Yueh Chi) from the borders of the Gobi desert. They occupied the greater part of the province and in later years, when the Parthians were in decline, they carved out a huge empire which extended from northern India to central Asia and the borders of Han China.

Had a less competent ruler than Mithradates come to power in 123 the other cities of Persia and the lands further west might have suffered the same fate as Bactria and it may not be ranking him too high to say that Mithradates the Great saved the civilized world of western Asia from destruction. In the ground-swell of the departing hordes he re-established Parthian rule across the plateau. At the same time he tapered his conquests to meet his defence needs by drawing the frontier along the Oxus and the satellite ranges of the Himalayas. On the western front, having established his suzerainty over Babylonia and followed the Euphrates upstream to its source, he invaded the kingdom of Armenia and took the king's son, Tigranes, hostage.

But, just as the Seleucids before him had discounted the warning signs which preluded the Parthian invasion, so Mithradates ignored the Roman eagles soaring into the western sky. He failed to see that he was entering their hunting ground and that if there was Armenian prey to be gathered the rulers of the great Roman republic were unlikely to be satisfied with the pickings.

The struggle for Armenia

By the beginning of the last pre-Christian century the shadow of Rome had moved eastwards into western Asia. She had fought her last Punic War, Carthage had been destroyed, Greece and Macedonia were in her grasp and Pergamum (known as the 'Province of Asia') had come into her possession. Mithridates[1], the warrior King of Pontus (120-63), ambitious, aggressive, the Napoleon of his time, had swept round the Black Sea coasts of Asia towards the west and was nudging Roman territory. The small kingdom of Armenia, subjugated over 500 years by the Achaemenids, by Alexander and the Seleucids, was seeking independence. In 95 Tigranes II had been released by Mithradates II and was king. But his mountain country was vulnerable, he needed an ally and he had married the daughter of King Mithridates of Pontus.

Against this setting Rome was to play on one end of destiny's concertina and Parthia the other bringing the two powers now together now apart and Armenia had to dance to one or other of their tunes.

But for a brief interlude the foreign clouds lifted and an Armenian sun shone directly on to the plains of Mt Ararat. The great Mithradates had gone to his tomb, the Arsacid monarchy had temporarily lost its grip and Tigranes had invaded North Mesopotamia and Syria. For two memorable decades in that country's unhappy history the tables turned in her favour and Tigranocerta was the imposing new capital of an empire, which extended from the shores of the Caspian Sea across to the Mediterranean and up to the Pontic Alps in the north.

Rome's initial problem lay with Mithridates of Pontus, when he invaded Pergamum and crossed the Bosphorus into Greece. In a series of Mithridatic wars (89-66) the Pontic king was defeated first by Sulla, later by Lucullus, whom he drew across the Anatolian plateau into Armenia, and finally by Pompey. On the last occasion Tigranes had refused Mithridates a refuge and the indefatigable fighter finally fled to the Crimea.

Pompey was now free to invade Armenia himself and he entered Tigranocerta unopposed. In the eyes of the admiring audience at home the great triumvir had scored another victory but on the diplomatic front he was less successful. Not only did Pompey humiliate the Parthians but he incurred their lasting hostility. When he arrived in the east Phraates III, at his request, had undertaken not to interfere in Roman military operations on the understanding that Parthian territory taken by Armenia would be restored. But in the settlement Pompey made with the vanquished Tigranes he reneged on the agreement. Nor did he accede to Phraates' request that the Euphrates should serve as the frontier between the two powers. 'The boundary . . . adopted would be a just one,' was the message relayed to the king through an equivocating Roman emissary.

The fact is that Pompey had miscalculated. He thought that by keeping the kingdom of Armenia as a buffer state firmly under Roman tutelage he could secure peace on the eastern front. Instead, by underrating the importance of Parthia, by his high-handed and provocative dealings and his duplicity he had ensured that, in the event of further Roman incursions into the region, Parthia would never again be party to a neutrality agreement.

But if in the eyes of the orient Pompey was seen to be an unreliable ally, he was nevertheless an astute statesman and a magnanimous victor. Plutarch describes his meeting with the Armenian king:

> Tigranes . . . set out of his own accord to surrender himself. When he rode up to the Roman camp, two of Pompey's lictors came to him and bade him

> dismount from his horse and go on foot; for no man mounted on horseback had ever been seen in a Roman camp. Tigranes, accordingly, not only obeyed them in this, but also unloosed his sword and gave it to them; and finally, when he came into the presence of Pompey himself, he took off his royal tiara and made as if to lay it at his feet, and what was most humiliating of all, would have thrown himself down and clasped his knees in supplication. But before he could do this, Pompey caught him by the hand and drew him forward . . . giving him a seat near himself.
>
> Plutarch, *op. cit., Pompey*, XXXIII.

Tigranes was allowed to retain his homeland and, for a consideration—enough to finance the war—he kept his Euphrates conquests. Roman honour may have been sacrificed on the altar of expediency but Pompey at a stroke had pulled off a double coup: Armenia, now vassalized, had replenished his coffers, yet at the same time she was ranged against Parthia and could serve her purpose as a buffer state.

For Pompey had formed a grand design. As Parthia could not at this time back her demands by force he was free to plan a political restructure of the Roman conquests in western Asia. Along the southern shores of the Black Sea and down the Mediterranean seaboard he formed a chain of Roman provinces. In 63 he entered Jerusalem and in line northwards, through the desert townships of Syria, now rid of their squabbling remnants of Seleucidae, he established garrisons that would serve as springboards for expansion to the east. He organized an administration, he regularized the collection of taxes, he introduced the rule of law. He sought in fact to bring about a peaceful settlement and to promote Roman civilization in the east.

To the Parthians Rome had done little more than show her face, but enough to sow distrust. Had Pompey acted honourably could some of the antagonism which was to entangle the two powers have been averted? Possibly not. But it was a bad start, for though the western world might wait 'the livelong day, with patient expectation, to see Great Pompey pass,' from now on the Orient viewed him and his successors with avid hostility. In solving one problem he had created another . . . and the waters of the Euphrates would flow through seven turbulent centuries of disputed ownership.

Military prowess was the favoured route to political power under the Roman republic. In 60 BC it took Pompey and Caesar into the all-powerful state triumvirate. Only the aging Crassus, very much the third member, had bought his way in. He longed for the 'trophies and triumphs' which the other two enjoyed and his appointment as governor of Syria offered him his chance. He saw himself heading the legions 'as far as Bactria and India and the Outer Ocean'. He was said, rather unfairly as it turned out, to be brave anywhere but in the field and many months of drum beating up and down Syria preceded the start of his campaign so that by the time he had his armies in battle order and on the march the enemy were ready for him.

Meanwhile in the Arsacid house Phraates had been the victim of a conspiracy by his two sons. After assassinating their father, the younger son, Orodes II, took control of the kingdom and his brother parricide, Mithradates, was forced to flee. In Syria, with some assistance from the Roman governor, he mustered an army, marched on Babylonia and succeeded in occupying Seleucia. The city fell in 55 after a siege to Surena, Orodes' general. Mithradates surrendered and was summarily executed. It was under Orodes that the Parthians so ably demonstrated that, given the right conditions, they were a match for Rome. Had Mithradates been able to hold out a while longer, Crassus might well have exploited the enmity between the two brothers to his own advantage by coming to Mithradates' aid and the fateful battle of Carrhae would never have taken place.

As it was, Crassus, having spurned the offer of military assistance and a passage for his armies through Armenia from Tigranes' successor, Artavasdes, crossed the Euphrates in May 53, into the more familiar territory of northern Syria. On the advice of an apparently friendly sheikh (who was in the pay of Orodes), he abandoned his river lifeline and marched westwards in search of the enemy. Plutarch tells how, many thirsty leagues and some days later, in the vicinity of Carrhae (Harran), the empty plain was suddenly filled with:

> a deep and terrifying roar . . . While the Romans were in consternation at this din, suddenly their enemies dropped the coverings of their armour, and were seen to be themselves blazing in helmets and breastplates, their Margianian steel glittering keen and bright, and their horses clad in plates of bronze and steel.
>
> Plutarch, *op. cit.*, *Crassus*, XXIII, XXIV.

Too late the hapless triumvir realised his mistake. He formed his men into a hollow square but an infinity of arrows from the darting horsemen rained on the human walls—they were an easy target. When Crassus saw that a camel train in the rear ensured an unlimited supply of the deadly weapons he ordered his son who was leading the cavalry to make a diversionary charge. The enemy withdrew and hope was restored but the day wore on and Publius did not return. Led on by the mounted bowmen, he had been brought up against the lances of the heavy armour. And it was not the Roman cavalry but the enemy who rode back in triumph carrying the head of Publius impaled on the tip of a Parthian lance.

Next day the Parthian commander-in-chief, the famous Surena, offered a truce. In the parley which followed, possibly through treachery, possibly towards retribution for Pompey's duplicity, more probably through misunderstanding, there was a scuffle and Crassus was killed.

Meanwhile, Artavasdes, after being rebuffed by Crassus, had formed an alliance with Orodes. The treaty had been sealed by a marriage and the two kings were attending the celebrations at Artaxata and watching a performance of Euripedes' *Bacchae*, when the head of Crassus was carried in. Catching it up the player chanted to a rapturous audience:

> We've hunted down a mighty chase today,
> And from the mountain bring the noble prey.
>
> D M Lang, *Armenia Cradle of Civilization*, London, 1980, p. 138.

Carrhae was the first milestone in the long catalogue of conflict between the two powers. For the Romans it was a disaster to be redressed. Mistakes leading up to the battle as well as the outcome of the contest itself called for a review of their tactics. Only a quarter of the 40,000 legionaries had struggled back to the Euphrates. Crassus in his ineptitude and conceit had rejected the advice of his lieutenants and his Armenian ally; he had abandoned his river defence, he had turned his back on the more suitable infantry-fighting hills of Armenia and struck out across the plain. He had allowed the Parthians to select open country for the battle, where their bowmen could ring the cohort ranks, and flat ground, where they could engage their heavy cavalry.

For the Parthians too there were lessons to be learnt. They had won a magnificent victory; they were now recognized as a great power and were free to draw their frontier along the Euphrates. Yet who could doubt that the legions would return, that the humiliation of Carrhae would one day be avenged and the eagle standards, lost in the battle, reclaimed? Orodes' proper course was to follow up the Parthian victory and consolidate their gains. He must have known that Caesar and Pompey, the two remaining triumvirs, were heading for civil war but it was not till the year 40, thirteen years after Carrhae, that he launched a serious full scale offensive across the Euphrates into Syria. The civil war by then was over, Pompey had been defeated and killed; Caesar had been assassinated and the two triumvirs at the forefront of the stage were Octavian (later known as Augustus) and Mark Antony, who ruled in the east.

Orodes meanwhile had executed his commander-in-chief. Next to the Arsacids, as Plutarch noted, the Surena was the most powerful family in the land. But their private army was too large for comfort and the victor of Carrhae, like others in their king's service who had gone before or were yet to come, had performed his tasks too well and aroused a lurking fear and jealousy in the mind of his master.

> In wealth, birth, and consideration, he stood next the king, while in valour and ability he was the foremost Parthian of his time'.
>
> Plutarch, *op. cit., Crassus*, XXI.

The invading forces were commanded jointly by Orodes' son, Pacorus, and Quintus Labienus, a renegade Roman general. At first all went well. Resistance was feeble. After taking Syria Quintus Labienus moved into Cilicia and overran much of Asia Minor. Pacorus invaded Palestine. He was welcomed in Jerusalem by Antigonus, a nephew of the High Priest, as a liberator from the heavy hand of Roman rule. He expelled Herod, an ally of Rome, and crowned Antigonus king of the Jews. But the invaders' success was short-lived. Mark Antony was moving his legions into Greece and by the autumn of 39, under the command of Ventidius Bassus, they had crossed into Asia Minor and were rolling the Parthians back into Syria. Labienus was taken prisoner and killed. The following year Ventidius marched on Syria. The decisive battle, that took place near Antioch at Gindaris, was in some ways reminiscent of Carrhae only this time it was the Romans who chose the site; it was the Parthians who were fed misleading intelligence and taken by surprise, and a Parthian prince who was killed. Pacorus fell fatally wounded, his horsemen retreated from the field and only a remnant of his army regained the east bank of the Euphrates.

For a brief interlude—a matter of months between 40 and 39—the Arsacids had presided over an empire of Achaemenid proportions. But after Gindaris their armies retired behind their river frontier and seldom ventured beyond.

Like Crassus, Mark Antony saw the conquest of Persia as his way to the Roman summit. Unlike Crassus he had some measure of Parthian tactics. Yet in the end he too failed. In 36 he led an army, possibly 100,000 strong, up the Euphrates across Armenia into Atropatene and besieged the city of Praaspa. He was forced to abandon the assault when his baggage train and siege equipment coming on behind were captured by the Parthians. As winter set in food was already running short and the army was forced to retreat. To have followed the more direct route across the plain would have courted disaster at the hands of the bowmen. So they took to the hills. But the bleak mountain borderlands of Armenia afforded little cover and the hungry soldiers were harried by the horsemen for nineteen days. By the time they reached the safety of Syria over 30,000 men had been lost, mainly through starvation and disease. After two more campaigns Mark Antony abandoned the attempt to subjugate Persia. He returned to Egypt in 33 and sought consolation in the arms of Cleopatra. His inability to secure even a foothold on enemy territory was the first step on the downward path of his career. It culminated two years later, after a sea battle off the bay of Actium, in his suicide and left Octavian virtually sole ruler of the Roman Empire.

As for the Parthians, the outcome of Mark Antony's disastrous sojourn in the east marked another milestone in their relations with Rome. Twenty years after Carrhae their frontiers remained intact; they were on reasonable terms with Armenia; they had repulsed the legions in the north and they were still the dominant power in Asia.

Dynastic difficulties

The reign of Augustus (Octavian) from 27 BC to 14 AD linked the last years of the old world to our own era and, though the Armenian question was a continuing problem, the five Caesars: Augustus, Tiberius, Caligula, Claudius and Nero, inclined to resolve their differences by diplomacy. 'Who fears the Parthian . . . while Augustus rules?' intoned Horace with some justification—for Rome came to the peak of her power under the first emperor. Negotiation suited the Parthian book too and the Euphrates more than once became the venue of negotiations between the two countries.

For Persia the lull in hostilities between east and west was particularly providential as a series of palace revolutions and succession disputes were beginning to shake the royal house. Most of the princes who found their way to the throne proved to be inadequate. There was friction between the monarchy and nobility and a resultant weakening of the Arsacids' standing, which did not pass unnoticed by the watchers in Rome.

Under Orodes the battle of Carrhae and the westward push had taken the Parthians to the high-watermark of their success. When Pacorus was killed the tide turned for the aging king and he abdicated in favour of his eldest son, Phraates IV. In the field Phraates had scored a great victory over Mark Antony in Atropatene but as a ruler he was universally hated. At the time of his accession he had executed his thirty brothers and his father to whom he owed the crown. When he singled out certain nobles for the same treatment some of them fought back and he was forced to flee. The Scythians in central Asia gave him a refuge and by the time, with their help, he had been restored to the throne he had learnt something of the wisdom of moderation. Relations with Rome improved too when Augustus, who held one of Phraates' sons hostage, agreed to return him in exchange for the eagle standards lost at Carrhae and the surviving prisoners.

However, it was Augustus who inadvertently sent the king to his death in 2 BC. He had given him a slave girl, Musa, and Phraates had married her. But the enclosed life that was the Parthian noblewoman's lot was not to her taste. She harboured ambition for power and persuaded the king to send his four sons by a previous marriage to Rome for their education. Once they were out of the way she poisoned her husband, placed her own son, Phraataces, on the throne and, as the coins of mother and son may testify, she married him. Incest had been practised in Persia in the time of the Achaemenids but the more refined sections of society were scandalised by this turn of events. Two years after their union in 2 AD, Phraataces lost his throne and fled to Syria where he died.

The dearth of suitable Arsacids determined a council of nobles to send to Rome to negotiate the return of one of Phraates' sons. This (about 8 AD) brought Vonones to the throne. Alas for the refining influences of a Roman upbringing! Parthian crudities and uncouth habits, their ignorance of such amenities as the baths, their orgiastic feastings and revelries, their love of horses and hunting—all these repelled the young king. For their part, the Arsacid court viewed Vonones' clean linen and cultivated ways as fastidious if not effeminate. Who but a Roman would ride around in a litter?

So Vonones was hustled out of the way by the next candidate, a distant Arsacid, a vassal prince from Atropatene, Artabanus III (c. 11-38). He too had an enforced stay with the nomads but for different reasons. Artabanus was a worthy monarch who made some attempt to strengthen the hand of the central government but he was a victim of Roman intrigue. The emperor Tiberius (with justification that could hardly be contested) pressed the claims of the Arsacids in the direct line in Rome. Enough of the Parthian nobility were won over to force the king to withdraw eastwards leaving the way open for a grandson of Phraates, Tiridates, to enter Seleucia and be crowned. Reaction among the loyalists was swift. A group of nobles went in search of their king and found him in Hyrcania dressed in the garb of a hunter and living by his bow. Helped by some local tribesmen and a gathering army, Artabanus ousted the pretender and resumed his seat on the throne. Relations with Rome were patched up and, after surviving another attempt to unseat him, he reigned altogether for twenty-seven years.

Every noteworthy Arsacid, it seemed, must seek to bring Armenia within the Parthian pale by establishing his nominee on that country's throne. Artabanus and the next two kings failed. But Vologoses I (c. 51-77) passed the crown to his brother, another Tiridates. This provoked armed retaliation from the Emperor Nero but in the end he agreed to accept Tiridates' claim on condition that the parties recognized him as Armenia's overlord. In 66 Tiridates travelled to Rome and at a ceremony in the Forum received the diadem from Nero. So an Arsacid dynasty came to Armenia, Roman honour was satisfied, Vologoses had won a signal victory and there was peace between the great powers for the next forty years.

The *Pax Romana* was needed. In Persia Parthian power was gradually seeping away from the centre towards the vassal kings. Hyrcania had severed its ties altogether and joined up with the northern nomads. Other nomads, the Alani, had broken through the Caucasus and were plundering the north of the country while the Kushans were making massive inroads in the east (see p. 75).

Had Nero proved less accommodating Arsacid dominion over Persia would have fragmented faster. As it was some of the practices of Phraates IV, the reigns of the several lesser kings who followed, the long drawn-out drama over Armenia, the Alani and Kushan incursions, the growing power of the vassals, all had contributed to a weakening of the monarchy. During the century of the Caesars, the Parthians' disputes with Rome had been relatively low-key affairs. But these developments on the home front had left them vulnerable to attack from the new militant breed of emperors who were about to take over. For them the Parthian empire would be a prime target.

The Parthian scene

While the Romans blazed a spectacular trail across the landscape of history and decorated it with impressive monuments, the Parthians left only occasional landmarks to record their passing. But they did bequeath a coined portrait gallery of their kings. In turn we see them frowning, determined, venerable, fiercely full-faced and in bearded profile. Their headgear over four centuries ranges from a simple diadem, similar in outline to the *'iqal* which holds the Arab headdress, to a series of splendid domed shapes akin to the Russian imperial crown.

Palace remains in some of their early northern capitals, such as Nisa, which was built by Mithradates I, Hecatompylos (Shahr-i Qumis) and Ecbatana, suggest that the Arsacids had yielded to the seductions of a sedentary life. The more primitive forms of shelter that had served their nomad ancestors translated into mud-brick and stone, into the arches and vaulted halls of the palace at Ashur, into the vast mountain fortress of Qal'ah-i Yazdigird at the western extremity of the Zagros mountains and the limestone city of Hatra on the plain below.

The culture of the Greek settlers attracted the new rulers. They learnt Greek, they absorbed elements of Hellenism into their architecture and they were captivated by drama—a novel art form—to which they did full justice by building special theatres. It was not until the later years that Greek influence began to decline. Pahlavi (a form of Middle Persian) which the Arsacids spoke became the national language during the Parthian and Sasanian periods and their script, which was derived from Aramaic, gradually replaced Greek on the coinage. At the same time Aramaic continued to be spoken in the west, especially in trading centres such as Hatra.

No town comparable to the city of Hatra has been found on the plateau itself. It was evacuated by the Sasanians and preserved for centuries in sand to emerge as the most complete urban survivor of the Parthian period. Built in a circle, perhaps at the time Christ, it housed a mixed population of Iranians, Aramaeans and Arabs. Its honey-coloured stone sun temple and palace are an amalgam of east-west styles that are in themselves unique. Like other large buildings it features that characteristic Parthian innovation, the *ivan* (an opening into a barrel-vaulted three-sided hall) which is seen on the grand scale in the Sasanian palace at Ctesiphon and which later became an important element in Islamic architecture. Unique too is the statuary whose figures emanate a curious detachment from each other as they 'face the spectator with an unblinking stare',[2] the arm upraised in prayer. This 'frontality' is paralleled later in the full-faced Christs-in-Majesty of the Byzantine mosaics.[3] No Persepolitan-type processions move along the walls, no darting horsemen even; only the occasional sculptured image: a guardian eagle, a crouching camel and a deity or two disturb the sunbaked surfaces.

Persia in Parthian times was less a nation, more a collection of vassalized states, city states and satrapies owing allegiance to a remote central monarchy. It has been said of their kings that, provided their commands were obeyed—that is so long as they received the tribute due and the manpower they needed to maintain the monarchy and service their armies in time of war—they left the people to lead their own lives. Sources of information are scarce and this may be an overstatement but it is indicative of the attitude of the Arsacids towards their subjects. They took little apparent direct interest in the art of government and, having carved the country up into eighteen vassal states and satrapies, they left the officials of the old regime to carry on. As the position of the monarchy weakened, the governors of the vassal states turned themselves into sub-kings, while the Greek city states continued to manage their own affairs. All peoples—whether they were Zoroastrians, Jews, Buddhists or, latterly, Christians—were permitted to practise their own religion.

The throne did not always pass from father to son. For instance, a brother could succeed, as Tiridates did when Arsaces, the founder of the dynasty, was killed.[4] Beyond that it is difficult to discern a pattern in the Arsacid succession. The new king had to be confirmed in his office by a council of nobles from the seven leading families (a legacy from Achaemenid times) and a secondary council of Magi and other eminent persons. Later, when dynastic struggles developed or there was no obvious successor, the council took it upon themselves to make the selection as they did in asking Augustus to return Vonones.

Parthian society conformed to a type of feudal pattern similar to that which prevailed in Europe in the Middle Ages. There were the landowning classes (many of them exempt from taxation): the great families, the lesser nobility, the priesthood and the knights; and the freemen: retainers, merchants and officials. Then there were the peasants, who were bound to work their lord's land as well as their own and to respond to his call to arms. At the end of the line came the slaves—small in number—probably ex-prisoners of war or peasants who had sold themselves into bondage to pay their debts.

Women in high society were not much in evidence. They lived and ate in their quarters guarded by eunuchs. But, unlike the Achaemenid nobility, they had their likenesses fashioned in stone. There is a portrait gallery at Hatra of vassal queens and noble ladies. The folds of their long carefully draped robes suggest they were made of silk; the veils over their turbans are thrown back. Like their menfolk they wear a great deal of elaborate jewellery. Necklaces, earrings, bracelets and torques (which the men wore) that have been recovered are finely worked in gold, with glass and semi-precious stones.

Following the arrival of an embassy from the Han emperor of China, Wu Ti, at the court of Mithradates II, that famous international highway, the Silk Road[5], as it came to be called, began to work its tortuous way into the trading history of the ancient world. From Ch'an An (now Sian) the main track lay through the pass of the Jade Gate and the Tun-huang oasis where it skirted round the 'moving sands' of the Takla Makan desert and finally emerged from the Pamirs on the Oxus plain. On the way it crossed trails coming in from Siberia and India. Samarqand, Balkh and Merv were some of the important centres where merchants exchanged goods and rested their animals in caravanserais before starting on the long and difficult journey home. From Balkh one of the trails continued across Persia via Hecatompylos and Ecbatana to Palmyra and the Syrian port of Antioch where goods were shipped to Rome. The Persians, whose chain of staging posts lay half way along the 5,000 mile route, found it advantageous to keep the customers at either end apart by providing 'protection' and other lucrative services to passing caravans.

Silk, was much prized, especially by the wealthy citizens of Rome where, as well as furs, ceramics, lacquer, cinnamon bark and jade, it was exchanged for wool and linen, precious stones, coral, amber, ivory and glass. The Parthians traded horses (the so-called 'heavenly' horses the Chinese needed for their wars with the Huns), the ostrich, the vine, the pomegranate, carpets and perhaps pearls from the Persian Gulf.

During the first century AD, when the empire of the Kushans spread out across the Oxus into central Asia as well as into Afghanistan and northern India, a section of the road came under their control. They were able to divert traffic through their own territory to the mouth of the Indus, where goods were shipped to Egypt. This benefited the Kushans and pleased the Romans, who had long wanted to cut off the route through Persia. And it was not until the Sasanians came to power in the third century that the Kushans were conquered and the overland route restored.

Arsacid armies

For a people whose avowed wish was to die fighting the Parthians were singularly unwarlike. Theirs was a defensive army or, more correctly, a collection of private armies, which seldom ventured across the frontiers in a spirit of wanton aggression.

Fig. x. The Parthian shot from a relief at Khaltchayan in Soviet Central Asia, probably c. 50 BC-50 AD

With little or no capacity for staging sieges in the deployment of their military skills they relied primarily on co-ordination between the light and heavy cavalry units, the accuracy of their archers and a battlefield in open country with plenty of room to manoeuvre.

The heavy cavalry, the *cataphractarii* with their great Nisaean warhorses was the armoured unit; both horse and rider were protected with iron mail. Their role was partly supportive as the weight of their armour restricted their mobility but the huge lance they carried could spike through two men at a time. The archers galloping up from the rear as they went into the attack would release a hail of arrows into the enemy ranks. Then, as they rode away, they would turn in the saddle to loose the backward 'Parthian shot', a tactic which moved Horace to exclaim: 'When Parthians flee, the legions are afraid of arrows.' This hit-and-run action, which they executed with consummate skill, was combined at Carrhae with that other famous Parthian ploy, the feigned retreat, when it brought the Roman cavalry up against the armed wall of the heavy horse.

The armies were mustered at the king's call for he himself had only a small standing army and if war threatened he would summon the feudal lords to call their men to arms. The barons brought their Nisaean horses; the lesser landowners and retainers were usually bowmen, having acquired their shooting skills in the chase. Peasants and slaves served in the infantry. But the main arm was the light cavalry:

> They fight on horseback either galloping into the attack or shooting backwards after they have passed. Often too they pretend to flee so that their pursuers think they are out of range of the arrows . . . They will sometimes withdraw from the fray only to return with renewed vigour later. Thus when the enemy believes victory lies within his grasp the greatest danger awaits him.
>
> Justin, *Historiarum Philippicarum Libri* of Pompeius Trogus

A confusion of cults

If the art forms that evolved in Parthian times were an amalgam of styles, the religious practices were no less varied. Old Iranian gods, Semitic gods, steppe-land gods, Indian and Greek gods and the

Zoroastrian god all feature in the observances of the period but, as always, sources of information are fragmentary.

The Arsacids may have venerated their Aryan ancestors, they may have brought their own deities—sun and moon gods—with them, they may have been what might be termed liberal Zoroastrians or they may have been caught up in the worship of syncretised divinities which had come to the fore under the Achaemenids. If at any time they followed the faith of Zoroaster they could hardly have been orthodox believers for their dead were buried in tombs.

Under the late Achaemenids fire altars dedicated to Ahuramazda, Anahita, the old Iranian Goddess of Fertility, and Mithra, the Sun God had begun to appear alongside those of Ahuramazda. Burnt fragments of bone tell of animal sacrifice—a practice which was not in line with Zoroaster's teaching. This triad must have been worshipped by the Parthians as the three altars appear on their coins. Anahita apparently enjoyed pride of place as a number of temples on the plateau were dedicated solely to her. But ultimately the cult of Mithra became more widespread as it was taken up by Pompey's legions and carried to Europe where at one time it rivalled Christianity.

The association of names played a part in the syncretising process. Thus some of the Greek deities worshipped in the Persian city states were linked with their oriental counterparts: Athena (Artemis) was identified with Anahita and with Nanaia, the Semitic goddess, while Mithra lent his name to the Arsacid Mithra-dates.

Burial practices were also diverse. They ranged from elaborate family vaults and communal tombs below ground to tomb towers and mausolea above. In their funerary chambers the dead were either laid out on benches till the flesh decayed and their bones could be scattered or they were placed in sarcophagi—'bathtub' or 'slipper' coffins—made of terracotta to the shape of a body, with a hole at the foot for the emission of gases from the decomposing corpse. The poor may have had to bury their dead in the walls or under the floors of their mud-brick houses.

From the outset the Parthians allowed the Greeks and other minority settlers, such as the Jews living in Babylonia who had been there since the time of Nebuchadnezzar, to practise their religions. They tolerated the Buddhists in the Kushan territories to the east, who carved giant effigies of the Buddha out of the rock in the Bamiyan valley, and the small Christian communities in northern Mesopotamia, which may have developed about that time.

In Fars, the Persian heartland, it may well be that through four

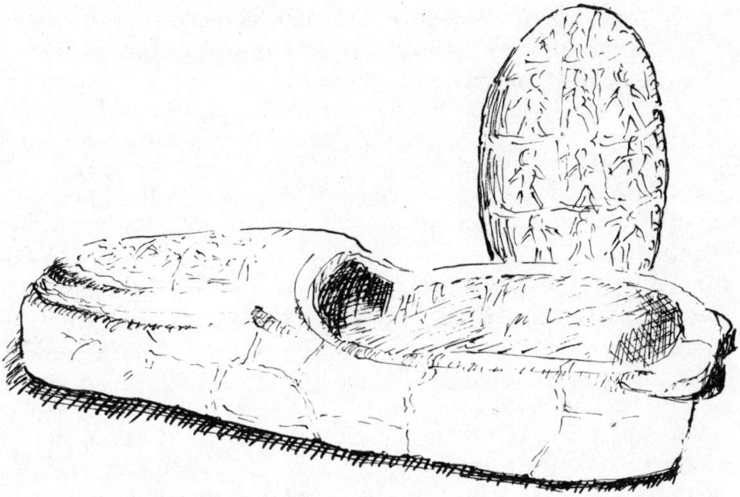

Fig. xi. Partian slipper coffin (British Museum)

centuries of Parthian rule the Magi followed more closely the preachings of Ahuramazda, that they rejected the claims of other deities, that they despised the observances of their rulers and awaited the day when the truth symbolized in the flame they tended would spread back into the outer darkness.

Keeping Rome at bay

During the second century the Roman empire held firm and her citizens enjoyed a relatively tranquil existence. The five emperors who spanned it did not indulge in the perversions of the Caesars who had followed Augustus—they were disciplined rather than dissolute, they wielded power with intelligence rather than through despotism. Nerva, Trajan and Hadrian along with Antoninus Pius and Marcus Aurelius (the two Antonines) were worthy of the purple.

But if on the home front conditions were relatively tranquil, on the perimeter, as Gibbon relates, the peace was:

> interrupted by scenes of war and conquest; and the legions, after a long interval, beheld a military emperor at their head . . . The praises of Alexander, transmitted by a succession of poets and historians, had kindled a dangerous emulation in the mind of Trajan.
>
> *The History of the Decline and Fall of the Roman Empire*, London, 1903, I, p. 6.

An acclaimed ruler, a brilliant soldier, majestic in appearance, austere in his life-style, for him the river boundaries in Europe, which Augustus had drawn and which had remained virtually intact for a century, were too constricting and he carried the Roman standards across the Danube. But the summit of Trajan's ambitions lay in the east. Where Alexander had turned back he would lead his men on to the outer ocean, the imperial army was ready to march and in 114 he invaded Armenia.

The young king, Parthamasiris, invited to the Roman camp, as he thought to receive the diadem at the emperor's hand, as his father Tiridates had from Nero, rode in and placed the crown at his feet. But Trajan made no move and Parthamasiris was seized and killed. With Armenia securely held and reduced once again to the status of a Roman province, Trajan disclosed his real objective. He turned south and entered Mesopotamia. After two seasons of campaigning the twin rivers were flowing from end to end through Roman territory. Ctesiphon, the Parthian winter capital at the time, had opened her gates. Osroes, the king, unable to confront the legions, had fled and Trajan himself by the summer of 116 was cruising down the Tigris. As he stood on the shores of the Persian Gulf watching a ship setting sail for India and pondering the next move, he called to mind the exploits of Alexander:

> If I were still young I would not rest till I too had reached the limits of Macedonian conquest'.
>
> Dio, *Roman History*, Epitome of Book LXVIII.

But he knew he was nearing his journey's end; he was ailing as well as aging. Mesopotamia was in revolt and Osroes was attacking his extended lines of communication. Reluctantly he turned back. The following year he evacuated Babylonia and he died in Cilicia on the long march home.

The Emperor Hadrian was content to withdraw the legions to the Augustan line and restore the Euphrates frontier. But his successors had Mesopotamia and Babylonia listed for conquest. The armies of Marcus Aurelius destroyed Ctesiphon, which Trajan had spared, and the soldiers were already plundering the nearby city of Seleucia when disaster struck. An epidemic of smallpox, hitherto unknown in the west, swept through the Roman ranks and much of their booty had to be abandoned. The Parthians would have been less susceptible to its ravages and on balance the disease must have assisted the king, Vologoses IV, to speed the passage of the frightened legions. But he failed to dislodge them from northern Mesopotamia, where they stayed on like pockets of snow waiting for more to come. As they assuredly did thirty years later.

In 198 it was the turn of Septimius Severus, successor to the Antonines, to follow the course of the Euphrates into Babylonia. He sacked Ctesiphon again, massacred the male population, enslaved the women and children and reoccupied the north. But he failed to take the desert town of Hatra. Its double circle of walls had already defied Trajan. Now catapulting jars of biting flies and bombs of burning bitumen, 'a mixture of biological and chemical warfare', sent Severus and his armies ignominiously away.

Vologoses V lacked the resources to follow up the Hatrenes' victory. Roman attacks were having a cumulative effect, having been launched, as the enemy well knew, over a period when the rifts between the vassals and the central monarchy were widening, when the Bactrian borderlands had been penetrated by the Kushans and when members of the ruling house were increasingly at odds among themselves. Coins of kings with overlapping dates point to disputes for the throne: the brothers Artabanus V and Vologoses VI, for instance, fought a civil war from which Artabanus—the last to hold the throne—emerged the victor.

But unlike the Achaemenids before them or the Safavids and the Qajars in later times, the Arsacids never became degenerate. Their courts, though luxurious, were not subject to the degrading or corrupting influences that permeated the tailends of so many regimes. Silken dalliance was not an important part of the Parthian wardrobe nor, so far as we know, did the excesses practised by some of their Roman contemporaries find favour with them. They continued their equestrian lifestyle, leading their armies of horsemen now against feuding vassals, now against the dreaded legions.

> To die fighting was the supreme happiness and death from natural causes ignominious and shameful.
>
> Ghirshman, *op. cit.*, p. 243.

Nor during their decline were they only on the defensive. Attacking was not a Roman monopoly and in 161 we find Vologoses IV reclaiming Armenia and advancing into Syria, an audacious action which boomeranged on him two years later, when the armies of Marcus Aurelius descended on Ctesiphon.

After some provocation Artabanus V too went over to the offensive and invaded Mesopotamia. He is said to have had a personal score to settle with the Emperor Caracalla, son of Severus, over a marriage alliance.[6] But by the time he encountered the Roman forces Caracalla had been murdered by his own officers. The new emperor, Macrinus, having rejected Artabanus' request for the return of the northern provinces, recommenced hostilities. The last battle fought over three days near Nisibis ended with the Romans fleeing from the field.

The Parthians had achieved a resounding triumph, only to fall victim to the enemies within. Termites had been eating away the ligneous interior of the Parthian house for so long that the walls were paper thin and when the vassal king of Fars revolted they pulverised. About 224 the government forces were routed at Hormizdegan in the south west. Artabanus was killed, his son hunted down. Ardashir, son of Papak of the family of Sasan from the plain of Murghab, seized power in Persia.

Notes

1 Spelt with an *i* to distinguish him from the Mithradates who were Parthian kings.
2 *New Enc. Brit.*, 'History of Iran', 15th ed., vol. 21, 1985.
3 In the twentieth century, as the visitor to Coventry Cathedral will recognize, the frontality posture is revived in the Sutherland tapestry of Christ.
4 In warlike societies, where the head of the tribe might be killed early on, an uncle or a nephew might equally well be chosen as leader.
5 The road was so-named by a German scholar in the 19th century. It was something of a misnomer as there were alternative routes; also silk was only one of a number of products that were carried.
6 Caracalla is said to have proposed a marriage with a Parthian princess. He visited the capital to claim his bride and during the celebrations the Romans turned on their hosts and massacred them. Artabanus escaped but Caracalla claimed he had won a victory. The authenticity of this story is doubtful.

CHAPTER 5
The Byzantine Challenge 224-651 AD

THE DEMISE OF THE CLASSICAL WORLD

The world of the third century, which witnessed the arrival of the new dynasty in Persia, had long expanded into the full orchestra of Eurasia, into a symphony of civilizations, whose ruling empires reached from the Atlantic Ocean to the China Sea. It was a world that had embraced both the distant splendours of the Han court and the imperial Rome of the Antonines. It was a world that had given birth to two great religions: to Buddhism, which had travelled the Silk Road from India to China, and to Christianity, which was spreading from the Middle East to communities in Persia and the west.

It was not a world whose armies afforded protection against persistent aggression from some northern barbarian: the Great Wall of China would be breached, the river defences of Europe, the mountain and desert barriers of central Asia—all would be crossed. The fourth and fifth centuries were a setback to civilization as a whole: the northern hordes saw into the gardens of Eden[1] and trampled them. Meanwhile in the Roman empire, decline, which had set in after the Antonines, escalated into anarchy. In 235 the civilian government collapsed and a series of military tyrants followed in rapid succession. Pre-occupied already with fending off the barbarians from northern Europe and Asia (and with keeping themselves in power) successive tyrants failed to tackle the enemy within. Rome had run into political and economic bankruptcy: her senate was impotent, her coinage debased and, as Gibbon recounts:

> The discipline of the legions, which alone, after the extinction of every other virtue, had propped the

> the greatness of the state, was corrupted by the ambition, or relaxed by the weakness, of the emperors. The strength of the frontiers, which had always consisted in arms rather than in fortifications, was insensibly undermined; and the fairest provinces were left exposed to the rapaciousness or ambition of the barbarians, who soon discovered the decline of the Roman Empire.
>
> *Op. cit.*, I, p. 223

At the turn into the fourth century the decline was arrested, when the reins of government were gathered into stronger hands. Diocletian established a dictatorship and although, as it transpired, the empire as a whole was beyond recall, his reforms paved the way for a rescue operation of the eastern half. The Emperor Constantine a generation later transferred the capital to Byzantium and when the crisis came his 'New Rome' survived. But only just. The beacon light flickered on the Bosphorus shore for 200 years before it prismed into the colourful spectrum of Byzantine pageantry, into the marble and mosaic of Justinian's Hagia Sophia, and left Rome ultimately to a different fate.

Interfacing the political turmoils were the religious crosscurrents associated with the demise of the classical gods. Constantine adroitly identified his New Rome with the changing pattern of belief and gave the kiss of life to Christianity in lurid technicolour:

> 'The very earth sweats,' he told an assembly of bishops, 'total darkness will close in, mountains topple, rivers run dry, a trumpet's voice will sound, and the Savior will appear.'
>
> Ramsay MacMullen, *Constantine*, London, 1970, p. 10

And the rulers of the house of Sasan? They saw Persia's traditional enemy undergo a metamorphosis and re-emerge in the new guise within sight of the Asian shore. They too were caught up in the web of world events; they in their turn failed to keep out the barbarians and, before the hordes were finally turned back, the face of Sasanian Persia had been badly scarred.

THE SASANIANS

Rome is repulsed

The northern invasions were two and three centuries on from the day in 224 when Artabanus V fell to a Sasanian sword on the plain of Hormizdegan and brought four hundred years of Parthian rule to an end. The victor, Ardashir, vassal king of Fars, who fought his way to the throne of Persia, faced a formidable range of enemies: the armies of the Arsacids, sub-kings of vassal states and nobles and, on the outer fringe the Armenian Arsacids, the Kushans, the nomads and the Romans.

Yet some fourteen years later, when his campaigning days were over, Ardashir had secured the Persian plateau as far as Merv and Sistan in the east, he had defeated or treated with the Kushans, he had driven the Romans from Nisibis and Carrhae in northern Mesopotamia and he had captured the Parthian city of Hatra, which had defied Trajan and Septimius Severus. Only Armenia it seems had eluded conquest, though her Arsacid king had been killed, probably with Sasanian connivance at the hand of a Persian nobleman posing as a refugee. His infant son, Tiridates, was carried to safety and lived to fight another day.

From the time of Alexander the rulers of Persia had been of mixed or foreign origin. Now the house of Sasan claimed descent from the Achaemenids and they made the most of their illustrious ancestry. Early on in his campaigns Ardashir had warned the Roman armies in Mesopotamia that 'he would win back everything that the ancient Persians had once held, as far as the Grecian Sea . . . this was his rightful inheritance from his forefathers' (Dio, *op. cit.*, Epitome of Book LXXX). The threat, as Dio ruefully admits, had its effect on the ebbing morale of the legions.

On the home front vassalage, that undesirable feature of the Arsacid landscape, was rooted out. Working from Ctesiphon, the capital, Ardashir appointed members of the royal family to key posts as governors. Their activities were monitored through a retinue of civil servants and secret police whose antennae, as in the days of Darius, reached to all parts of the realm. The army was reorganized, trained, equipped and disciplined into a regular fighting force ready to serve on the frontiers and to maintain internal security.

Centralism was the theme: government and defence were controlled by the king. The church too was made subservient, 'Mazdaism' became the state religion and the priesthood was harnessed to help turn the monarchial waterwheel. 'Consider the altar and the throne as inseparable', Ardashir counselled his son. Here too he was adopting a useful ancestral device as by receiving the royal diadem from Ahuramazda, God's representative on earth was himself elevated to divinity.

If centralism was the theme of the Sasanids then power was the keynote they sounded: incontrovertible, god-given sovereign power. It reverberated through their palaces and echoed along the sculpted cliff-faces of Fars. Once in control no challengers, no lingering vassals, it seems, disturbed their early years, no doubts, no introspections, no shades of grey. Well might they have said like the Medici, 'Now that God has given us the papacy let us enjoy it.'

The thick walled barrel-vaulted palaces of Ardashir and Shapur I have more affinity with the battlemented buildings of Assyrian Nineveh than with the lofty residences of their Achaemenid forefathers; they are functional with fewer concessions to refined decoration.

Similarly, in contrast to the quiet dignity, the flowing elegance and folding draperies in which Darius and Xerxes grace the walls of Persepolis, the cliff face reliefs that portray Sasanid coronations and triumphs are martial, pugilistic even, rather than regal. But if these testimonials were overwritten they were nevertheless indicative of the character and achievements of their authors, of Ardashir and his son Shapur.

Shapur I (240-270) in his turn subjugated the Kushans, then he marched against the Romans. In a long series of campaigns the Emperor Gordian was killed and his successor Philip defeated; Armenia was ceded and Antioch successfully besieged. In northern Mesopotamia the fortress city of Edessa fell, Nisibis and Carrhae—which Gordian had retaken—were won back. These and the other northern stronghold Amida,[2] were to suffer a chequered history as they were reclaimed first by one side, then the other. Shapur's *coup de bonheur* was the capture of Valerian before the walls of Edessa in 260. It probably owed less to tactical skill than to the treachery of the Emperor's lieutenant, Macrinus, who played Iago to his master's Othello. At this stage of Rome's decline, when there was a high turnover in emperors, the off-loading of one of them on to the enemy presented a new way of creating a vacancy for a dangerous but popular office. Before turning for home, Shapur gave his armies a good rampaging time. 'We burned, devastated and plundered Cilicia and Cappadocia.' And any lack-lustre element in the triumphant arrival at Ctesiphon, due to having been relieved of some of their booty en route by the prince of Palmyra, would have been offset by the acquisition of their royal captive and a labour force of several thousand prisoners.

It was hardly to be expected that the son and co-emperor of Valerian would make any attempt to rescue him and the old man appears to have lived out his remaining years in abject humiliation. He was probably kept at Bishapur ('the Good Deed of Shapur') for display. Reason (and inclination perhaps) leads us to believe that he was not treated as a slave or used as a mounting block to the royal charger but it is doubtful if he fared as well as Croesus did at the hands of Cyrus. On the rock faces of Fars he and Philip were placed on exhibition for all time. We see them as diminutive, entreating pathetic figures held in the king's grasp or kneeling in supplication, while the body of Gordian is trampled by the king's horse. Better to have been a common soldier labouring on public works, on 'Caesar's dam' across the river Karun at Shustar, which survives as one more testimony to Roman engineering skills and as a monument to a successful reign.

Religious cross-currents and a Byzantine invasion

Following the death of Shapur the standing of the monarchy declined. The six lesser kings who reigned over the next forty years, Hurmizd I, Bahram I, II and III, Narseh and Hurmizd II, were denied the right to name their successors. Such undulations became a feature of the royal landscape. With each downturn the nobility and their allies, the *eminences grises* of the priesthood, who hovered in the shadows of the throne, while remaining outwardly deferential to the tenets of absolute monarchy, infiltrated the chancellery bringing dissension to the centre, unrest in the provinces and trouble on the periphery.

For instance in 297, when Narseh was defeated by a Roman army under Galerius, he was forced to surrender Armenia and the northern provinces. Tiridates III (the Arsacid prince who had been wrested from the clutches of Ardashir) was acclaimed Armenia's king and—worse still—as a convert to Christianity the royal missionary led the nation towards the new faith.

Weakling kings were the magis' opportunity to press for pogroms and persecutions. One Kartir, who appears to have exercised political as well as religious influence at court, records with relish how 'Jews, Buddhists, Brahmins, "Nazoreans" Christians . . .

were struck upon.' (*New Enc. Brit.* 'History of Iran', 15th ed., 1955, vol. 21). With the exception of Mithraism, the religious movements that affronted the champions of orthodoxy had their origins in other countries of Eurasia. That Persia was caught in the crosscurrents was partly her rulers' doing as many of the 'non-conformists' were descended either from prisoners of war or from enslaved civilians: Buddhists from the Kushan territories, Jews and Christians from the Levant and Rome. Others were of Greek origin and their forefathers had marched with Alexander or come as colonists in Hellenistic times. Now, as the clouds covering Mount Olympus carried the old classical gods away towards the realms of mythology, the civilized world of the third century was looking elsewhere for spiritual enlightenment, to mysticism and astrology, to new oracles and omens, to other religious faiths, to Judaism, Buddhism, Christianity, Mithraism and to Zoroastrianism.

To this cauldron of proliferating cults and creeds Mani of Babylonia had added yet another. Declaring himself the Apostle of Light, he proclaimed a universal faith which embraced aspects of Zoroastrianism, Buddhism and Christianity. Shapur, who had received the prophet in audience, was said to have been impressed. He encouraged Mani in his missionary work and the prophet carried his message to India and central Asia. But Bahram I, persuaded probably by Kartir that Mani was a dangerous heretic, handed him over to the magi for execution. Even so his teachings lived on. They spread from North Africa to China and continued to be an important religious force for centuries after the death of the movement's founder.

When Hurmizd II died in 309, the Magi confidently predicted that his widow:

> had conceived, and would safely produce, a son. Obedient to the voice of superstition, the Persians prepared . . . the ceremony of his coronation. A royal bed, on which the queen lay in state, was exhibited in the midst of the palace; the diadem was placed on the spot which might be supposed to conceal the future heir . . . and the prostrate Satraps adored the majesty of their invisible and insensible sovereign.'
>
> Gibbon, *op. cit.*, II, p. 254

The 'Magic' prophecy was validated and the infant Shapur II

(309-379) was duly delivered to the throne.

Once free from the confines of the harem, the youth began to assert his authority. Early on his rejection of cosmetic power—his relegation of ministers, priests and nobles to compliant subordination—indicated the strength of his personality and his firmness of purpose. During his first essay into war—a naval expedition across the Persian Gulf against marauding desert nomads from the Arab mainland—it is said he brought the tribesmen to heel by filling in the wells with sand.

Meanwhile on the Roman front Constantine was moving his capital to the ancient city of Byzantium on the Bosphorus and Christianity under his patronage was spreading freely eastwards, especially to Armenia whose royal house were converts. In a letter to Shapur he expressed pleasure in learning that there were Christians living in Persia but exhibited concern for their welfare. To Shapur such patronising sentiments savoured of provocation. 'They live in our midst and share the sentiments of Caesar', he commented (A J Arberry (ed.), *The Legacy of Persia*, Oxford, 1953, p. 334)

For him such exchanges were all part of the build up to a renewal of hostilities. He was not tolerant towards the peoples of minority faiths and when he needed money to help finance his campaigns he singled out the Christians and doubled their taxes.

Yet, tempted though he must have been, Shapur did not venture to declare war on the great Constantine. But when the 'Caesar's' death in 337 resulted in a temporary partition of the empire among his sons and a weak succession in the east under Constantius, Shapur led his armies northwards. Armenia as always was the coveted Golden Fleece and northern Mesopotamia the battleground with its shield of fortresses which Diocletian and Constantine had striven to render impregnable.

In the east of Persia Shapur succeeded in keeping the Huns—a new wave of nomads—in check but on the Roman front long years of campaigning won him only marginal success. Nisibis, a major arsenal and the greatest immediate prize, was besieged three times but Shapur never took it by force. At Amida, where he fared better, Ammianus Marcellinus, the soldier historian, witnessed from within the arrival of the Persians:

> And when the first gleam of dawn appeared, everything so far as the eye could reach shone with glittering arms, and mail-clad cavalry filled hill and dale. The king himself, mounted upon a charger

> and overtopping the others, rode before the whole army, wearing in place of a diadem a golden image of a ram's head set with precious stones, distinguished too by a great retinue of men of the highest rank and of various nations . . . The power of heaven . . . had driven the king to an enormous degree of self-confidence, and to the belief that all the besieged would be paralysed with fear at the mere sight of him, and would resort to suppliant prayers. So he rode up to the gates attended by his royal escort.
>
> Ammianus Marcellinus, tr. J C Rolfe, London, 1950, XIX, 1.

But the high command were not impressed by the pageantry, they refused to parley and the siege began. Seventy-three days later Amida fell. Ammianus, who escaped, described the hard-fought battles and the carnage which included 30,000 Persian dead.

The year 361 ushered in a new Roman emperor, a man of a different order from his predecessors: scholar, philosopher, orator, an intellectual, indifferent to the trappings of power that were nourishment to lesser men, a courageous commander, an experienced soldier, in government a reformer, in religion a throw-back (he rejected the Christian ethic for its moral softness). Julian the Apostate was also an enigma. Among his more inexplicable actions was his renewal of hostilities in the east, when Shapur for once had offered to negotiate. Perhaps like Trajan he saw himself as some latter-day Alexander.

Following a year of intense and detailed preparation Julian set out with his army (Ammianus and his notebook with them) from Antioch. His route lay along the Euphrates. He met only local opposition until he was within sight of Ctesiphon, where a battle before its walls ended with the surviving Persians fleeing for the safety of the citadel. Victory boosted morale in the ranks of the Romans who, despite the midsummer heat, now contemplated an assault on the capital with increasing confidence. But the order to attack never came. A council of war had voted against a siege and Julian had bowed to the majority.

Why did Julian agree to hold back when his men were buoyed up to make the final assault? Why did he wheel his armies away consigning 11,000 valuable river transports to the flames as he did so? Why did he undertake such a costly campaign if he was not prepared to see it through? Various explanations have been offered. It has been suggested that agents within the walls had been expected to open one of the gates; that having seen the massive defences Julian decided he could not take the city; that intelligence revealed that another Persian army might attack the Romans in the rear.

Whatever the reason, the siege was abandoned. Harried by the enemy on all sides, starved as he burnt the crops ahead of them, tormented by flies and the intolerable heat, the Roman armies battled northwards towards the greater safety of the hills. Ten days out from Ctesiphon Julian was killed during an engagement:

> [He] rushed boldly into the fight. His guards, who had scattered in their alarm, were crying to him from all sides to get clear of the mass of fugitives, as dangerous as the fall of a badly built roof, when suddenly—no one knows whence—a cavalryman's spear grazed the skin of his arm, pierced his ribs, and lodged in the lower lobe of his liver. While he was trying to pluck this out with his right hand, he felt that the sinews of his fingers were cut through on both sides by the sharp steel. Then he fell from his horse.
>
> Ammianus Marcellinus, XXV, 3.

Jovian, commander of the household troops, was hurriedly elected his successor and the new emperor, preferring dishonour to death, accepted Shapur's terms for a safe conduct to the frontier. Armenia was to be ceded, the northern territories lost by Narseh returned and certain strongholds restored. And that was how Shapur won the fortress of Nisibis.

In common with so many other oriental kings of antiquity, Shapur is known to us mainly by his actions. There was no Ammianus Marcellinus among those around him to reveal to us the mind of the man who so firmly controlled both the civil and military affairs of his kingdom throughout his lifetime. Coins, scenes on silver plates and a stucco bust of the period suggest he had regular features, a long nose, curly hair, a moustache, a beard and a determined expression. He is said to have shared with members of his house a proclivity for building: several cities, a university, a hospital and a small palace or hunting lodge at Sarvistan in his Persian homeland may perhaps be associated with him. Originally set in a garden, its columns and archways lead the eye upward to the domed and vaulted roof of the great hall. Perhaps in his later years as he walked in its shade he recalled some of the deeds which earned him the title, Shapur the Great. He died in 379, his seventieth year, secure in the knowledge that the central government was in the hands of the king and that the frontiers had been restored to the line established by his great-grandfather, Shapur I, a hundred years before.

The battle order

> The Persians opposed to us serried bands of mail-clad horsemen in such close order that the gleam of moving bodies covered with closely fitting plates of iron dazzled the eyes of those who looked upon them, while the whole throng of horses was protected by coverings of leather. The cavalry was backed up by companies of infantry, who, protected by oblong, curved shields covered with wickerwork and raw hides, advanced in very close order. Behind these were elephants, looking like walking hills.
>
> Ammianus Marcellinus, XXIV, 6.

This was Shapur's defensive line-up before the walls of Ctesiphon from which it appeared that the heavy cavalry had moved up to the front line. There was no scope here for the hit-and-run tactics of the Parthian light horse; instead the bowmen, whether mounted or on foot, shot from behind. The battle order had changed but the weapons were those used at Carrhae 300 years before. Maybe the elephants were something of a status symbol but, as we have seen, they instilled a certain irrational fear in the Roman ranks and they made useful troop carriers.

But the nature of the conflict between Rome and Persia took on a new dimension as the battles that had previously ranged over open country gave place to siege warfare. For assaults on the northern fortresses the Roman engineers hauled up their artillery: the battering ram for holing walls, the tormentum that hurled missiles, the ballista which could shoot metal balls and iron-tipped arrows. And to meet the challenge, which they did with some success, the Persians had to resort to the time-honoured method of capturing enemy machines.

Gunpowder had not yet been invented and the strong arm of the cavalry still retained pride of place. One of the later rock reliefs features a prince mounted on a charger resplendent in chain mail and high plumed helmet. Had he travelled down the years into the not-so-distant age of chivalry, with his jousting lance on one arm and shield on the other, he might have passed for a crusading knight of medieval Europe.

The bow and arrow was used by all ranks; even the armoured prince sported a quiver. Before battle commenced the soldiers paraded in front of the king and each man, as he passed before him, threw an arrow into a basket. Those who returned from the field drew one out. In this way the king kept a tally of the casualties. Losses in the Roman wars, especially from the sometimes fruitless assaults on the northern fortresses, may have run into many thousands. But to the king, so long as replacements could be found, this was of small account. A soldier's life was cheap.

Huns, Ephthalites and Mazdakites

By the early part of the fifth century successive waves of Eurasian nomads had broken through to the Mediterranean and spread from end to end along civilization's shore. Vandals thrusting through Spain landed in north Africa, other Gothic peoples crossed the Danube into Roman territory, as Huns sweeping in from the steppes of central Asia pressed in. Another group of Huns had invaded Persia in the north-east (p. 101) and in China cities had been attacked by the Hsiung-nu, a powerful alliance of nomad tribes from central Asia, who had been a source of trouble in the time of the Han.

The crushing defeat of a Roman army at Adrianople in 378, when the Emperor Valens was slain by the Visigoths, hastened the inevitable partition of the empire. In 410 Rome was sacked. But the eastern capital survived and Arcadius (395–408) became the first ruler of the partitioned east.

In the face of this growing threat from the north it was as well that relations between the New Rome and Persia did not deteriorate into war on a Shapurian scale. The Byzantines themselves were in no shape to stage a full-scale invasion and the Euphrates frontier held. Relations between the two emperors even took an encouraging turn as, according to the historian Procopius, when Arcadius lay dying he committed his seven year-old son to the guardianship of the Persian king. Yazdigird I, who ruled in the first two decades of the fifth century, was known to be tolerant towards the Christians and the fact that there was peace between the two powers while Theodosius II grew up, and indeed for the rest of Yazdigird's reign, lends credence to the story.

In Shapur's last years there had been trouble over Armenia before the greater part of that country was abandoned by Rome to her oriental fate. After his death a small predominantly Christian area in the region of Mt Ararat was handed back and Persia retained the remaining four-fifths. For the two great powers this was the diplomatic way out of an otherwise intractable problem. The Arsacid kings continued to rule in 'Persarmenia' as vassals of the Sasanians until 428 when, at the request of a group of Armenian nobles, the king was deposed and a Persian governor was installed.

In 350, when the Hunnic vanguard had overrun the Kushans in Bactria and the north-east, Shapur had been able to suspend hostilities in the west while he brought the invaders under control. But during the critical fifth century Sasanid attempts to fend off the hordes met with diminishing success and one king, Peroz, was captured, ransomed and later killed fighting them.

Like the Saka before them most of the Huns were nomadic. Their life-style was plunder and destruction. They were squat and bow-legged, their faces yellow-skinned and hairless, with slit eyes, high cheek-bones and flat noses. But the White Huns or Ephthalites, who invaded Persia in the fifth century were a degree more civilized. According to Procopius they had settled in lands to the north of the country. They were, he says, 'the only ones . . . who have white bodies and countenances which are not ugly.' (*History of the Wars*, tr. H B Dewing, London, 1914, I, iii).

Bahram Gur (420–38) was the one king at this period who repelled the Ephthalites. In a surprise attack near Merv he is said to have killed their chief with his own hand and chased the escaping remnants back across the Oxus.

Possibly at the instigation of the magi, Bahram resumed Shapur's policy of persecuting the Christians and he requested Theodosius (now emperor) to repatriate the refugees who had found asylum in Constantinople.

A brief clash of arms ended in a treaty under which Bahram agreed to adopt a conciliatory attitude towards religious minorities and Theodosius promised to help improve their joint defences in the Caucasus. And later, when the Persian Christians distanced themselves from Byzantine orthodoxy by joining the Nestorian sect, they were at last able to allay suspicions that their political loyalties were to Constantinople rather than to Ctesiphon and a century-old problem with its attendant persecutions receded for a while.

After his death Bahram, as one of the hero kings, was immortalised into popular folklore as a poet and musician, a dashing fighter and a courageous hunter—a Persian Adonais—for he supposedly died when his horse plunged into quick sands chasing after the wild ass:

> Why didst thou leave the trodden paths of men
> Too soon, and with weak hands though mighty
> heart
> Dare the unpastured dragon in his den?'
>
> Shelley, *Adonais*

Nevertheless it must also be said that Bahram was one of a second group of eight undistinguished rulers. The death of his grandson, Peroz, at the hands of the Ephthalite Huns and the heavy tribute that was subsequently exacted by them as the price of peace was doubly humiliating. The monarchy once again was in a period of decline. Bahram, like the other kings who followed Shapur II, lost the right to select his successor and power spread back to the nobility and the priesthood.

Not till the nobles selected Kavadh in 488, who reigned twice, was the decline halted and then after a turbulent reign. Adventurous, energetic, adaptable even, he saw that if the invader was to be ousted, if national sovereignty was to be restored, the king must regain undisputed control. But how?

A new religious sect, which had evolved out of Manicheaism and which offered the people some improvement in their lot in hard times was attracting country-wide support. It was led by Mazdak, a revolutionary and a social reformer, who opposed the feudalism which a rigid class structure imposed (see below p. 112). He preached vegetarianism, he antagonized the nobles by calling for greater equality among men, for a fairer share-out of wealth, for the unlocking of the harem doors and for a more equal distribution of the women. Kavadh, casting off custom and convention, came down on the side of the Mazdakites. But he went too far and too fast. The nobles and priests combined against him, there was a palace revolution and he was deposed in favour of his more pliable brother. But his life was spared and he was consigned to the Castle of Oblivion, a Sasanid Colditz in Susiana for erring royalty and notables. His fairy tale escape is documented by Procopius, who recounts how the fortress came to be named:

> If anyone is cast into it, the law permits no mention of him to be made thereafter, but death is the penalty for the man who speaks his name.
>
> Procopius, *op. cit.*, I, v.

These restrictions did not prevent Kavadh's 'exceedingly beautiful wife' from seducing the governor and gaining access to her husband. He escaped in her clothes and his impersonator remained unrecognized for several days. Procopius draws a veil over her fate but in the meantime waiting horses had carried Kavadh far to the east. He took refuge with the Ephthalites who received him well (as a youth he had been their hostage). They supplied him with a replacement wife and an army which restored him to the throne. With the Ephthalite guards at his elbow Kavadh regained his authority in the palace. His problem now was how to satisfy his new masters for services rendered? How was he to pay the tribute they demanded when seven years of drought had added to an already depressed economy, when decades of devastations by nomadic northerners had disorganized whole tracts of country and the state coffers were empty?

Tapping the Emperor Anastasius for payments owed for the joint defences of the Caucasus passes proved unrewarding and Kavadh retaliated somewhat irrationally, it seemed, by resuming hostilities. With Ephthalite help he besieged Amida (now back with the Byzantines). It fell in 503, with the usual appalling casualties, after eighty days.

Yet another nomadic inroad across the Oxus diverted Kavadh to the north-east. But fortunately for the now aging king the Byzantines failed to retake Amida and they negotiated for peace. They agreed to pay a thousand pounds weight in gold for possession of the fortress, enough (presumably) to satisfy the Ephthalites for the rest of his reign. The siege had served a purpose after all.

At home the Mazdakites, frustrated by their sovereign's more circumspect attitude towards them the second time round, resorted to extremism. They antagonized not only the Zoroastrians and the Nestorians but allegedly the crown prince as well and at his instigation Mazdak and many of his followers were massacred. The survivors went underground but, unlike the Manichaeans, they had little or no following abroad and the movement gradually petered out. The Nestorians on the other hand took advantage of their greater freedom. They built churches, founded monasteries and established bishoprics as far east as Herat and to the north beyond the Oxus in Samarqand.

By the time Kavadh died (531), after thirty-two years of almost incessant wars he had got the measure of the northern hordes. Had he lived in less turbulent times his reformist outlook might have yielded more positive results. Instead, he had to direct his indomitable spirit and untiring energy to turning the Hunnic tide and it fell to his younger son, Khusraw, the most illustrious of all Sasanids, to carry the country into calmer waters. But this time it was the king—and not the nobles—who selected him for office.

The Sasanid Meridian and the Social Order

Over nearly half a century (531-579) Khusraw introduced far-reaching reforms and built up the empire from within. Ask an Iranian: 'who was the greatest king of antiquity' and he will probably name either Cyrus or Darius or Khusraw of the Immortal Soul.

As invasion threats receded roads were repaired, villages restored, *qanats* and waterways dug out. Land reforms enabled derelict fields to be brought back into production: all agricultural land was surveyed and the tax system adjusted so that the cultivators, who bore the main tax burden, paid a fixed annual sum based on the yield of several years' harvest. Law and order was restored and, as the 11th century poet, Firdawsi, put it: 'the Shah covered the face of the earth with his justice . . . Any man, small or great, could lie down to sleep in the open.'

The king presided over a magnificent court; he introduced a wide-ranging building programme and sponsored activity in the arts. Halls and palaces were constructed and embellished, rocks carved, special coins minted, jewellery fashioned, textiles transformed into apparel. The metal worker took up his hammer, the sculptor his chisel, the potter returned to his wheel. For defence the country was divided into four military commands. Conscription was introduced and the village headmen, or *dihqans*, as well as the ranks were paid from the central exchequer. This encouraged loyalty to the crown (rather than the nobility) and eased the burden on the small landowner.

Confidence gradually returned and in time Khusraw judged his position strong enough to stop paying tribute to the Ephthalites.

Finally, in 557, with help from Turkish tribes to the east of the Caspian Sea, he drove the nomad remnants—Huns, Ephthalites and all, back over the Oxus into central Asia.

So ended a series of invasions spread over two centuries which had threatened the existence of the state. And the king shared the victory with his people by issuing a commemorative coin bearing the inscription 'Iran Free from Fear'.

Taken as a whole Khusraw's wars with Rome were a qualified success and he fared better (as Kavadh had done) when not opposed by Justinian's brilliant captain, Count Belisarius. While the Count was serving his master's imperialist ambitions in Italy and North Africa, Khusraw, uninhibited by a treaty of eternal peace signed only seven years before, spearheaded an attack across Syria. Twenty years of intermittent fighting ended in a Persian victory and in 562 the beautiful city of Antioch was captured, plundered and reduced to a smoking ruin. Such was Justinian's need for peace on his eastern front at the time that he accepted the terms offered and paid over a large sum in gold. And Khusraw, who wanted craftsmen for his building activities deported the Antiochans to Veh az Antiok (Better-than-Antioch), a cynical replica city near Ctesiphon,

> constructing for them a bath and a hippodrome and providing that they should have free enjoyment of their other luxuries besides. For he brought with him charioteers and musicians both from Antioch and from other Roman cities.
>
> Procopius, *op. cit.*, II, xiv

To the south Khusraw's conquests down the sleeve of the Gulf and round the southern shores of the Arabian peninsula yielded commercial advantages. His warships gained command of the east-west sea routes. By infiltrating the ports along the west coast of India and the Red Sea, Persian middlemen carefully contrived to keep buyer and seller apart. They also took their cut as the Parthians had from merchandise travelling along the Silk Road. Trade flourished irrespective of hostilities and whether the destination was Alexandria or Antioch, the Bay of Naples or the Golden Horn, the cargoes that sailed in from the Yellow Sea via Egypt to the Mediterranean took up to four years to complete their journey.

At Ctesiphon from the unparalleled splendour of the Taq-i Kisra, 'the palace of Khusraw', the king governed, dispensed justice, received emissaries and held court. He ruled through a regimented bureaucracy whose scribes beavered away in the adjoining complex of halls, courts and corridors that were his Whitehall. Under the aegis of the grand vizier or chief minister who presided over the *divans* or departments of state, the functionaries administered the royal commands.

In the throne hall, under the great parabolic *ivan*, that massive arch which is still prominent on the skyline, the king held audience. There to witness the arrival of a foreign envoy, we may surmise that the grand vizier would take his place by the king, the princes of the blood, the noble families, the chief *mobed* (high priest) and the captain of the guard. Other dignitaries ranged in order at specified distances by the grand usher and the chamberlains included the sword bearer, the guardian of the curtain, the master of the hunt, the chief falconer, the keeper of the gates, the master of the robes, astrologers and physicians; lower down the line came the poets, musicians and story tellers and, crowding the open-ended approaches, the general public.

Witness the arrival of a new ambassador. Conducted from the frontier by a special escort he approaches the city along the east bank of the Tigris and enters the palace through the hunting park (or garden paradise). As he passes under the massive archway he exchanges the heat and glare without for the cool shade of the throne hall with its myriad shafts of sunlight filtering through the vaulted roof on the mosaic and white marble of the walls.

Crossing the floral silk carpet 'a garden embroidered with gold thread and sewn with pearls', he advances between the assembled courtiers towards the curtain, he arranges an anti-pollutant white handkerchief across his mouth and the curtain is drawn aside.

Such is the awe with which many visitors behold the king's face that they involuntarily prostrate themselves before him. Hopefully our ambassador is not quite so overcome and, after making suitable obeisance, is able to take in the scene before him.

Khusraw wears a gold embroidered white tunic over blue trousers, he is bejewelled with earrings, necklaces, bracelet and belt, his hands rest on the hilt of a sword that stands on end in front of him. His gold throne is supported by winged horses and cushioned in brocade. The elaborate battlemented crown encrusted in emeralds, rubies and pearls must be excessively heavy but on closer inspection our visitor perceives that it is suspended just above the king's head on a thin gold chain.

Invited to speak, the ambassador expresses the hope as etiquette requires that His Divinity will live for ever. He identifies himself, explains his mission and, when the audience is concluded, he retires backwards bowing as he goes till he is beyond the confines of the curtain.

Society in Sasanian times was rigidly structured into four main classes, each with its own sub-classes. There was little movement between one main class and another and many of the categories were in any case hereditary. In descending order below the royal family, the seven great families and the nobility, came the first main class which was confined to the clergy and included the chief *mobed*, lesser *mobeds, herbeds* (teacher priests and guardians of the sacred flame), the magi and others. They issued penances to offenders against the state religion, they inflicted punishments on Christians and other infidels, they were versed in law and they probably assisted in the administration of justice.

Then came the army: the commander-in-chief, professional soldiers, cavalry knights and the lesser knights or *dihqans,* whom Khusraw brought into prominence as a sub-class and who also acted as tax collectors.

Third were the government servants: ministers with their attendant retinue of draughtsmen, letter writers, sealers, archivists, scribes and others, also poets, musicians and physicians. And fourth came the merchants, farmers and craftsmen.

Under the Sasanids the practices of incest and polygamy and the seclusion of women were carried over from Achaemenid times, but, following in the wake of the Mazdakite movement, the position of women had deteriorated further. Hitherto, though once within the confines of the harem a woman lost her identity in the world outside, lifelong subservience to one master did afford her some security. When the Mazdakites 'freed' her from its latticed shades she lacked protection and could be passed from one 'husband' to another. Khusraw decreed that women should have one owner (usually the first husband), that they owed obedience to him alone and that widows and orphans must be protected.

The cultural legacy

The Sasanians were builders on a monumental scale. Some of the cities they founded were designed to serve their own residences: Ardashir, Shapur I and Shapur the Great, delighting in the new-found style, explored its possibilities through the vaulted corridors, domed halls, open courts, *ivans* and pavilions of their Fars palaces at

Firuzabad, Bishapur and Sarvistan.[3] Their architects, some of the earliest to grapple with the problem of placing the dome on the square, effected the union with receding semi-domes (squinches) to the corners. The early compact solid-walled structures gave place under the later kings to larger, loftier, more grandiose designs, the great *ivans* at Ctesiphon (there were two) being nearly twice the size of the one at Firuzabad. Among the several palaces of Khusraw Parviz, the last of the great, whose building megalomania was in the Assyrian class, were Dastagird north of Ctesiphon and Qasr-i Shirin in the Zagros foothills, which he built for his wife.

Then there was Takht-i Sulayman (Throne of Solomon), a fire temple high up in the Azarbaijan hills, where the sacred flame had perhaps burned since Achaemenid times. Khusraw Parviz (and probably his predecessors) made a pilgrimage there on foot after his coronation. The processional way led from the main gate through a colonnaded hall to the fire altar and on to the lake outside, which was 'unfathomable' and whose azure depths were thought to have magical properties. From this eminence where earth and sky met the king could invoke the aid of heaven and from its sanctuary the sacred flame was carried to all the temples in the land.

As befitted this celestial seat Khusraw spared no expense in renovating and refurbishing its precincts. It is said that:

> its balustrades and steps were . . . gold-plated and only gold and silver nails were used throughout. A dome representing the sky, was inlaid with lapis lazuli and turquoise, heavily encrusted with jewels, stars being indicated by rubies set in golden astronomical tables, and the sun and moon rendered in gold and silver.
>
> (Arthur Upham Pope, *Persian Architecture*, London, 1965, p. 74)

The famous larger-than-life rock sculptures (there were about thirty, most of them in Fars) were devised to glorify the dynasty. We see Ardashir, its founder, thrusting his lance at Artabanus, the Parthian king, who falls from his horse; we see him again (and his successors) at his investiture as Ahuramazda hands him the royal diadem and we see Shapur I (repeatedly!) parading his trio of defeated Roman emperors. Scale and design help convey the message: god and king, whether on horseback or on foot, are on equal terms, the vanquished are dwarfed. In later scenes a king is seen jousting with his enemies, another makes a kill at the hunt while musicians play background music.

Though the king's face (which the sculptor probably never saw), in accordance with oriental custom, is only vaguely delineated in the sculptures and on the coins, the silver drachmas describe some interesting trends in royal headgear. Each king had his own crown and some had more than one. Ardashir, for instance, who first of all appropriated the tiara of Mithradates II, later blossomed out in a korymbos or hairnet enclosing a bun held to the top of the head by a skull cap, which in its turn was secured by a diadem. This evolved into a fluted crown and later into the battlemented crown of a playing card king. When further additions or wings, stars and crescents made the whole structure too heavy for the human head to bear, it was suspended like a candelabra just above the king's head as he sat on the throne (see p. 111).

Sasanian craftsmen excelled in metalwork and there must have been an enormous demand for their skills from the monarchy alone, as well as from members of the court and the wealthy classes for arms and armour and the many varied forms of jewellery worn by men. But the art history of the Sasanians is best known for its spectacular silver vessels, for the bowls, dishes, vases, jugs and ewers that were produced in quantity. Raised in relief they picture royal hunting scenes, dancing girls, youths, lute players, animals, birds and flowers. Much of the style and subject matter is characteristically Sasanian but Roman influences can also be seen. Emperors would exchange craftsmen to decorate their palaces or take them by force as Khusraw did when he deported them from Antioch.

Stucco was an art form that was used to decorate palace walls and other large surface areas. Repeated into all-over patterns and sometimes into friezes it could be worked equally well into geometric, floral and animal designs. A favourite subject was that curious mythical creature, the dog-bird or *senmurv*, which had the head of a dog and the tail of a bird.

As well as being moulded into stucco the *senmurv* was chased in silver and woven into fabric. The secret origin of the silk thread is said to have been discovered when two Nestorian monks smuggled some fertile eggs out of China inside a wooden staff and took them to Justinian. The story may be apocryphal but it is certain that by the sixth century, if not before, raw silk was being produced in western Asia. Demand by then had spread from clothing to furnishings for Persian and Byzantine churches. Some of the silk fragments that

Fig. xii. Sasanian *senmurv*, partially gilded silver dish, 7th century AD (British Museum)

have survived the passage of time were wrapped around Christian relics. But the enveloping fabric was not woven, as one might expect, into designs of a religious or even a naturalistic theme. These beautiful silks, which are variously coloured in shades of red, blue, green and yellow portray the pagan image of the senmurv!

The poet Firdawsi should be mentioned here as, although his national epic, the *Shahnama*, was written after the Arab conquest, he dwells at length on the Sasanian kings (he will be referred to later – p. 154, 157). His work opens almost in the style of Genesis:

> In the name of the Lord of the soul and of wisdom, than Whom thought can conceive nothing higher; the Lord of all things nameable and of all space; the Lord who grants sustenance and is our Guide; the Lord of the universe and the revolving sky, who kindles the Moon, Venus and the Sun . . .
>
> (*The Epic of the Kings*, tr. Reuben Levy, London, 1977, p. 1)

He takes us from the creation to the Arab conquest. He mingles fact and fiction, history and legend, as he describes the glorious deeds of the shahs and his romantic hero Rustam, the Saka, who lived through three centuries, who 'grew to the height of eight men' and who flew from one heroic deed to another on his (apparently jet-powered) horse, Rakhsh. Firdawsi touches down on reality too, for instance, in describing Khusraw's land reforms:

> The expert and the warriors, the nobles and keen-minded priests, assembled together with the princes to distribute the land after measuring it with the cord. They levied an impost of one dirham on all, being on their guard that no villager should be reduced to distress. He that had no seed or cattle when the time came for cultivation was provided with them from the king's treasuries.
>
> (*op. cit.*, p. 322)

But he reverts to the language of fairy tale as he describes a kind of Chinese puzzle sent by the 'Rajah of India' to the court of Khusraw. The envoy, received in audience, handed the king the gift of a chequer-board and some pieces with a message inscribed on silk:

> Bid those who have been most engaged in the pursuit of science to place the chequer-board before you and let each man express his opinion as to how this subtle game is played . . . If they discover . . . this . . . they will have surpassed all other sages.

After studying the board for a day and a night the king's vizier (much to the envoy's chagrin) came up with the solution:

> The sage has invented a battlefield, in the midst of which the king takes up his station . . .
>
> (*op. cit.*, pp. 328-9)

And the vizier went on to identify the pieces and their moves in the game of chess.

Thanks in part to their secure foundations, to the strong central government and the regular army introduced by Ardashir, the House of Sasan had maintained its hold over Persia for four centuries. On the frontiers they had triumphed over the Romans and their Byzantine successors, they had thrown the Asian hordes back across the Oxus while, at home, they had weathered the extremist movements of the Manichaeans and the Mazdakites and religious orthodoxy—so closely identified with the monarchy—remained well entrenched.

For his part Khusraw gave his people both a respite from war and renewed hope for the future. (Though he went out of his way to attack the Byzantines he fought them on foreign soil and left the homeland in peace.) He worked to improve the lot of the different classes within the social order and to create conditions by which each man could better pursue his calling. The armed forces—trained and equipped by the state—received regular pay; merchants carried their wares into markets overseas and craftsmen found new openings for their skills. Nor were the needs of the weaker members of society overlooked: widows and orphans received assistance from the state, land reforms helped the workers in the fields. Yes, even for the peasants, the Sasanid meridian was a better time for them too.

The door begins to close on the age of antiquity

By 633 Khusraw had been dead for fifty years, fifty of the most turbulent years in the history of western Asia. Once again—and for the last time—the Persians had waged war with the west. Their armies had invaded Asia Minor, they had conquered Syria and Palestine and swept down into Egypt: the entire eastern seaboard of the Mediterranean from the Bosphorus to Alexandria had come into their possession.

But it is the last battle that counts and the final outcome was decisive, even more so than Carrhae had been some 700 years before. The armies of the west had triumphed.

Yet this last great conflict proved fatal to victor and vanquished alike. Preoccupied with their internecine wars both sides had ignored the fires smoking up from the south. The mountain defences of the Fertile Crescent, which once shielded the Asian uplands from the Semitic nomad, could not contain the flames fanned by religious fanaticism and when the holocaust came Persia and Byzantium were consumed. The fire altars of the Zoroastrians melted into obscurity and Christendom alone survived for 800 years, beleaguered in its Constantinople citadel until the great city too fell before the sword of Islam.

Khusraw's son, Hurmizd IV, was an intellectual who lacked

political acumen and let the reins of power slip from his hands. He was deposed and cast into prison (this time blinding ensured his non-return). The cause of his downfall was Bahram Chubin, his commander-in-chief, a Garibaldi figure of Arsacid descent, a man of great presence and valour who had fended off the Turkish tribes pressing in from central Asia. Hurmizd, jealous of his captain's popularity with the army and alarmed by his mounting power, recalled him. The nobles, taking the view that kings—unlike valuable generals—were expendable, deposed Hurmizd and placed his son on the throne. But the army wanted Bahram Chubin as their king and they marched on the capital at Ctesiphon.

In this situation the newly crowned young Sasanian was forced to flee. He took refuge in Byzantine territory, where the Emperor Maurice (after some deliberation) treated him as an honoured guest and for a consideration—the return of Persian Armenia and two northern fortresses—lent him an army which in 591 restored him to the throne. Bahram fled to the Turks and was later killed. Such was the inauspicious beginning of the eventful reign of Khusraw Parviz ('the Victorious').

His first decade in power was given to consolidating his position and smoothing over affairs on the home front. His undertakings to Maurice were faithfully honoured and the promised territory was ceded. Only in the south-west were there serious disturbances when Khusraw deposed the ruler of Hira, a friendly border state of settled Arabs, and left the frontier undefended. Heading up from the Arabian peninsula the beduin had broken through Shapur's old desert defences and defeated a Persian frontier force. Though discounted at the time as nothing more than a border raid the reversal suffered by the Persians at Dhu Qar was to have far-reaching consequences.

In 602 Maurice was assassinated and Khusraw, taking advantage of the turmoil within Byzantium and claiming that he must avenge his friend's death, set his armies on the march and took back the northern fortresses and Armenia. In 610, when the new emperor Heraclius was crowned, he made overtures for peace but received no response. Khusraw by now was seized with imperialist ambitions and was starting on a career of conquest. In 612 he marched into Syria and sacked Antioch. His general, Shahin, invaded Asia Minor and captured Chalcedon, from whose cliffs a Sasanian army looked across the Bosphorus at the gateway to Europe, to Constantinople itself. In the south General Shahr-baraz besieged Jerusalem (from which the relic of the 'True Cross' was removed to Ctesiphon) and by 619 he had crossed the Sinai desert into Egypt, occupied Alexandria and marched up the Nile to the borders of Ethiopia as Cambyses had done 1,000 years before.

Khusraw now was at the peak of his power. He alone had fulfilled Ardashir's pledge that the Sasanians would win back the lands the Achaemenids once held. For three years he 'trod the sunlit heights' but Heraclius with commendable courage had resolved to rescue the Byzantine empire from the clutches of the Great King and he went over to the offensive.

From the outset Heraclius had one important advantage: the seas were open to him. General Shahin had no warships with which to launch an attack on the Byzantine citadel; his forces were landlocked in the 600 mile cul-de-sac of the Anatolian peninsula and the citizens of Constantinople, who had at first trembled at the sight of the smoke spiralling up from the smouldering townships of Chalcedon a mile away across the Bosphorus, realised with relief that its waters would protect them. In 622 Heraclius sailed out of the Golden Horn in full view of the enemy and rounded the Hellespont unchallenged. Facing east he followed the coast to Cilicia and landed at Issus (site of the great battle between Alexander and Darius Codommanus) and somewhere in the vicinity of the Armenian frontier he won his first victory.

So began a hard fought five year campaign which ranged from the southern shores of the Black Sea through Armenia, Asia Minor and Azarbaijan to Mesopotamia, which culminated in 627 in the defeat of the Persians, in the reconquest of Armenia, in the destruction of the fire temple at Takht-i Sulayman, in the flight of the royal family and the sack of the king's palace at Dastagird, north of Ctesiphon.

Khusraw Parviz has his allies among historians. He has been accorded 'a distinguished rank among the kings of Persia through the majesty and firmness of his government, the wisdom of his views . . .' and so on. It is more probable that success warped his judgment and perhaps even his reason; that for firmness we should read intolerance, for wisdom folly, for majesty paranoia. He had no call to massacre 50,000 Christians after the sacking of Jerusalem, no call to revile or order the execution of General Shahr-baraz, as he did when the tide turned against him. As to the display of 'majesty', this was all part of the furniture of despotic government which Khusraw carried to excess. Consider his Dastagird palace:

> Six thousand guards successively mounted before the palace gate; the service of the interior

> apartments was performed by twelve thousand slaves; and in the number of three thousand virgins, the fairest of Asia, some happy concubine might console her master for the age or the indifference of Sira [Shirin] . . . The voice of flattery, and perhaps of fiction, is not ashamed to compute the thirty thousand rich hangings that adorned the walls, the forty thousand columns of silver, or more probably of marble, and plated wood, that supported the roof; and the thousand globes of gold suspended in the dome, to imitate the motions of the planets and the constellations of the zodiac.
>
> (Gibbon, *op. cit.*, V. p. 87)

In the circumstances of 627 it is not surprising that the people rebelled. War weary, overtaxed to fund the army and the monarchy, and stricken by an outbreak of plague that carried away a third of the population, they sided with the nobles against the king. Khusraw was seized, cast into a house of darkness and murdered.

The one redeeming gesture that colours the career of this unfortunate monarch is his lifelong fidelity to his Armenian wife, Shirin. She was a Christian who was renowned for her piety and for the monasteries she founded all over Persia. The story of their courtship is part of the national epic. A section of the twelfth century work, the *Khamsa* of Nizami, relates how they had fallen in love with each other from a distance. So enraptured was the young prince by a description of her beauty that he rode off to Armenia to find her while the princess, attracted by the portrait he had sent her, journeyed to Iran.

> Shirin rode her night-black horse, Shabdiz, for seven days and nights, until at last, dusty from travel, she bathed in an inviting pool. While she was doing so, Khusraw, en route to Armenia, chanced upon the disarming scene, upon which he gazed as though in a trance. For a moment, in extreme embarrassment, each sighted the other. And although each sensed the other's identity, they were both too overcome to speak. They rode on.
>
> S C Welch, *Royal Persian Manuscripts*, London, 1976, p. 82)

The inglorious scenario of the last decades plays on as Khusraw's son, Kavadh II, who has connived at his father's death, dies of the plague and his infant son is deposed and killed when Shahr-baraz (who has survived) stages a military coup. But this time the nobles are determined to maintain the royal house. As a result a succession of unsuitable men (and two women even) climb the royal dais only to be discarded and government gives way to anarchy.

But some semblance of order is restored when Yazdigird III is persuaded to accept the crown. Peace terms have been negotiated with Heraclius, who has settled for the return of the pre-war territories, along with Armenia, the northern fortresses, and the exchange of prisoners. Retribution is not part of his creed; he prefers the role of saviour of Christendom and stages a victorious entry into Jerusalem to restore the relic of the 'True Cross'.

But Heraclius' triumph is shortlived, we are into the year 633 and the Arabs are at the gate. Two beduin armies from al-Madinah are advancing northwards into Syria and towards the Euphrates. Persia and Byzantium reluctantly resort to arms.

Judged by appearances the oncoming hordes made a poor showing. They were ragged, undisciplined and ill-equipped. On the other hand the desert beduin had greater powers of endurance than those reared in the comforts of civilization. 'Victory or Paradise' was their battle cry as they ranged behind their tribal leaders and the value they placed on life was so low that if they lacked weapons (bows and arrows or stones, supplemented by an occasional lance) they threw themselves into the fray. But the overwhelming advantage that they carried with them was the built-in warhead of the new faith. Whereas the northern nomad from central Asia had nothing to offer—he thought only of destruction and plunder—his Semitic counterpart brought a message which classed him as a conqueror, not a mere invader. And he wrote it in the indelible script of the Qur'an across the face of western Asia.

The opening thrusts were centred on Syria. In 635 Damascus fell. Heraclius withdrew to the north and the Caliph 'Umar ordered the army to cross the desert to the border region of Hira. There they were joined by forces from al-Madinah and any others that could be gathered in from the tribes.

The terrible four-day battle of Qadisiya to the west of the Lower Euphrates followed. It culminated in the 'night of fury', as tribesmen accustomed to moving in the dark harassed the enemy lines, and as a sandstorm next day drove into the faces of the Persians. Exhausted, they fell back leaving the road to Ctesiphon open.

Later the Arab forces moved north. As the massive edifice of the Taq-i Kisra loomed up among the palm trees on the skyline, as they passed under the palace archway and saw the furnishings, the gold and silver objects and the jewelled carpets, they marvelled at it all and praised the Lord for delivering the great capital city into their hands.

In 642, six years later, the Persians made a final stand on the homeland plateau of Nihavand, south of Ecbatana. Theirs was the larger army but they were outmanoeuvred by the Arabs, who spread the rumour of the caliph's death and, feigning retreat, inveigled the Persian forces out of their fortified positions into open country. 'O God! make thy religion glorious and thy people victorious', they chanted as they charged the massed enemy ranks. The Persians, very much on the defensive, were soundly defeated. Many thousands perished; the others—the king among them—fled the field.

Yazdigird, now a fugitive, fled eastwards and died later at the hands of a robber. Like Darius Codomannus nearly a thousand years before, he had not sought power, like him he suffered for the follies of his predecessors and like him he was the last of his line. Yazdigird was also the last Zoroastrian king. As such, perhaps appropriately, he has a memorial. It is enshrined in the calendar of the Indian Parsees whose ancestors fled from Muslim Persia to north-west India. To this day they number the years from the date of the death of their king in 651.

Qadisiya and Nihavand were the graveyards of the Sasanian era. But for the Arabs the Persian plateau was a stepping stone to the plains of northern India, to southern central Asia and the Caucasus. From Egypt the black banner of Islam was carried along the north African coast and into Spain till Arab conquests reached from Cordoba to Kashmir, from the Yemen to the Oxus and beyond. This was the groundplan for a new era in the affairs of human history.

For 800 years the route of the royal road is lost to the Persian monarchy though it constantly re-appears in different guises. Glancing back at the landscape through which it has travelled since Daiaukku built his fortress at Ecbatana—at the tall grandeur of the Achaemenids, at the hellenizing heirs of Alexander, at the Parthian enigma, at the muscular splendour of the Sasanians—we recall how certain characteristics of one age were passed to another. So now, though the door begins to close on the age of antiquity, it never quite shuts. Certain landscape features will re-appear. And not in outward expression only, for the caliphs learnt from the cultural refinements of their subject peoples.

Persia too in her own inimitable way took what the conquerors had to offer—in particular the new found faith—and when the royal progress was resumed the road entered that colourful Islamic scenery which is the supreme glory of Iran to this day.

Notes

1 The original was traditionally at the confluence of the Tigris and the Euphrates.
2 Respectively modern Urfa, Nusaybin, Harran and Diyar Bakr in southern Turkey.
3 The dating to this period has recently been queried.

PART II
THE AGE OF ISLAM
629–1979

CHAPTER 6
The Coming of Islam 652–1040

THE MESSENGER OF GOD

> There at last it lay, the bourn of my long and weary Pilgrimage, realising the plans and hopes of many and many a year. The mirage medium of Fancy invested the huge catafalque and its gloomy pall with peculiar charms. There were no giant fragments of hoar antiquity as in Egypt, no remains of graceful and harmonious beauty as in Greece and Italy, no barbarous gorgeousness as in the buildings of India; yet the view was strange, unique—and how few have looked upon the celebrated shrine! I may truly say that, of all the worshippers who clung weeping to the curtain, or who pressed their beating hearts to the stone, none felt for the moment a deeper emotion than did the Haji from the far-north. It was as if the poetical legends of the Arab spoke truth, and that the waving wings of angels, not the sweet breeze of morning, were agitating and swelling the black covering of the shrine.
>
> Richard F. Burton, *Personal Narrative of a Pilgrimage to Al-Madinah and Meccah*, London, 1919, II, p. 160.

Makkah! Such was the rapture of one man who reached the sanctuary in 1853. And, infidel though he was, the reader who follows Burton through the pages of his journey, will surely understand his emotion and marvel at the devotion of the pilgrims who braved the hazards and harships of those early caravans to submit themselves to the will of God.

The sacred precincts are said to date back to the dawn of recorded history, to the time of Abraham. For it was his son Ishmael who raised the first house of God and received the black meteorite from the angel Gabriel, the hallowed stone housed in the Ka'bah wall. But by the sixth century AD (some 2,300 years later) an assortment of idols had gathered about the house. Female deities, animals and birds, stones and pieces of wood, all were objects of veneration. Makkah had become a cult centre where take-home images could be bought to set up in the tribal tent.

The promoters of this lucrative trade and the guardians of the sacred house were members of the wealthy Quraysh tribe. Muhammad was born into the tribe about the year 570 but he did not have an easy start. His parents were poor relations, his father died before his birth, his mother soon after and the small boy was left an orphan.

The beduin took him in and he earned his keep as a shepherd, until a kindly uncle adopted him and he returned to Makkah to work with the caravans that plied the Spice Road between the Yemen and Syria. His job brought him into contact with a wealthy client, the Quraysh widow Khadijah, whom he later married. It was a happy union and during her lifetime he took no other wife. They had six children of whom only a girl, Fatimah, outlived him.

Age 25 then, found him in comfortable circumstances with an interval of fifteen years before his first vision. It is doubtful whether he had any premonition of his calling, yet he must have pondered the mysteries of life and of death and, though he was probably illiterate, he no doubt studied the faiths of other peoples in the world about him.

Perhaps in the course of managing his wife's business he crossed the Red Sea and met the Egyptian Copts or the Christians of Abyssinia, where some of his followers later found refuge. Perhaps he travelled the Spice Road and talked to the Jews of the Yemen and al-Madinah. Perhaps he took the northern route and listened in the temple and the churches of Jerusalem. Perhaps he visited the Zoroastrians in furthest Persia.

Wherever his journeys took him and whatever course his meditations followed, they led him to despise the nature gods, the demon spirits and the idols lauded by his fellow Quraysh. He came to believe in the monotheist teachings of the biblical prophets and of Christ, the Nasrani, whom he also regarded as a prophet.

His first vision came on the hillside of Mt Hira outside Makkah in

اَللهُ لاَ اِلٰهَ اِلاَّ هُوَ الْحَىُّ الْقَيُّوْمُ لاَ تَأْخُذُهُ سِنَةٌ وَلاَ نَوْمٌ لَهُ مَا فِى السَّمٰوَاتِ وَمَا

فِى الْاَرْضِ مَنْ ذَا الَّذِى يَشْفَعُ عِنْدَهُ اِلاَّ بِاِذْنِهِ يَعْلَمُ مَا بَيْنَ اَيْدِيهِمْ وَمَا

خَلْفَهُمْ وَلاَ يُحِيطُونَ بِشَيْئٍ مِنْ عِلْمِهِ اِلاَّ بِمَا شَاءَ وَسِعَ كُرْسِيُهُ السَّمٰوٰتِ

وَالْاَرْضَ وَلاَ يَؤُدُهُ حِفْظُهُمَا وَهُوَ الْعَلِىُّ الْعَظِيمُ *

Fig. xiii. The Qur'an, the Throne Verse (ii, 257) (Courtesy World of Islam Festival Trust, from S H Nasr, *Islamic Science*, London, 1976)

in the year 610. During a period of meditation the angel Gabriel appeared and bade him:

> Recite in the name of your Lord who created . . . "[1]
>
> Qur'an, 96:1, tr. Dawood

Other revelations followed telling him that God is the creator of the universe, that he is one and indivisible, that he is compassionate and merciful, but that there is a day of judgment and men must submit to attain a state of paradise. Perhaps an answer to his own searchings came in this revelation:

> By the white forenoon
> and the brooding night!
> Thy Lord has neither forsaken thee nor hates thee
> and the Last[2] shall be better for thee than the First
> Thy Lord shall give thee, and thou shalt be
> satisfied.

> Did He not find thee an orphan, and shelter thee?
> Did He not find thee erring, and guide thee?
> Did He not find thee needy, and suffice thee?
>
> Qur'an, 93:1-8

He was urged to preach:

> O thou shrouded in thy mantle,
> arise, and warn!
> Thy Lord magnify.
>
> Qur'an, 74:1-3

Yet he hesitated. For a year or more he hesitated. Only his intimate circle, among them Khadijah, his cousin 'Ali, his friend Abu Bakr and Zayd, a freed household slave, were party to his experiences. And they believed.

The ridicule he encountered when he began to preach soon turned to hostility and the Quraysh, not daring to assault a member of their own tribe, began attacking his followers. His first converts, the city's beggars, slaves and the poor were easy targets for persecution. But, rather than renounce their new-found faith, the tiny band left the city and found their way to Abyssinia where they were allowed to settle.

The gap they left gradually filled: merchants and other townspeople joined, among them 'Umar (a man of strong character who was to follow Abu Bakr as guardian of the faith) and a group of visiting elders from al-Madinah. They invited the Prophet and his followers to make their home with them.

So began the famous *Hijrah* of 622 which 'Umar later fixed as the start of the Muslim calendar, Anno Hegirae 1. The community—a hundred or so in all—left secretly; Muhammad himself went into hiding and followed later by a circuitous route. Khadijah was not among them as she had died three years before.

Al-Madinah, the second holy city of Islam, lies more than 200 miles north of Makkah in the Hijaz. 'Walled habitations, green fields, running water, every blessing', according to one traveller, had been lavished on the city. And the immigrants exchanged the searing summer heat, the sterile soil, the mountain wastes, and the gloomy rock ridden valleys surrounding Makkah for a town set in a plain of palm groves as famous for its dates as Basra is today.

Here, following a friendly reception, Muhammad carved out for himself a position as civic leader. He was called upon to settle minor disputes between one section of the community and another. Such was the power of his personality, the appeal of his eloquence, the wisdom of his judgments, that the visionary was generally regarded as both statesman and lawgiver. Al-Madinah became a micro-Islamic state, a theocracy, in which religion, politics and the law were indivisible.

He went over to the offensive. The revelations called for *jihad*, a holy war, and this was waged against the Makkans, when he attacked a caravan passing through the oasis of Badr. In military terms it was only a skirmish but for Muhammad it provided the triumph that he needed. It enhanced his prestige among his followers and won him some support beyond the city gates. Nor were the effects of this initial victory in any way diminished by subsequent encounters in which the faithful were repulsed, not even when al-Madinah itself was attacked. For Islam encompasses an attitude of acceptance (the word itself means submission) and if defeat was God's will so be it:

> that Allah may know the true believer . . . that He may test the faithful and annihilate the infidels
>
> Qur'an, 3: 141 tr. Dawood

Later Muhammad sought to bring in the Jews but without much success and they were dispossessed of their lands or forced to pay a tax, the *jizyah*. This tax was later extended to tolerated religious minorities in Persia and elsewhere.

The day came when Muhammad judged he was strong enough to treat with the Makkans. Adroitly he had already declared Makkah the foremost holy city and he negotiated a truce which allowed him to return. Eight years after the *Hijrah*, he marched the faithful back. The Quraysh surrendered without bloodshed, their idols were thrown out and the Ka'bah was declared a sanctuary. The days of ignorance had gone for ever:

> The Truth has come and falsehood has been overthrown.
>
> (Qur'an, 17:81, tr. Dawood)

Five times a day for over 1,300 years the voice of the muezzin has called to the people thronging the concourse of the Ka'bah:

> God is most great.
> I testify there is no God but Allah.
> Come to prayer, come to security.
> God is most great.

In the year after his victory, when he led the pilgrimage from al-Madinah, Muhammad preached to the faithful assembled on the slopes of Mt Arafat. At the conclusion of his sermon he turned away from the assembled multitude and raised his voice to the unseen audience above:

> O Lord, I have delivered my message and discharged my Ministry.

He died four months later in 632. In the same year the last Sasanian king, Yazdigird III, was crowned king of Persia.

> 'O Messenger of Allah, what is Islam?', the Prophet was asked one day and he replied: 'Islam is to believe in Allah and his Prophet, to recite the prescribed prayers, to give alms, to observe the fast of Ramadan and to make the pilgrimage to Mecca.'
>
> Sykes, *op. cit.*, I, p. 521

The Qur'an (the word means 'recitation') embodies the revelations at Makkah and al-Madinah. It was first compiled after the Prophet's death and the authorised version followed in the time of the third Caliph, 'Uthman. It recites the word of God as relayed by the angel Gabriel and its *surahs* (chapters) detail a code of conduct ranging from commercial law to punishments for criminals, from the division of the spoils of war to the treatment of women:

> Men are the managers of the affairs of women
> for that God has preferred in bounty
> One of them over another, and for that
> they have expended of their property.
> Righteous women are therefore obedient . . .
>
> Qur'an, 4: 38

But they have rights of inheritance and it is the duty of a man to protect his wives (whose numbers were later limited to four). Widows, children and orphans must be cared for and slaves may be granted manumission. In a society which regarded women as chattels and in which girl babies were buried alive, the message of Muhammad was enlightened and humane.

For centuries scholars have been interpreting the Qur'an's 114 *surahs* into other languages but the Arabic rhetoric and rhythm make the task extremely difficult. Here is A J Arberry's rendering of a prayer in the second *surah*:

> Our Lord,
> take us not to task
> if we forget, or make mistake.
> Our Lord,
> charge us not with a load such
> as Thou didst lay upon those before us.
> Our Lord,
> do Thou not burden us
> beyond what we have the strength to bear.
> And pardon us,
> and forgive us,
> and have mercy on us;
> Thou art our Protector.
> And help us against the people
> of the unbelievers.
>
> Qur'an, 2: 285

THE RASHIDUN CALIPHATE

The 'Rightly Guided' Caliphs

News of the Prophet's death had repercussions across the peninsula. Some tribes reverted to their idolatrous practices, others listened to the claims of upstart prophets, many discontinued the giving of alms and murdered any Muslim tax gatherers who ventured near.

The people of al-Madinah elected Abu Bakr as caliph, that is 'successor' as guardian of the faith. He also controlled the army and despatched flying columns into every region which bore down on the defaulters and brought them to heel. So successful were these task forces that within twelve months order had been restored. Arabia had acquired a centralised—if somewhat rudimentary—government, and 'church' and state were under the black banner of the caliph.

In the north the famous warrior Khalid b. al-Walid, 'the Sword of Allah', invaded the borderlands of Syria and Persia. The people of Hira came over and joined the swelling tide which broke, as we have seen, on many distant shores. Yet it is doubtful whether the Arabs originally intended to cross the Zagros mountains or the Nile.

Almost inadvertently, as it were, within a span of twelve years they found themselves masters of an empire which extended from the Oxus to Egypt.

Their extraordinary success was due to a combination of situations which developed in the early part of the seventh century, which, in the context of world history, were in themselves unremarkable. The Arab advance into Iraq and Syria was not the first (Semitic nomads in antiquity 'yearning after bread and dates' had frequently overflowed into the pasturelands of the Fertile Crescent). Nor was the downfall of two mutually hostile empires by any means the last. The trauma of the seventh century was one of those accidents of history. On the one side an impoverished and expanding population was caught up in a compulsive religious movement. On the other two great powers had fought each other to a standstill, their empires were disintegrating, their armies in disarray.

During the caliphates of Abu Bakr and of 'Umar, who followed, when the Arab armies were catapulted on to the civilized world, they were faced with the many and varied problems that conquest can leave in its wake. How were a people in a relatively primitive stage of development, whose experience of government was traditionally limited to tribal rule, who were nomadic, who were largely illiterate, who despised agriculture and education—how were they to administer the countries they now had to govern?

In Persia a sound administrative framework already existed and 'Umar's solution was to make use of it. At the same time the Arab soldiers were instructed to hold themselves aloof as integration between Muslim and unbeliever would not be tolerated. Officials of the former regime were reinstated and in rural areas the *dihqans* went about collecting taxes as before. Military base camps were set up at Basra and among the sands of Kufa, where scribes and other government servants from the *divans* of Ctesiphon were set to work to apply their expertise. Regional commands in tented towns were pegged out along the desert fringes; to them the *dihqans* delivered the revenues and the cultivators paid their taxes in kind. In this way 'Umar adroitly sidestepped the many tasks which the Arabs were incapable of performing and at the same time he ensured the supply of pay and rations to his armies.

The fiscal system that was adopted over the years was also masterminded by 'Umar. The taxes imposed were heavy but not extortionate. In the occupied territories a *kharaj* or land tax, payable in cash or in kind, was charged on the productivity of the area under cultivation. In addition non-Muslims, who were exempt from military service, paid a poll-tax, the *jizyah*, in return for the protection the armies accorded them.

Though proselytising was not an article of the Muslim faith, the imposition of the *jizyah* served as an inducement to receive the new message. The peasant, if he was prepared to accept military service, had little to lose by coming over; indeed in the restructured society he had some slight status to gain. On prisoners of war too the pressures were strong: for them conversion bought freedom from slavery, a price which many thousands thought worth paying. But to ensure the preservation of the master race converts—*mawali*—were kept at a distance. They were regarded as second-class citizens and they served in the armies for a lower rate of pay. This treatment, which persisted, became a serious source of friction in later years.

Zoroastrians, Jews and Christians—the gentiles as it were of the Muslim world—who paid the *jizyah*, were classed as *dhimmis*. As 'People of the Book', that is as believers who had their own scriptures, they were tolerated. Since they could hardly be subject to Qur'anic law, they were permitted to have their own judiciaries.

Thus the class structure of Iran's imperialist days based on birth and occupation (the nobility, the priesthood, the army, and so on), gave way to a society that was categorized by race and religion: Arab Muslims were the new élite, then came the non-arab Muslims (*mawali*), and the tolerated religions (*dhimmis*).

Marriage for the Arabs in the occupied lands posed a problem. How was their separate identity to be safeguarded when few of the women—local girls, camp followers, captives and slaves—could claim to be of Arab origin? This local difficulty was overcome by the happy expedient of a declaration that the children of these unions would be Arab.

Following the decisive battle of Nihavand in 642, Rayy (now on the outskirts of modern Tehran) and Isfahan fell, the provinces of Azarbaijan in the north-west and Fars were overrun and Khurasan in eastern Iran invaded. The Arab armies, when they had first overflowed into Lower Iraq and the Persian borderlands, had had no coordinated plan of campaign but now, operating from their garrisons at Basra and Kufa, the remaining centres of population on the plateau were systematically attacked. Within a decade the provinces surrounding the great central deserts, the heartlands of Persia, had been conquered. The fiercest fighting centred round the cities. Once defeat was conceded, agreements were negotiated between the Arab commanders and leading citizens which stipulated the amount of *jizyah* to be paid.

News of the murder of Yazdigird in 651 must have been received with satisfaction in al-Madinah. But the weapon that killed the king struck deep into the Zoroastrian faith. With his death the last forlorn hope of a return to Sasanian rule perished. Some of the communities, as we have seen, abandoned their homes for another shore where the sacred flame could burn undimmed. But in Persia over the centuries their numbers dwindled and today only two Zoroastrian communities of small farmers around the desert towns of Yazd and Kerman survive.

But if the death of the last Sasanian was a tragedy for the Zoroastrians it held out no immediate prospect of a victory for Islam, although it was heralded as such. A century or more was to pass before the new faith began to gain more general credence. Sporadic revolts broke out especially in the east and towns that had fallen once had to be re-taken. In Iraq the people more readily accepted the new regime but on the plateau the Arabs faced an Aryan race well inured to putting up long-term resistance to invaders. And though to the caliphate Persia was but one country among others to be reduced to the status of a province, she had been an independent sovereign state too long and she was culturally too far advanced to lose her national identity.

Meanwhile in al-Madinah signs of the religious strife which was to tear the Arab world apart first appeared during the caliphate of the aging 'Uthman (644-656). During his tenure of office the Arabs pushed northwards: they invaded Armenia and reached the river Oxus. They desperately needed a firm hand to organize and manage their territories. But 'Uthman, though a man of undoubted piety, was weak, easy-going and indolent. The hours he felt called upon to devote to the study of the Qur'an left him insufficient time to supervise the administration of the great empire he headed. Unlike the first two caliphs, 'Uthman lived in comfort, he appointed his relations to lucrative posts and he accepted presents. And, despite high levels of taxation, income was not always sufficient to meet the needs of his expanding armies; there was a widespread belief that some of the revenue was reaching the wrong pockets but little was done to remedy abuses.

Discontent spread through Egypt and the garrison towns. It came to a head among the extremist elements in Kufa, who expelled their governor (the caliph's half-brother) from the city. 'Uthman, instead of punishing the rebels and reinstating his brother, tried to appease them by appointing a new governor. The Kufans responded some months later by marching on al-Madinah. The holy city was undefended, 'Uthman refused to leave and he met his end bravely. The rebels broke into his house as he sat reading the Qur'an and fell on him with their swords.

The wilful murder of the caliph by members of the faith just twenty-four years after the death of Muhammad marked the first significant loosening of the bonds of the brotherhood which the Prophet had laboured to bring about.

'Ali, a cousin and Companion of the Prophet, was proclaimed caliph. As a cousin of Muhammad and the husband of his only surviving daughter, Fatimah, he was the obvious candidate. Many of the faithful believed he should have been the first rather than the fourth successor. He faced a difficult situation. Had he been as autocratic as Abu Bakr or as hard as 'Umar he might have merged the discontented elements. But, though he had fought with great distinction beside Muhammad, Ali was at heart a devout peace-loving man. He tolerated the young hotheads who claimed to be his supporters, even if he was not always in sympathy with them, while his refusal to punish the rebels laid him open to accusations of favouritism towards his followers and of complicity by his enemies, especially from among the members of 'Uthman's family. Some of them he dismissed from their posts but a nephew, Mu'awiya, powerful governor of Syria, refused to go and 'Ali was forced to act against him. After some months of civil war each side appointed an arbitrator and 'Ali was judged to have been in the wrong. His sphere of influence was confined to Arabia and the eastern territories, while Mu'awiya ruled over the richer lands of Syria and Egypt. Five years after 'Uthman's murder 'Ali too was struck down and killed by the sword of an assassin.

'Ali was the last of the so-called 'Rightly Guided' (Rashidun) Caliphs. His death was a prelude to the schism which has tormented the Muslim world throughout its history: the division between his own followers and the orthodox (Sunnis). But to 'Ali himself death brought a martyr's crown and lasting fame as the first Imam and the founder of the Shi'ah sect, the Party of 'Ali:

En ma fin est mon commencement.

THE UMAYYADS—SHI'ISM AND THE IMAMS

With the death of 'Ali, Mu'awiya became the undisputed ruler of the

Arab world. Under the Umayyad dynasty, which he founded, he and his successor caliphs advanced the march of Islam in two important respects. They introduced a system of organized government appropriate to the needs of a nation state and they carried the faith to Spain and the shores of the Atlantic, to the Turkish speaking peoples of central Asia and the fringes of the Indian sub-continent. On the debit side they failed to bring the followers of ʻAli back into the fold and they succeeded only in widening the rift between the orthodox Sunni and the non-orthodox Shiʻah minority.

Muhammad had been dead for thirty years when in 661 Muʻawiya took over the eastern provinces of Iraq, Arabia and Persia. The holy war, which the Prophet had waged from al-Madinah against the infidels, had already been followed by a civil war among the faithful and the young militants in the camps at Kufa and Basra were showing signs of fomenting another as supporters of other would-be caliphs sharpened their swords.

Muʻawiya had, however, shown himself to be shrewd, subtle and skilled at achieving his aims by manipulating others. He had discredited ʻAli, he had moved the centre of the Arab Kingdom to the north, he had governed Syria without bloodshed:

> 'I apply not my sword,' he reportedly said, 'where my lash suffices, nor my lash where my tongue is enough.'
>
> Philip K Hitti, *History of the Arabs*, London, 1982, p. 197.

Here then was a man who could attempt to unite the disaffected. If he was less a person of principle then ʻAli, if he was more ambitious to win power than to attain piety and if secularity rather than theocracy was the hallmark of his administration, could he succeed where ʻAli had failed?

The elders of al-Madinah, piqued at the relegation of their city in favour of Damascus, were another brooding source of discontent. But Muʻawiya saw that the time had come to dispel the homely image of the early barefooted caliph, who governed from the courtyard of a mosque in the far south and who sat after evening prayers patching his shirt, accessible to all.

So the year 661 ushered in a new era in which a start was made in setting up the machinery of government and the conduct of Islamic affairs took on a more sophisticated dimension. Muʻawiya modelled the administration on Byzantine lines with separate bureaux (*divans*) to manage state finances and the needs of the army. He placed the three eastern provinces under the command of his formidable and ruthless viceroy, Ziyad b. Abihi. Through him the army was reformed, the malcontents split up, the narrow tribal affiliations discouraged to make way for the wider concept of loyalty to the caliph.

Mu'awiya built a fleet and went to war with the Byzantines (a popular move), which kept his forces occupied and in fighting order. But he failed to take Constantinople from the sea and on land his armies did not advance beyond the Taurus mountains. Far to the east Ziyad's armies carried the banner of Islam over the desert and mountain barriers of southern and central Asia, where they made contact with the Turkish tribes: they crossed the Oxus, they entered Bukhara and the important trading centre of Samarkand, while in Afghanistan they traversed the Hindu Kush and invaded the plains of northern India.

The success of Mu'awiya's expansionist policies went some way to restoring unity; but the mark of his failure lay in his choice of a successor. Muhammad, like Alexander, had omitted to lay down a system of succession and the selection had hitherto devolved somewhat arbitrarily on the citizens of al-Madinah. Mu'awiya's decision to introduce the hereditary principle was not well received, especially as his eldest son, Yazid, was not of a religious disposition. He was a pleasure-loving man who was more interested in hunting than in assuming the cares of office.

During his three year reign (680-683), Yazid's attempt to destroy the seed of Shi'ism, which 'Ali had sown, led to its successful germination. 'Ali's first son, Hasan, had died and his younger brother Husayn declared that, if the caliphate was to be hereditary, it should descend in direct line from the Prophet. He refused allegiance to Yazid and, urged on by his sympathisers, accepted an invitation from the Kufans to lead them against him. Husayn was honest, tolerant and devout; he was motivated by belief in the rightness of his cause rather than by personal ambition. Against the advice of his Makkan supporters he took the Kufans on trust and accepted the asurances he was given that they had the forces to back him.

In August 680, with his family and a small band of seventy-two supporters, Husayn set out from Makkah on the fateful journey. Some six weeks later they sighted the Euphrates but no guard of honour came to escort the new leader into Kufa. Yazid's army had already subdued the city and was marching to attack him. Husayn refused to surrender.

Beleaguered now with only his family, his few followers and his faith to support him against impossible odds, Husayn rode towards the enemy cavalry calling as he did so:

> Oh God, Thou art our trust in every danger, our hope in every extremity.
>
> John B Glubb, *The Empire of the Arabs*, London, 1963, p. 53

But the arrows came; his supporters were picked off one by one; his two small sons were killed and he carried their bodies back to his tent. For Husayn himself the end came slowly; though badly wounded he was left to the last. As he stood at bay even his enemies hesitated, each afraid to end the agony of the dying man. The order had to be given before a merciful lance pierced his body. Only the women and children were spared.

Back in Kufa the seventy-two heads were laid before the governor. As he turned the head of Husayn with his sword an old Arab cried out:

> Gently! it is the grandson of the Prophet. By Allah! I have seen these very lips kissed by the blessed mouth of Mohamed.
>
> Sykes, *op. cit.*, I, p. 541.

Yazid, on being presented with the trophies, is said to have condemned the massacre and disclaimed responsibility for it. He returned the head of Husayn to his family, he treated the women and children well and sent them all back to Makkah.

In the courtyard of the mosque in the modern city of Kerbela, near where the action took place, Husayn's body is entombed; his father rests at Najaf some fifty miles to the south. Kerbela has become a holy city, a place of pilgrimage, where each year on the tenth of the Muslim month of Muharram the tragedy of the House of ʻAli is enacted. Husayn's martyrdom swept the Shiʻite movement into being.

Having lost the caliphate, Husayn's supporters appointed their own Imam (spiritual leader). Muhammad, they believed, had decreed that he must be a lineal descendant of ʻAli and Fatimah. The Imams were credited with a mysterious inherited power which they passed on down the line to the twelfth and last of their number,

Muhammad al-Mahdi. He disappeared in obscure circumstances from the great mosque at Samarra leaving no heir. But he is said to be immune from death and will one day reappear to 'fill the earth with justice after . . . it has been filled with iniquity'. (E G Browne, *A Literary History of Persia*, Cambridge, 1956, II, p. 195)

During the century of Umayyad power 'Abd al-Malik (685-705) proved to be the most worthy of the successors to Mu'awiya. Each were capable administrators, each extended the bounds of empire and each, with the help of iron-heeled viceroys, held the dissident elements in the eastern provinces in check. Al-Hajjaj, a colourful and even more fearsome character than his predecessor, had a taste for the dramatic. Arriving at Kufa in disguise to take up his appointment, he entered the mosque, raised the veil from his face and addressed the astonished congregation, taking the words of the poet as his text:

> I am he who scattereth darkness and climbeth lofty summits.
> As I lift the turban from my face ye will know me.

He continued:

> O people of al-Kufah! Certain am I that I see heads ripe for cutting, and verily I am the man to do it. Methinks I see blood between the turbans and the beards.
>
> Hitti, *op. cit.*, p. 207

He was as good as his word. If his methods were drastic he nevertheless served his master's interests well. He disposed of a serious rival for the office of caliph and he either executed the Shi'ite troublemakers or drafted them into his foreign legion where, instead of fomenting civil war, they brought yet more territory under the Commander of the Faithful.

During the reigns of 'Abd al-Malik and his son al-Walid the Umayyads reached the high watermark of their power and splendour. In the west their armies swept along the coast of North Africa and crossed into Spain; in central Asia al-Hajjaj consolidated and extended Ziyad's gains till the mantle of Muslim rule had spread from the Pyrenees to the borders of China. The vicars of the Prophet had long since exchanged the simple dwellings of the Madinah days for marble palaces, homespun had given way to brocaded silk, desert fare to culinary delicacies. They presided over elegant courts and surrounded themselves with regal ceremonial. They had become accustomed to the material amenities of civilization and were themselves contributors, especially in the field of architecture. The great Umayyad mosque erected by al-Walid on the site of a Christian church, though much restored, is the crowning glory of Damascus to this day.

During the Umayyads' tenure of office Persia remained a province of their empire. Though not forced to adopt the new faith, her people, in common with the many thousands of the caliphs' subjects, genuflected to the arabizations which the new theocracy imposed, notably the introduction of Arabic as the official language. But belief in 'divine' kingship was deep-rooted and it is not clear how many converts there were to the new faith. Those who did come over would have been attracted to the Shi'ite honeypot in the belief that Sasanian blood ran in the veins of the 'Alids and that Yazdigird's daughter, Shahr-banu, had been married to Husayn. This apocryphal story was carefully cultivated among the Shi'ah and incorporated in the passion play which they loved to enact:

> . . . in my father's palace once at night
> In sleep to me came Fatima 'the Bright';
> 'O Shahr-banu'—thus the vision cried -
> 'I give thee to Husayn to be his bride!'
>
> E G Browne, *op. cit.*, I, p. 132.

Just as in Damascus the caliphs modelled their government on that of the more sophisticated Byzantine north, so in the province of Persia the conquerors adopted the administrative practices that were already in force. Consequently Arabs who displaced *dihqans* and other functionaries found it necessary to be literate and numerate—thus education could no longer be despised, nor could agriculture. For the shaikhs who took over the estates of the Persian nobility were in effect coming into the ownership of property and of land which required cultivation.

Like other dynasties the Umayyads in their turn followed the footsteps of history into decline. Their strength was dissipated in succession quarrels and, as they sank back into the cushioned comforts of their palaces, their vision clouded, their control over state affairs slackened and expressions of discontent grew until in time almost every section of society was voicing grievances. The devout elders among the Arabs, who revered the asceticism of the early caliphs, were affronted by the indulgencies of their successors, by their disregard of the scriptures, by their addiction to wine and by their adoption of that undesirable feature of affluent society in the orient, the harem; peasants and small farmers protested at the extortionate demands of Arab tax collectors; the *mawali*—another substantial body—resented their low social status, while, among the Arabs, a long-standing conflict between the Yemenis and the tribesmen of the north was renewed. The most serious disturbances were in Khurasan and it was there that the bubble burst.

The revolt was masterminded by the 'Abbasid branch of the Prophet's family. They were orthodox Muslims but like the Shi'ah they regarded the Umayyads as usurpers. Their leader, Abu'l Abbas, and his commander in the field, Abu Muslim, planned the operation with great care. They fanned the feud among the Arabs, they rallied the disaffected *mawali* and they made common cause with the Iraqi Shi'ites. Abu Muslim with a following of 2,000 men raised the 'Abbasid standard and occupied the important city of Merv. From there his army marched across the Persian plateau. On 30 October 749 the capital of the eastern provinces opened its gates and the rebels entered the city of Kufa. Abu'l 'Abbas emerged from hiding and headed a procession through the streets to the great mosque where he addressed the congregation:

> Praise be to God . . . who has given us ties of relation and kinship with the Messenger of God, and has brought us forth from his fathers . . . and has placed us in respect to Islam and its people in an exalted position . . . He has informed them of our excellence and made it obligatory for them to render us our right . . .
> Oh people of Kufa, you are the object of our love and affection. You have been constant in that love, your mistreatment by the oppressors has not turned you from it until you reached our time and God brought you our turn in power . . .
>
> *Cambridge History of Iran*, 1975, 4, p. 57

Elated at their delivery from the Umayyad yoke, the Kufans were easily swayed by the rhetoric of the man who stood before them and they hastened to offer their allegiance. Yet he was a Sunni with no connection with the House of 'Ali. Abu 'l-'Abbas was a great-great-grandson of the Prophet's uncle, a man who was crafty, cruel and untrustworthy, who by a carefully timed coup had ridden to the summit of power on the backs of the Shi'ah and pre-empted the claim of the Imamate to command the faithful.

Three months later 'Abdallah b. 'Ali, an uncle of Abbas, defeated the Umayyad armies on the banks of the Great Zab. Damascus fell soon after and Marwan II, the last of the their Caliphs, fled to Egypt where he was hunted down and killed. As part of his mopping up operations, and with 'Abbas' connivance 'Abdallah invited some eighty members of the Umayyad family to an amnesty ceremony and a banquet. At a given signal his men turned on the guests and clubbed them to death. Leather covers were placed over the bodies and the hosts feasted to the sound of the groans from the dying beneath them. Henceforth the executioner and his leather carpet formed part of the caliph's suite. Not without reason Abu'l 'Abbas acquired the sobriquet al-Saffah, 'Shedder of Blood'.

With the passing of the Umayyads the Arabs relinquished their monopoly of the caliphate. They had carried the Muslim faith from its birthplace within the remote and narrow confines of the Arabian peninsula across the desert sands into three continents. Now as their armies were disbanded, their government dismembered, their capital demoted, the new leadership assumed a more cosmopolitan outlook and racial considerations were of little or no account.

Once again the course of the Tigris lay through the capital of an empire. From its banks the new caliphs while proclaiming the religious nature of their authority were content to delegate much of the daily administration to a bureaucracy which came increasingly under Persian control.

THE 'ABBASID SHADOW OF GOD UPON EARTH

A traveller who arrived in al-Madinah in the early days of the caliphate stopped a passer-by and asked how he might gain an audience of 'Umar.

> 'There is no door,' the stranger replied, 'between him and the people. You can speak to him every day in the streets and in the mosque.'
>
> J B Glubb, *The Great Arab Conquests*, London, 1963, p. 269

1 Monument on which Shalmaneser III recorded in cunieform script his encounter with the Persians and the Medes; black obelisk from the citadel at Nimrud, c. 825 BC, in the British Museum.

2 Detail of plate 1, showing Shalmaneser receiving the tribute of Jehu, King of Israel.

3 Ashurbanipal and his queen drinking in a garden to the sound of music. The head of the defeated Elamite king hangs in a tree above; stone relief from the king's palace at Nineveh, c. 645 BC, in the British Museum.

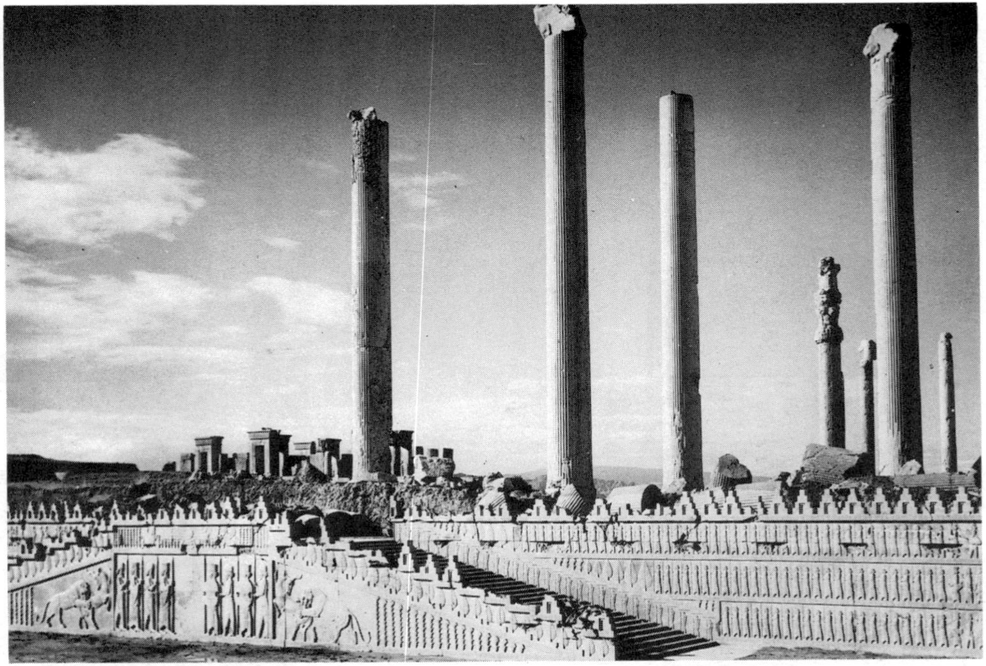

4 Persepolis: stairway leading to the Audience Hall (Apadana) with the palace of Darius in the background (Courtesy of the Oriental Institute of the University of Chicago).

5 Persepolis: detail of a relief of the Great King Darius

6 Alexander the Great; marble bust in the British Museum

7 Hatra: facade of the Parthian temple-palace

8 Hatra : limestone relief from the sun temple of a Gorgon's head, with snakes in place of hair

9 Shapur I commemorating his victories over two Roman emperors, the captive Valerian and Philip the Arab who sued for peace. One pleads for mercy, the other is held in the king's grasp; rock relief from Naqsh-i Rustam.

10 Takht-i Sulayman: landscape view (collection of Michael Roaf)

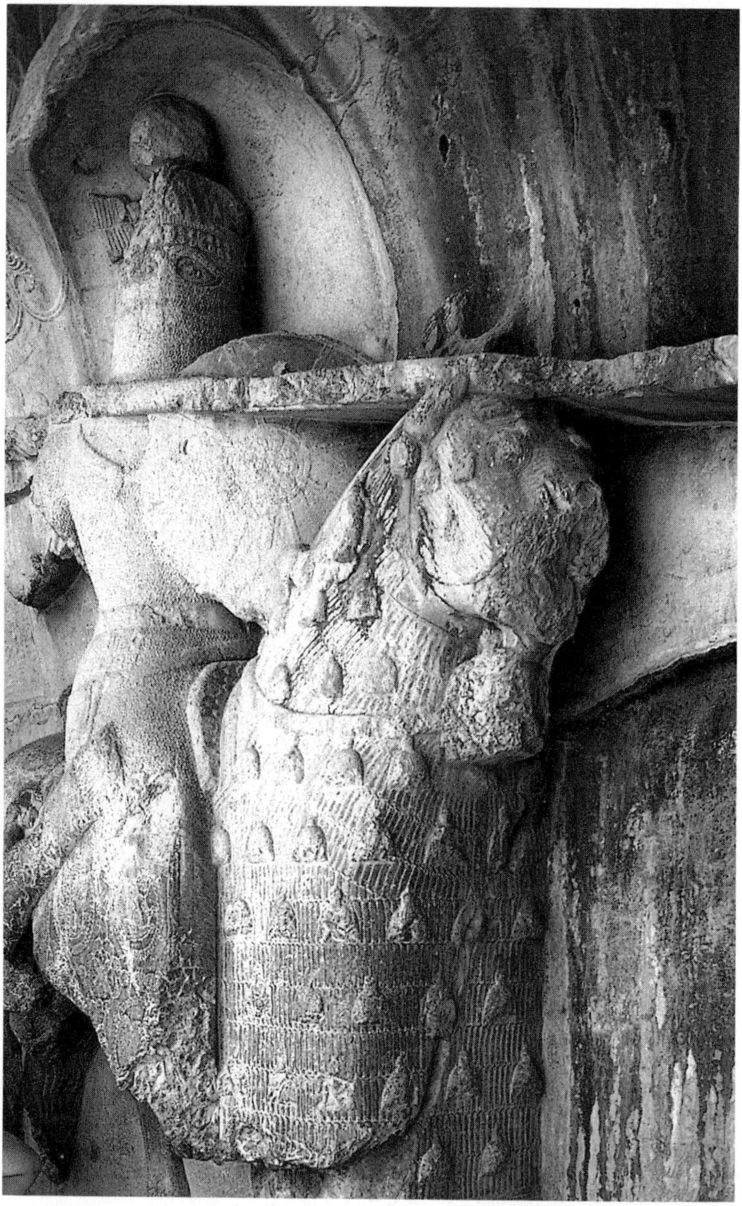

11 Bas relief of royal mail-clad Sasanian cavalryman from Taq-i Bustan (photo: Warwick Ball)

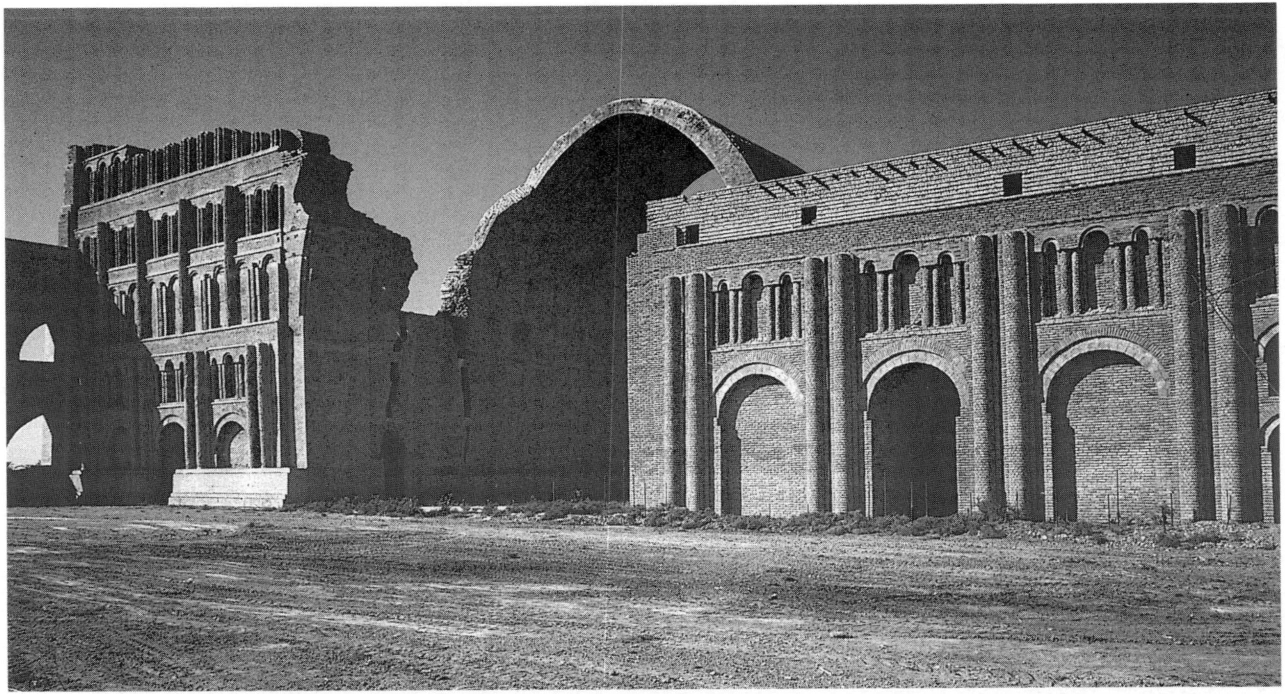

12 Taq-i Kisra (palace of Khusrau I), said to be the largest unsupported mud brick arch build without centring (photo: Warwick Ball)

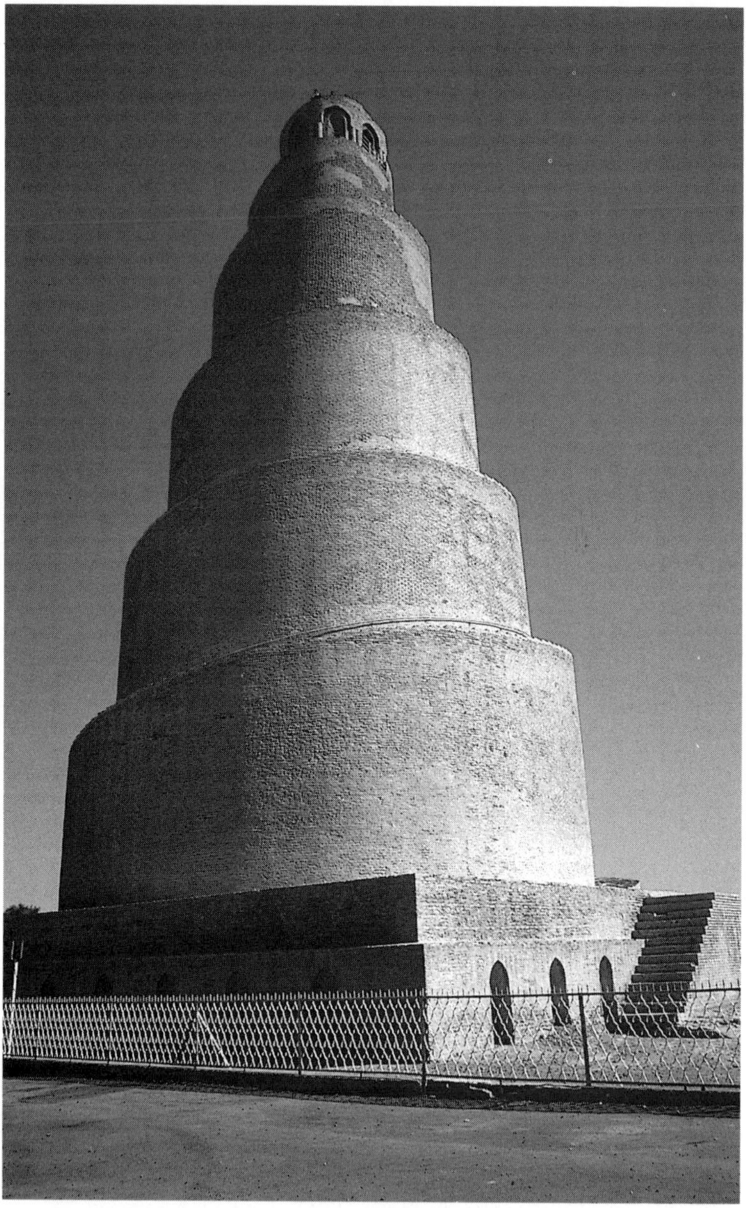

13 The spiralling munaret at Samarra, near where the Twelfth Imam disappeared in 873 (photo: Warwick Ball)

14 Saljuq Minaret at Sava (photo: Antony Hutt)

15 Ghengis Khan admonishing the people of Bukhara; Persian miniature of 1397 in the British Library

16 Tamerlane, from F R Martin *Miniature paintings of Persia*, Macmillan, London, 1912

17 Portal of Jami 'mosque, Yazd (photo: Antony Hutt)

18 Mahan : shrine of Shaykh Ni'matallah, 15th to 19th centuries (photo: Antony Hutt)

19 Shah 'Abbas; Mughul school late 17th century, British Museum

20 Isfahan : Madrasa Madar-i Shah, early 18th century (photo: Antony Hutt)

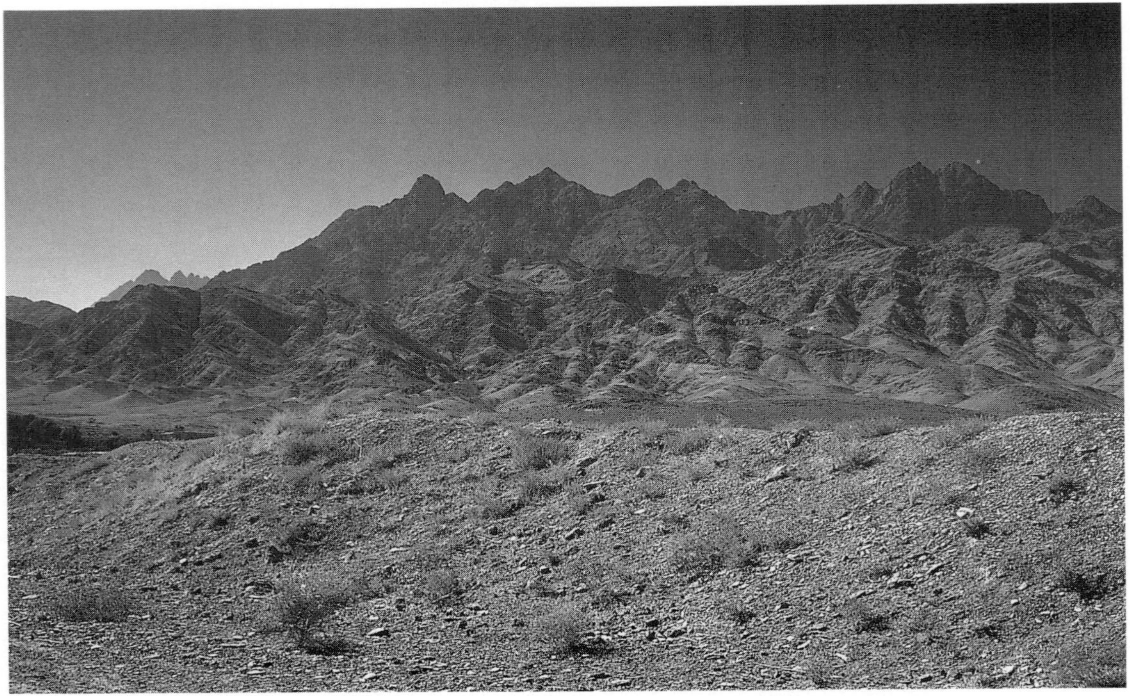

21 The timeless landscape of the Iranian plateau

And he pointed to a circle of men seated on the ground in the square. They wore the customary garb of the desert; their clothes were patched; they had no shoes. Among them was one of the most powerful men in the world.

A century and a half later a traveller on the same mission presenting himself at the golden gates of the caliphal palace in Baghdad would have found the doors to the audience chamber guarded by chamberlains, eunuchs and a host of other lackeys. Gone were the days when the caliph mingled with the people after the midday prayers or when he distributed food to the poor, as 'Umar did in the alleys of al-Madinah.

Abstemiousness had given place to indulgence, the conviviality of the courtyard to the elegant formality of the court. The sanded alleyways, the mudded walls and hovels that furnished the city of al-Madinah had been discarded during the caliphate's two-stage journey to the east in favour of paved precincts and houses. Simplicity had surrendered to elaborate ceremonial, frugality had been outmoded by magnificence.

Scientists, artists, philosophers, writers and scholars from distant lands mingled with religious sages, merchants, soldiers, sailors, craftsmen—the men and women of Harun al-Rashid's brilliant city. Not surprisingly, the poet who lingered in imagination one evening at the 'Gate of the Sun' as members of a caravan assembled (our traveller among them perhaps), was anxious to know why they wished to depart:

> 'Is not Bagdad the beautiful? O, stay.
> . . . For what land
> Leave you the dim-moon city of delight?'
>
> J E Flecker, *The Golden Journey to Samarkand*

Back on that day in 749, when al-Saffah had been acclaimed in the mosque at Kufa, Baghdad was just another hamlet on the banks of the Tigris. Yet its time of greatness was only thirty years or so away. How did the city so rapidly reach its prime?

The 'Abbasids, unlike the Umayyads, were not set on extending the perimeters of empire. They sought to merge the disparate elements over which they governed into an orthodox (Sunni) state and to create a climate in which trade and industry could flourish. That is not to say that there were no wars beyond the frontiers or that merchants and traders always enjoyed a free hand to pursue their occupations; indeed the Jews and other *dhimmis*, who acted as money changers (usury was forbidden by the Qur'an), were persecuted from time to time. But in general the upsurge of economic growth stemmed from the reign of the second caliph, al-Mansur. He built Baghdad, he had the vision to locate the capital at a cross-roads that would develop into a centre for international trade, he started a programme of roadway and waterway improvements. Moreover, he and his successors, with their cosmopolitan outlook, did not regard the Arab people as an élite. In the provinces garrison towns became market towns from which *mawali* merchants and craftsmen, freed now from the stigma of social inferiority, could explore wider markets for their goods and services.

And so it was that in the latter part of the eighth century the 'Abbasids came into their golden age. Once more the turbines of oriental despotism were churning the waters of the Tigris as they filtered through the fabled city. Within two generations the 'Abbasids had established themselves as the undisputed rulers of a great empire. Yet their effective power endured for barely a hundred years. Theirs was a tadpole shaped dynasty which shook the world and then tailed quickly into four centuries of decline,. which survived at times in name only until it was obliterated altogether by Hulagu's Mongol hordes in 1258.

The Tigris-Euphrates river systems chiselling their way south towards the waters of the Gulf formed a fertile borderland between the foothills of the Zagros mountains and the Syrian-Arabian deserts, between Aryan Persia and Semitic Asia, a sleeve-shaped country, with Baghdad at the elbow, elongating into a narrow sea which (depending on the location of the inhabitants who lined its shores) was known either as the Persian or as the Arabian Gulf (as it still is today).

Baghdad became the undisputed nerve centre of the Islamic empire; the basic tenets of the faith were never challenged and the language of the Qur'an acted as a unifying influence across the state. But Arab influence in the conduct of civil affairs declined. Nor were their armies with their Umayyad loyalties welcome to the new regime and some of the Kufa units were phased out.

As the flood tide of Arab nationalism ebbed away Persian influences filtered in. The Khurasan army, which had helped the ruling house to power formed the caliphal bodyguard and in government circles Persian and Iraqi *mawali* under a Persian vizier staffed the *divans*. For those who frequented the court it became fashionable to marry into Persian families and to adopt Persian dress.

The 'Abbasids in their heyday used the revenues they exacted to buttress their own position, to clothe the caliphate in luxury and to support an increasingly heavy bureaucracy. But when power began to slip from their grasp they leaned yet further on the faith. They claimed that their authority to rule had been bestowed on them from above and arrogated to themselves the title: the Shadow of God upon Earth.

The Golden Age

When in 754 al-Saffah died of smallpox and his brother al-Mansur succeeded, he did not attain office without bloodshed. His uncle, the infamous 'Abdallah, disputed his claim and the services of Abu Muslim had to be enlisted to eliminate him from the contest.

Abu Muslim had served his 'Abbasid masters not wisely but too well. Al-Mansur now revealed himself in his true colours: to his dark and devious mind the man who had secured him his throne had become his rival. He summoned Abu Muslim to an audience and, as he stood before him, he ordered his bodyguard to cut him down. Treachery compounded by corruption became part of the family stock-in-trade and on this occasion some carefully directed gratuities were distributed to silence Abu Muslim's own men.

Al-Mansur was the archetypal grand inquisitor: a lean lugubrious humourless man, he was also calculating and careful with money and he amassed a vast treasury. He introduced the office of vizier (originally a Sasanian innovation) to supervise the *divans* and ensure the smooth running of the administration. He was interested in the Arabic language and literature and sponsored translations from the Greek of the works of Galen and Hippocrates. But he is remembered above all as the builder of Baghdad. Kufa had proved to be an unsuitable venue from which to direct the affairs of a Sunni government and his selection of the site on the banks of the Tigris for his 'city of peace' was a shrewd choice of which he was rightly proud:

> This island between the Tigris in the East and the Euphrates in the West is a market place for the world . . . ships that come up the Tigris . . . anchor here; wares brought on ships down the Tigris . . . and along the Euphrates from . . . Syria and the border marshes, Egypt and North Africa will be brought and unloaded here. It will be the

> highway for the people . . . Praise be to God who preserved it for me and caused all those who came before me to neglect it. By God, I shall build it. Then I shall dwell in it as long as I live and my descendants shall dwell in it after me. It will surely be the most flourishing city in the world.
>
> Bernard Lewis, *The Arabs in History*, London, 1950, p. 82

He built a round moated city. Set within its double walls were four equidistant gates, starting points on the roads to Damascus, Kufa, Basra and Khurasan. In the centre stood the Golden Palace with its green domed audience chamber and the Great Mosque.

Al-Mansur supervised much of the building work himself. He used the old Sasanian palace at Ctesiphon as a quarry. Thinking that the advice of his Minister of Finance, Khalid b. Barmak, must be biased because of his Persian origins, he at first rejected his suggestion that he could cut costs by baking bricks on the site.

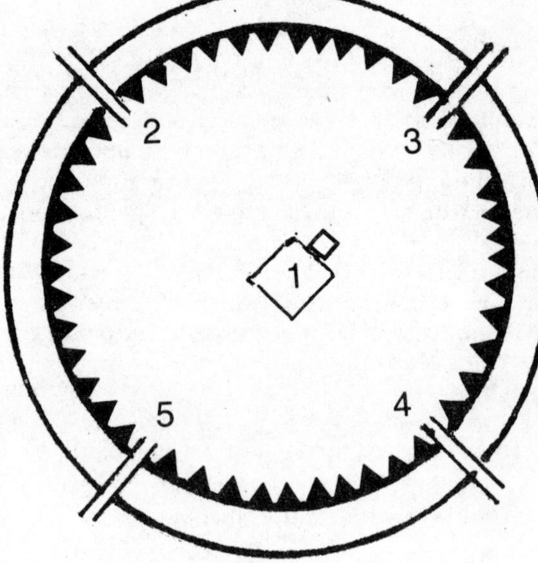

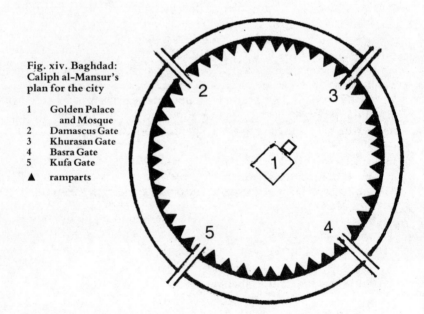

Fig. xiv. Baghdad: Caliph al-Mansur's plan for the city

1 Golden Palace and Mosque
2 Damascus Gate
3 Khurasan Gate
4 Basra Gate
5 Kufa Gate
▲ ramparts

Fortunately the minister's calculations proved to be correct and Khusraw's audience hall was spared for posterity.

Khalid b. Barmak was the first of the famous Barmecides to gain political power. They were a *mawali* family from Khurasan. Khalid's father had been chief priest in a Buddhist monastery at Balkh, he himself had served Abu Muslim in the revolution and his son, Yahya, who became the boyhood friend and counsellor of Harun al-Rashid, was the first to hold the office of vizier.

To the succession problems endemic in dynastic history in general and Islamic history in particular, al-Saffah had introduced yet another by designating 'Isa, a nephew, as successor to al-Mansur. This nomination exercised al-Mansur in his old age for he wanted his own son, al-Mahdi, to follow him. Inducements of several sorts—bribes, threats and attacks on his person—failed to persuade 'Isa to renounce his right. But where 'Abbasid guile was of no avail the resourceful minister of finance succeeded and in the end 'Isa retired from the political scene.

Under al-Mahdi wars were resumed over frontier disputes with the Byzantines but in a lower key than before. His younger son, Harun, conducted a successful campaign against them which won him the accolade 'al-Rashid' (follower of the right path).

A number of disturbances with which al-Mahdi had to contend were fomented by extremists on the heretical fringe of the faith. Among them was the rising led by Muqanna', one of a number who claimed to be the incarnation of God. For several years Muqanna' defied the 'Abbasid armies and ruled an area beyond the Oxus. His disciples were not privileged to see the features of their saviour as in public he wore a white shroud over his face. This device served to heighten the mysticsm of the movement, to awe his peasant followers and to spread his fame as 'the veiled prophet of Khurasan'.

The ninth century was also a time of philosophical argument and serious theological debate 'about it and about'. Just as the Christian churches, once they had gained acceptance, were beset with schisms and heresies so Islam, already rent by the Sunni-Shi'ite division, turned in upon itself as elders and others pondered those questions to which there are no certain answers this side of the grave, questions that were to exercise future generations and ultimately to divide the believers themselves still further.

> There was a door to which I found no key:
> There was a veil past which I could not see.
>
> *Rubaiyat* of 'Umar Khayyam

Meanwhile overlaying these besetting doubts the outer world continued on its colourful course and Harun al-Rashid was proclaimed caliph in 786. His father had been killed in a hunting accident and his elder brother, al-Hadi, after a brief inglorious reign, had died, poisoned some said by their Persian mother who favoured Harun.

The tarnishing affect of the al-Hadi interlude soon faded and one of Harun's first acts as caliph was to release his Barmecide friend, Yahya, from the prison in which his brother had incarcerated him and to hand him the keys of the office of vizier:

> I have placed the responsibility for my subjects on your shoulders. Rule them as you think best . . . Here is my signet ring, which I entrust to you.
> J B Glubb, *The Empire of the Arabs*, 1963, p. 271.

Armed with this authority the new vizier took over and, as the administration grew in size and complexity, some of the ministerial openings were filled by members of his family. Under the Barmecides the prosperity of the 'Abbasid empire increased and Baghdad, as al-Mansur had intended, became an important centre for trade and commerce. But Harun's hand remained on the tiller. His armies kept the Byzantines at a distance and, nearer home, where due to al-Hadi's clumsy handling of the Shi'ah problem the 'Alids staged several revolts, he suppressed them without mercy.

Storytellers have portrayed Harun as a glamorous prince, who was regaled during the day by fawning courtiers and who sloped off incognito to indulge in incredible escapades through a 'Thousand and One Nights'[3]. But he was also an intellectual and a poet in his own right. His evenings were frequently devoted to conversation, to recitations and to music. He was a devout Sunni (the taking of wine being perhaps his only indulgence) and he is said to have habitually spent many hours at prayer.

Though clearly of a sunnier and more generous disposition than al-Mansur, Harun's treatment of the Barmecides suggests that he was almost as ruthless as his grandfather. Yahya had been his boyhood tutor and friend; under al-Hadi he had suffered imprisonment for his loyalty and as vizier he had directed the machinery of state for seventeen years. On the other side of the coin he had placed his three sons and other members of the Barmecide family in important government posts, they had amassed enormous wealth, they had built themselves grandiose palaces, they had dispensed largesse on a lavish scale. They had made enimies too and in their parade of pomp, power and partronage they had come near—too near—to being more royal than their master. Maybe Harun harboured a lurking jealousy of their success in office, maybe he resented their display of opulence, maybe they had passed too many favours to their fellow Khurasanians. Whatever the reason he had undoubtedly been casting around for an excuse to be rid of them, when an episode leaked from the harem reached his ears.

In the early part of his reign during his evening revels, Harun had sometimes called for the company of Yahya's son Ja'far, and his own favourite sister, 'Abbasa. To observe the proprieties Ja'far and 'Abbasa had agreed to go through a form of marriage which, they promised him, would be purely platonic. When Harun learnt from a disgruntled harem servant that during a pilgrimage to Makkah 'Abbasa had borne a child, the fate of the Barmecides was sealed. Ja'far was summarily executed and parts of his body displayed around the city and Yahya was taken back across Baghdad's bridge of sighs to the prison from which Harun had rescued him, with the rest of his family. Such was the tragic fate of a house that with all its faults had rendered the caliph notable service.

After announcing his plans for the succession Harun realised—too late—that he had set the country on course for civil war by partitioning it between his two elder sons, al-Amin and al-Ma'mun. Relations between the brothers were far from fraternal, the only aim they had in common being a desire for power. And when at the age of forty-five their father fell ill they awaited his death like vultures gathering round a prospective kill. The end came in 809 when he was visiting Khurasan. 'My sons', he is said to have told an aide, 'are watching the hour of my decease'. Harun was buried in the village where he died in what is now the holy city of Mashhad.

Back in Baghdad al-Amin succeeded as caliph and governor of Iraq, while al-Ma'mun, son of a Persian slave girl, established his eastern capital at Merv. There he held court and bided his time while consolidating his hold over Khurasan. Al-Ma'mun was a tolerant deep-thinking religious man and altogether a more worthy successor than his elder brother. He told a Khurasanian assembly:

> 'Oh people, I have taken it upon myself before God that, if he gives me charge of your affairs, I will obey him in dealing with you. I will not purposely shed blood except in lawful punishments and obligations imposed by God.'
>
> *Cambridge History of Iran*, 1975, 4, p. 72

Four years later his armies under the command of General Tahir marched on Baghdad. The city surrendered after a long siege and al-Amin was killed. Inexplicably al-Ma'mun himself made no move but stayed on in Merv for another four years. Meanwhile, for lack of firm leadership, the situation in the western provinces deteriorated, especially in Shi'ite areas, and Iraq, now virtually rudderless, drifted into anarchy.

Sufficiently alarmed at last, al-Ma'mun set out towards the capital. He had tried to pacify the Shi'ites by nominating the Eighth Imam, 'Ali al-Rida, as his successor, a courageous but imprudent measure, as it enraged the Sunnis and created further disturbances, especially in Baghdad. By the time al-Ma'mun reached the capital the elderly al-Rida had died, according to popular Shi'ite belief, from eating poisoned grapes. The Shi'ites chose to believe that al-Ma'mun had been responsible for al-Rida's death and declared the Imam a martyr to the 'Alid cause.[4] So, just as Alexander II, the one reforming Russian Tsar who had liberated the serfs, suffered assassination, the only caliph who attempted to reconcile the Shi'ites, was vilified by the very people he tried to help. Nevertheless, once al-Ma'mun had established himself in Baghdad, calm was restored. Under his wise and tolerant rule the scars of the civil war faded and the city settled down once again.

When al-Mamun died, on a sortie against the Byzantines, the caliphate passed to a younger brother. Al-Mu'tasim, the son of a Turkish concubine, was a man of action with little time for cultural pursuits. He stepped up the import of Turkish slaves from central Asia to replace the dwindling Khurasanian element in the army. As their numbers grew so did their confidence, their conduct became overbearing and by 836 the civilian population in Baghdad was threatening to rebel. Rather than face an uprising, al-Mu'tasim moved up the Tigris and took up residence in Samarra. In doing so he unwittingly laid a trap for his successors and it was not long before the Turks had the caliphs in their clutches. A period of anarchy followed until al-Mu'tamid, fifty-six years and seven caliphs later, returned to Baghdad. By then the empire was breaking up. Minor dynasties were establishing themselves in the east and the 'Abbasids had lost the power to govern effectively.

After the Samarra interlude the caliphs had no regular army. They became puppets in the hands of whatever military clique was riding high at the time and any lingering authority attached to the office was symbolic rather than actual.

During Baghdad's golden prime the 'Abbasids fostered the many

Fig. xv. Scene on the Tigris

and varied forms of human creativity and learning by attracting men of distinction from Europe and Asia to their city. Harun himself corresponded with Charlemagne and with the Tang emperor.

The introduction of paper from China enabled writers to record a wealth of prose and poetry which had hitherto been handed down mainly by word of mouth, while translators made available philosophical and historical writings of the classical age as well as treatises on medicine, mathematics and astronomy, among them the works of Plato and Aristotle, Euclid and Archimedes.

In the visual arts, though the human face was seldom portrayed, the word of God was written in the new art form of calligraphy. Floral and geometric designs were described on textiles, lustre, ivory, wood and metal and in traditional hand-woven rugs and carpets.

Virtually nothing now remains of al-Mansur's city, with its palace and mosque, its libraries and courts, where scholars studied and deliberated. The spiralling minaret of the great mosque at Samarra is the most spectacular surviving monument of the period in the area. The tales of *The Arabian Nights*, though probably deriving mainly from Cairo, sketch in the everyday social scene in Baghdad's golden age as well: the shopkeeper with his wares in the bazaar, the narrow shaded alleyways, the door in the wall, the courtyard with the fountain playing within.

Caliphs might come and go but life in al-Mansur's city continued on its course and the waters of the fountain played intermittently on through five centuries until the forces of destruction returned once more to attack the civilized world.

The Minor Dynasties

The region of Baluchistan is an inhospitable land of waterless wastes and jagged rocky hills. It lies in the furthest corner of south-east Iran segregated by mountain ranges and by deserts: the Dasht-i Lut (Lot's Desert), the great central sand desert, the Makran in the south, the Helmand Desert and the Dasht-i Naumid (the Desert of Despair) in the east. It is said of these desolations that when God created the world he left Baluchistan to last and formed it from the dregs.

Sistan, which lies to the north of the area, is a country which the world has passed by, where time has stood still, where myth merges with reality, legend with history. Along with Khurasan to the north it was the *Shahnama* land of the heroic Rustam, who championed the great kings of antiquity, and of his horse, Rakhsh, who transported him on the instant to the scene of battle wherever he was needed.[5] Except towards the east, where the Helmand river flows the year round, it is a land which has little to offer, where men must needs prey on each other, where the wise man moves on, where the traveller is counselled darkly:

> Conceal thy gold, thy destination and thy creed.
>
> E G Browne, *A Year Amongst the Persians*, Cambridge, 1927, p. 570

Muqaddasi was a traveller in the tenth century who braved the crossing of the Dasht-i Lut and lived to tell the tale. He described the people who roamed its wilderness as:

> 'a people with savage faces, evil hearts, and neither morals nor manners.' None could escape meeting them, and those they overcame they would stone to death 'as one would a snake, putting a man's head on a boulder, and beating upon it, till it be crushed in'; and when Mukaddasi enquired why they so barbarously put men to death he was answered that it was in order not needlessly to blunt their swords.'
>
> G Le Strange, *The Lands of the Eastern Caliphate*, repr. London, 1966, p. 323.

Yet it was the members of just such a band, the Saffarids, who first came near to restoring sovereignty over Iran after the Muslim conquests.

During the Samarra period of the caliphate, a century before Muqaddasi arrived in Sistan, the country was under the overlordship of the Tahirids,[6] semi-independent governors in Khurasan to the north-east. The Saffarids took their name from Ya'qub b. al-Layth, a coppersmith (Ar. *saffar*), who joined a group of these roaming brigands and established himself as their leader. He deposed the Tahirid governor and in 861 declared himself ruler of Sistan. Ya'qub too was a robber but he generally spared the lives of his victims.

Once he had consolidated his position he led his bands to the north-east where he gained control of Kabul and the silver mines beyond. His magnanimity won him recruits from the ranks of the Tahirid army and by 873 he felt himself strong enough to march westwards to regions more closely allied to the caliphate. When Ya'qub died six years later he had conquered the greater part of the plateau and had won the recognition of the caliph to whom he sent regular tribute. But it was a short-lived victory and in the years following his death the Saffarid kingdom shrank back towards Sistan.

Ya'qub b. al-Layth was a successful robber baron but he had a greater claim to fame: he restored a degree of national consciousness to the people for he is associated with promoting the Persian language in literature. Since the Arab conquests 200 years before, Arabic had been the medium of written and verbal communication for the educated, rather as Latin was in Europe in the middle ages. But Ya'qub spoke no Arabic; he spoke only Persian and it was probably in his day and with his encouragement that the language was adapted to the Arabic script and the 'New Persian' of modern times, in its various dialects, began to form. As well as 'Middle Persian' (see p. 85), the language includes elements of Kurdish, Pashto (which is spoken in Afghanistan) and Baluchi.

The tenth century witnessed the creation of other minor kingdoms. Of these the greatest, the longest surviving and the most enlightened was the Samanid, which flourished for 125 years (874-999). Unlike their less refined neighbours to the south the Samanids were of noble origin. Their founder, Nasr, owned extensive estates in the region of Balkh and his successors, having ejected the Saffarids from Khurasan, expanded northwards into Transoxiana. Under their patronage men of letters turned to writing in their native language as well as in Arabic. Scientists, artists and scholars converged on their capital at Bukhara which a chronicler was moved to describe as:

> 'the Focus of Splendour, the Shrine of Empire, the Meeting-place of the most unique intellects of the Age, the Horizon of the literary stars of the Worlds, and the Fair of the greatest scholars of the Period.'
>
> E G Browne, *op. cit.*, I, p. 365

Among the most illustrious was Avicenna (Ibn Sina). Physician, philosopher and poet, he was born near Bukhara in 980. At the age of ten he knew the Qur'an by heart and while still in his teens he was fortunate enough to cure the king, Nuh II, of an ailment. This gained him admission to the court and access to the royal library. Avicenna's medical treatises were written in Arabic, his poems in Persian.

Like the Saffarids, the Samanids were Sunnis. In their heyday their influence extended from the plateau to the plains between the Caspian and the Aral Seas, where trading relations were established with the Turkish tribes. Many were persuaded to adopt the Muslim faith—a development that was to have far-reaching consequences in western Asia—and which at the time won favour in Baghdad. In their dealings with the caliphate the Samanids were punctilious in observing the proprieties: they sent regular tribute and in return the caliphs recognized their right to govern. None of the eastern rulers entered the city of Baghdad (though in Ya'qub's case it was not for want of trying). The prize of the capital went to the Buyids, a minor Persian dynasty from the hills of Tabaristan (Mazandaran) in the north. After over-running the southern provinces of the plateau they spread down into Khuzistan and in 945 one of their leaders entered the city. He was received by the caliph, who was 'invited' to confer on him the title, Mu'izz al-Dawlah, 'He who renders the state mighty'.

During their century of power (932-1055) the Buyids, who were Shi'ites, could, theoretically, have installed a descendant of 'Ali in the holy office. But none of their rulers was prepared to face the repercussions that such a provocative step would have had, either within or beyond their frontiers, across a land that was predominantly Sunni. Their devotion to Shi'ism was in any case only moderate and they were content to allow the 'Abbasids to stay on in the caliphal palace with what religious authority they retained.

'Adud al-Dawlah was the most noteworthy of the Buyids. In his day their rule extended from the Caspian Sea to the Persian Gulf, from Iraq to the borders of Khurasan. He devoted some time to building activities. Near Shiraz, the administrative capital, which he embellished, he constructed the Band-i Amir dam across the river Kur. He built roads, waterways, bazaars and hospitals as well as mosques, libraries and a palace for himself in Baghdad. And he restored 'Ali's tomb at Najaf. But after his death in 983 the dynasty went into decline.

In Bukhara meanwhile the Samanids had emulated the follies of the early 'Abbasids. They had opened the doors of their courts and the ranks of their armies to large numbers of Turks from the north. In 962 a Turkish officer seized the town of Ghazna south of Kabul in Afghanistan and his successors rapidly carved out yet another kingdom in the eastern marches. Forty years later the armies of Mahmud, the great Ghaznavid conqueror, who was also of Turkish origin, turned west and swept the Samanids out of Khurasan. It was said that the owls wished him a long life because he left the towns in such a terrible state of desolation.

In this turbulent period the poet Firdawsi, author of the epic *Shahnama*, (see pp 115-116 and 154) was born, probably about 970. He was an impoverished *dihqan* from Tus in Khurasan. Cut adrift by the invaders from his Samanid moorings, he was forced to seek the patronage of the Ghaznavid court. He dedicated his life's work to Mahmud but so meagre was the reward he received that he composed a daring satire on his 'benefactor' and fled into hiding:

> Long years this Shahnama I toiled to complete,
> That the King might award me some recompense
> meet,
> But naught save a heart wrung with grief and
> despair
> Did I get from those promises empty as air!
> E G Browne, *op. cit.*, II, p. 81)

Browne records that years later, after a friendly minister at the court interceded successfully on Firdawsi's behalf:

> Mahmud ordered that sixty thousand *dinars* worth of indigo should be given to Firdawsi, and that this indigo should be carried to Tus on the King's own camels, and that apologies should be tendered to Firdawsi. . . . The Minister . . . caused the camels

> to be loaded, and the indigo safely reached Tabaran [Tus]. But even as the camels entered the Rudbar Gate the corpse of Firdawsi was borne forth.
>
> *Op. cit.*, II p. 137-8

In these lines from the *Shahnama* which precede the murder of his hero, Rustam, the poet soliloquizes on death. Browne's translation follows the Persian rhyme and metre:

> Should Death bid thee fare to thy long home with speed,
> And constrain thee to mount on pale Destiny's steed,
> Think not that for Justice Injustice is sent,
> And if Justice, then wherefore bewail and lament?
> In Destiny's sight Youth and Age are as one;
> Thus know, if ye want not Religion undone.
> If thy heart is fulfilled with Faith's light, then I trow
> That silence is best, for God's servant art thou.
> Be thy business to supplicate, worship, obey,
> And order thine acts for the Last Judgement Day.
> In thy heart and thy soul hath the demon no lot,
> Then to fathom this secret of God's seek thou not.
> Seek now in this world of religion a share;
> That alone will support thee when hence thou shalt fare.
>
> *Op. cit.*, II p. 145

During the first thirty years of the new millennium Mahmud conducted a series of raids on northern India which brought the Punjab within the orbit of Islam. But, so intent was he on plundering the infidel temples of Hindustan that he under-estimated the gathering menace in the north. The Saljuq Turks, crossing the Oxus in their thousands, were moving into Khurasan. At Dandanqan (near Merv) in 1040 they defeated the Ghaznavid forces under Mahmud's son, Mas'ud. Their leader, Tughril Beg, set up his capital at Merv and fifteen years later he entered Baghdad peacefully. The caliphate was back once more in the hands of Turks.

In the four centuries since the armies of Islam had first carried their message into western Asia and along the coast of north Africa the caliphs had not effectively united the believers under their own rule and the issue of temporal and religious leadership among the faithful had yet to be resolved. On the other hand the establishment of the minor dynasties in Persia had shown that loyalty to a monarchy was not incompatible with allegiance to the faith. In following the Shi'ite route to God Iranians would one day work out their own solution. And when that time came these minor dynasties would be seen as staging posts along the 800-year road leading from the great kings of antiquity and on again towards national sovereignty.

Notes

1 A J Arberry, *The Koran Interpreted*, London 1963 2 vols. I have used this translation unless otherwise stated.

2 I.e., the last part of the Prophet's life.

3 *The Arabian Nights* was a collection of tales that were written up and, when later they were translated, they fired the imagination of people in the West. E W Lane, among others, translated them into English (1839-41).

4 Al-Rida was buried beside Harun and to this day Mashhad is revered as the resting place of the Eighth Imam rather than as the site of the tomb of the great caliph.

5 The *Shahnama* or 'The Epic of the Kings' by Firdawsi (see pp. 115-116).

6 Descendants of General Tahir. He had been granted the governorship of Khurasan and the eastern provinces by al-Ma'mun in 820.

CHAPTER 7
The Northern Hordes
1040-1500

CIVILIZATION UNDER ATTACK

The new millennium witnessed the Saljuq conquests of Muslim Asia. Other tribes followed Qara-Khanids, Ghuzz, Qara-Khitai, Khwarazmians, Ottomans and Uzbegs. With the exception of the Qara-Khitai all shared the same ethnic origin, all were Turks and nearly all were orthodox Muslims.

Then came the holocaust. An explosion of barbarians from central Asia blasted on to the civilized world and the Muslim countries suffered the greatest destruction in their history. Beside such a disaster the crusader occupation of the western littoral was of small account.

Yet ultimately the faith triumphed. The Mongols like the Saljuqs before them were converted, the frontiers of Christendom were rolled back into Europe and, 500 years after the first Saljuqs crossed the Oxus, Islam reigned supreme among the peoples of south-west and central Asia—from Aden's shore to the borders of China and from India to Asia Minor, where in 1453 the Ottoman flag was hoisted over Constantinople.

And Persia? She lay right in the path of the invader and she too suffered the most terrible devastations. Yet in the end even the Mongols were won over by the civilization they had set out to destroy and, not for the first time or the last, Persia triumphed over her conquerors.

THE SALJUQS

The Great Saljuqs

The Saljuq leaders throughout their term maintained an unshakeable devotion to orthodoxy. For the caliph their arrival in Baghdad in 1055 was providential. Not only did the occupation rid him of the Buyids but it protected him from other heretics, notably the Fatimids. These powerful Shi'ite rulers, who claimed descent from the Prophet's daughter, had spread along North Africa into Egypt. From their new capital at Cairo their armies had crossed the Sinai desert into Arabia and were preparing to move further east.

But if the 'Abbasids were to recover credibility, after the expulsion of their Shi'ite overlords, some semblance of authority had to be restored to their house. How was this to be achieved when the Saljuqs also believed they had a divine right to rule? As one of them put it:

> We received from the lord of the world . . . the kingship of the world, and we received this by right and inheritance.
>
> A J Arberry (ed.), *The Legacy of Islam*, Oxford, 1979, p. 169

It was a problem that drew the intellectuals into 'great argument', but eventually a division of authority was agreed between the two parties. Tughril Beg, the tribal leader, was accorded the title of 'sultan'. He was authorised to exercise political sovereignty over the empire while the caliph, as spiritual head, was recognized as the sole interpreter of the laws of God. There was of course no gainsaying the sultan's power to appoint the caliph but, having done so, he owed him allegiance. In this way some lingering prestige that still attached to the trappings of the holy office was preserved and honour too was outwardly satisfied.

A ceremony was held to instal the new sultan. Amid scenes of great splendour the caliph formally invited him to govern on his behalf. Two crowns were suspended over his head to symbolise his authority over the east and the west. The gift of a Saljuq princess was accepted by the caliph but Tughril's request for the hand of his daughter was less well received. It was regarded by the Successor of the Prophet as an affront to the sanctity of his office and granted only with the greatest reluctance.

Tughril was succeeded in 1063 by his nephew, who was a man of many qualities. Valiant in battle, magnanimous in victory, yet modest in his manner of living, Alp Arslan was a knight in Saljuq clothing, a 'chevalier sans peur et sans reproche'. He was immensely tall, he wore a high hat (*kulah*) and he cultivated a long tapering moustache, the distance from the top of the hat to the tips of the moustache was said to be six feet.

Alp Arslan rescued Makkah and al-Madinah from the clutches of the Fatimids, he captured Herat in the east and Aleppo (another Fatimid stronghold) in the west. But he is remembered most of all for his triumph over the Byzantines in 1071. For them the battle of Manzikert north of Lake Van was a catastrophe. For the Saljuqs it paved the way for the conversion of Asia Minor to Islam; it was the first step on the long road to Constantinople and it led ultimately to the occupation of the peninsula by the Ottoman Turks.

During the battle the Emperor Diogenes Romanus was taken prisoner. Alp Arslan treated him with great courtesy and returned him—on payment of a ransom—with a military escort to his own people. Eight hundred years before when Valerian was taken by the Sasanid king not 200 miles away such magnanimity would have been almost inconceivable.

The third great ruler, Alp Arslan's son, Malikshah (1072-92) extended the Saljuq hold on Asia further. In the old Samanid kingdom his armies crossed the Oxus and brought the cities of Bukhara and Samarqand, as well as Kashgar on the borders of Tang China, into his empire. In the west he extended Saljuq influence into Syria while in Asia Minor another branch of the tribe infiltrated the plateau and established the Sultanate of Rum (Rome), as it was called, first in the region of Nicaea south of Constantinople and later at Konya.

Malikshah was interested in engineering and building; he improved the roads and made them safe for the traveller; he built caravanserais, he dug wells along the pilgrim route to Makkah and in Isfahan, his capital city, he turned his attention to the old Friday Mosque. Erected on the site of a Sasanian temple, enlarged by the 'Abbasids and the Buyids, it was rebuilt by the Saljuqs. Over eight centuries it sustained alterations and additions but the inspiration of its Saljuq architects has placed the Jami' Mosque among the great monuments of the Islamic world. Two dome-chambers dating from the time of Malikshah have had the plaster of a later period removed. In the larger of the two—the sanctuary—where 'twelve massive piers engage in a Promethean struggle with the weight of the dome', the finely calculated stresses have successfully withstood the test of time. The smaller chamber was a tomb tower. Here, because of its more modest scale, the economy of design in the arches and squinches that support the dome is more apparent. To Robert Byron their balance and proportion was the 'perfection of architecture' (*The Road to Oxiana*, London, repr. 1981, p. 172-73).

The need for a more unified control over the civil and military functions became apparent during the succession disputes that followed the death of Malikshah. The illustrious vizier, Nizam al-Mulk, who had first been appointed by Alp Arslan, co-ordinated their activities and supervised the administration. He curbed the excesses of the Turcomans, nomad offshoots of the unruly Ghuzz tribe who had entered Persia with the Saljuqs. He prevented military commanders, who were granted land in return for services (a system known as *iqta'*), from treating their tenant farmers as serfs and he checked extortionate tax collectors. In the provinces he kept an eye on the governors and others in coveted posts, Saljuq princes or the sons of leading tribesmen, some of whom were too young to take up their duties and had to be placed under the care of *atabegs* (guardians). So long as Nizam al-Mulk was at the centre the system worked and law and order was maintained among the population.

Nizam al-Mulk was a Persian. He instructed his royal masters in court procedure and the niceties of gracious living. They were probably illiterate but they thirsted for culture and they approved the establishment of theological colleges (*madrasas*) which he set up in the cities. He was also anxious to promote the Persian language and at the college he founded in Baghdad Persian literature was included in the curriculum. This Nizamiyyah was later merged with another institution, the Mustansiriyyah. It stands to this day beside the Tigris. Though heavily restored it is the only noteworthy remnant there of an 'Abbasid building to survive the Mongol devastations.

After thirty years of loyal service the great vizier was dismissed by Malikshah. Like the Barmecides he had placed his relations in lucrative posts, he had made enemies, he had become arrogant and, when called to account by the sultan, he had retorted:

> 'He who gave thee the Crown placed on my head the Turban, and these two are inseparably connected and bound together.'
>
> E G Browne, *op. cit.*, II, p. 185

—a riposte that was presumptuous as it was unwise. His life was spared but Nizam was endowed with a superstitious nature and he believed that death was imminent. He recalled that he had ousted his predecessor, al-Kunduri, from office and that from his death cell the condemned man had issued this message:

> 'Say to the King, "Lo, a fortunate service hath your service been to me; for thy uncle gave me this world to rule over, whilst thou, giving me the martyr's portion, hast given me the other world; so, by your service, have I gained this world and that!" And to the Wazir [Nizam al-Mulk] say: "An evil innovation and an ugly practice hast thou introduced into the world by putting to death [dismissed] ministers! I pray that thou may'st experience the same in thine own person."'
>
> E G Browne, *op. cit.*, II, p. 174

Al-Kunduri's prayer did not apparently go unheeded. Nizam was murdered shortly after his disgrace—knifed at the order of one Hasan-i Sabbah, founder of the fanatical movement known as the Assassins.

The religious spectrum

Among the problems which troubled the Saljuqs the most dangerous and the most persistent were the splinter movements among the Shi'ah. After the death of 'Ali, the Imams followed each other in lineal descent until the year 873 when the Twelfth Imam, Muhammad al-Mahdi, mysteriously disappeared from the mosque at Samarra. The majority of his followers have always believed that he is not dead but hidden, that he is the Mahdi, the Guided One, who will return in the last days 'to fill the earth with justice'.

The main schism among the believers came about when the Sixth Imam disinherited his heir, Isma'il, in favour of his second son possibly on account of his addiction to wine. A minority held that Isma'il was divinely guided, that he could do no wrong and that the Imamate ended with him. These were the 'Seveners' who founded a number of secret societies.

The group that appropriated Isma'il's name were among the more militant. They linked up with the Qarmatians, a clique of uncertain origin based on Bahrain, and with the upstart Fatimid dynasty in

North Africa; they too were Seveners, who claimed descent from the Prophet's daughter. In 969 the Fatimids occupied Egypt intending the new city of Cairo as a springboard for an assault on 'Abbasid Asia. They captured Jerusalem but were thwarted in their advance on Baghdad by the arrival of Tughril and his armies in 1055. By the end of the century they were running to fat, being too comfortably installed on the banks of the Nile to give active support to their erstwhile allies.

The Isma'ilis meanwhile had been gathering strength. Their initiates were lean intellectuals who read obscure inner meanings into Qur'anic texts, who formulated esoteric doctrines and abstruse theological hypotheses. Much of their literature was lost but their agents, carefully trained and disciplined, worked with jesuitical fervour to infiltrate their teachings into the strongholds of orthodoxy. Their undercover missions carried them the length of the Saljuq empire and beyond; no corner of Islam was too remote for them to penetrate.

One agent who returned to Persia from his training school in Egypt was Hasan-i Sabbah, a Shi'ite from Qum who sought to advance the Isma'ili ideology yet further. In 1090 he and his followers seized the fortress of Alamut in the Alburz mountains to the east of Qazvin and two years later, during some infighting between Malikshah's sons, they captured a succession of fifty or more strategic fortress sites, most of them in the north.

Hasan no doubt aimed to create a state of his own but first he had to dispose of 'the enemies of God'. Membership of his movement, the 'New Preaching', was open to those who accepted its dicta with unquestioning obedience and had only a qualified respect for human life. The communities that inhabited those mountain fortresses were highly structured. At their head stood the grand master, below him the grand priors, each in charge of a district, each with his cadre of 'Companions' and 'Adherents'. The 'Assassins', the so-called hashish-eaters, came at the end of the line but it is unlikely that they were drugged before being sent out on their murderous missions.

One of their victims was Nizam al-Mulk. Sultans, caliphs, emirs, eminent men, even Crusaders—all were vulnerable. But assassination was about the sum of their achievements. They failed to capture any of the larger towns (though they came near to taking Isfahan).

After Hasan's death the movement continued for 130 years until Hulagu's Mongol armies arrived in the Alamut valley. Fifty or more Assassin castles were destroyed by the Mongols and the Isma'ili movement disappeared from the political arena. Survivors today live peacefully in Syria where they have split into different sects. Others, perhaps 150,000, are resident in India. They look to the Agha Khan, who is descended from Isma'il through the last grand master, as their leader.

Nevisar Shah, 'perhaps the most impressive castle of all', guards the eastern end of the Alamut valley. As the crow flies it lies some forty miles east of Qazvin and is sufficiently intact to show the sophistication of their engineering and building systems. Standing on the side of a mountain 10,000 feet high, it had stabling for 60 to 80 mules or horses, a barracks and citadel above with a complex intercommunicating water system.

Marco Polo, the Venetian who passed through northern Iran after Hulagu's invasion in the thirteenth century, describes how the youths, whom 'the Sheikh of the Mountain' recruited as killers, were let into a secret garden where they sampled the delights that awaited them in paradise:

> No one ever entered the garden except those whom he wished to make Assassins. At the entrance stood a castle so strong that it need fear no man in the world, and there was no other way in except through this castle . . . damsels stayed with them all the time, singing and making music for their delight and ministering to all their desires . . .
>
> When the Sheikh desired the death of some great lord . . . he would take some of these Assassins of his and send them wherever he might wish, telling them that he was minded to dispatch them to Paradise: they were to go accordingly and kill such and such a man; if they died on their mission, they would go there all the sooner. Those who received such a command obeyed it with a right good will . . . Thus it happened that no one ever escaped when the Sheikh of the Mountain desired his death.
>
> *The Travels of Marco Polo*, tr. R E Latham,
> Harmondsworth, 1980, p. 40-42

The century of Saljuq domination was not a propitious period for the Sevener sects to spread their doctrines. The new *madrasas* were strongholds of orthodoxy and the vigorous body of scholars they sent into the world were well versed in the doctrine of Sunnism.

In the Nizamiyyah Madrasa at Baghdad, the chair of theology, was held in 1091 by Abu Hamid al-Ghazali. He was much revered and students flocked to his lectures but the time came when conventional dogma no longer satisfied him. He craved a release from 'the bond of conformity' and sought a deeper, more spiritual relationship with God. So after four years al-Ghazali abandoned the comfortable life of the academic, left his family and took to the road. Years of wandering led him to Sufism.

Sufism has many definitions. G M Wickens sums it up as being the state of 'the soul's exile from its Maker and its inborn longing, nourished or supressed in the face of other attractions, to return and lose itself in Him' (*Legacy of Persia*, Oxford, 1953, ed. A J Anberry, p. 159).

The way to God then was by the *via purgativa*, by asceticsm and the denial of self or, as the poet Abu Sa'id b. Abi 'l-Khayr expressed it:

> To lay aside what thou hast in thy head (such as desire and ambitions), and to give away what thou hast in thy hand, and not to flinch from whatever befalls thee. The veil between God and His servant . . . is neither earth nor heaven, nor the Throne nor the Footstool: thy self-hood and illusions are the veil, and when thou removest these thou hast attained unto God.

But God is also revealed to man through beauty and the path follows in that direction:

> By whatsoever Path, blesséd the Feet
> Which seek Thee; blesséd He who strives to meet
> Thy Beauty; blesséd they who on it gaze,
> And blessed every tongue which Thee doth greet!
> E G Browne, *op. cit.*, II, pp. 268, 266)

Ultimately the quest is for the return of the soul to a mystic union with God. Jalal al-Din Rumi, the most famous of all Sufi poets, writing in the 13th century, expresses this relationship in his *Divan-i Shams-i Tabriz*:

> Up, O ye lovers, and away! 'Tis time to leave the
> world for aye.
> Hark, loud and clear from heaven the drum of
> parting calls—let none delay!

The cameleer hath risen amain, made ready all the camel-train,
And quittance now desires to gain: why sleep ye, travellers, I pray?
Behind us and before there swells the din of parting and of bells;
To shoreless Space each moment sails a disembodied spirit away.
From yonder starry lights and through those curtain-awnings darkly blue
Mysterious figures float in view, all strange and secret things display.
From this orb, wheeling round its pole, a wondrous slumber o'er thee stole:
O weary life that weighest naught, O sleep that on my soul dost weigh!
O heart, towards thy heart's love wend, and O friend, fly toward the Friend,
Be wakeful, watchman, to the end: drowse seemingly no watchman may.

E G Browne, *op. cit.*, II, p. 524–5; tr. R A Nicholson

In donning the Sufis'[1] mantle al-Ghazali conveyed their mode of thought to a wider audience. Through him Sufism came to rest on orthodox foundations, he opened the doors of Sufi mansions for mystics to explore and for writers to describe, the poets Jalal al-Din Rumi and Sa'di among them.

Nearly 170 years before al-Ghazali's own mystical experience al-Hallaj, one of the first Sufi martyrs, believed that he had attained unity with God. To the religious order of the time this was blasphemy and al-Hallaj was led out to a terrible death. But this expression of his state of ecstasy survives:

I am He whom I love, and He whom I love is I.
We are two souls dwelling in one body.
When thou seest me, thou seest Him:
And when thou seest Him, thou seest us both'.

Hitti, *op. cit.*, p. 436

Flowers and tears in Khurasan

Following the death of Malikshah twenty-five years elapsed before

Sanjar, the last of the Great Saljuqs, won the throne in 1117. They were damaging years: the central government, so carefully built up by Nizam al-Mulk, lost its grip; Sanjar's three brothers fought each other for the crown and emirs of the Saljuq house staked out their own principalities.

Sanjar himself held aloof from the fraternal feuds. He remained in the east and bided his time. If he was anxious for power, as he surely was, he contained his ambition and contented himself with the governorship of Khurasan. His court at Merv became the cultural capital of the empire. There men versed in the arts and sciences gathered and there, in the sheltered calm of palace precincts, poets could exercise their literary talents:

> I will go my way, I will find the goal of this world in Khurasan;
> I am thirsty, I will find the source of benefits in Khurasan.

So sang Khaqani, one of the great poets of the time, though it is not known if he made the journey. Among those who did apply for admission to the court was Anwari:

> Save at thy threshold in the world no resting-place have I;
> Except this gate no place is found whereon my head would lie.

These beguiling words won Sanjar over and it seems the new recruit did not disappoint him:

> The Lord of the world called Anwari
> Before him, gave him his hand, and caused him to be seated;
> Called for wine, and asked him for poetry ...
>
> E G Browne, *op. cit.*, II, pp. 395, 367, 381.

Nishapur, one of the great cities of Khurasan, was the home of the astronomer and mathematician, 'Umar Khayyam. He computed a calendar, which began on 15 March, 1079. It was adopted and proved to be more accurate than the Gregorian calendar. Though 'Umar is known to English readers for his poetry, not all the quatrains, which Edward Fitzgerald so colourfully translated and which caught the imagination of Victorian England, are now attributed to him. Perhaps it was in recognition of his scientific work that a shrine was erected in his memory. In this account of 'Umar's burial place, the authentic and the romantic for once join hands. It is told by a pupil, Nizam-i 'Aruzi. Mindful of the aridity of the Khurasanian soil, he first recalls a meeting with 'Umar which took place:

> in the city of Balkh, in the Street of the Slave-sellers, in the house of Amir Abu Sa'd . . . In the midst of that friendly gathering I heard that Proof of the Truth . . . Umar say, 'My grave will be in a spot where the trees will shed their blossoms on me twice a year.' This thing seemed to me impossible, though I knew that one such as he would not speak idle words.
>
> When I arrived at Nishapur in the year AH 530 (= AD 1135-36), it being then some years since that great man had veiled his countenance in the dust, and this lower world had been bereaved of him, I went to visit his grave . . . his tomb lay at the foot of a garden-wall, over which pear-trees and peach-trees thrust their heads, and on his grave had fallen so many flower-leaves that his dust was hidden beneath the flowers. Then I remembered that saying which I had heard from him in the city of Balkh, and I fell to weeping, because on the face of the earth, and in all the regions of the habitable globe, I nowhere saw one like unto him'.
>
> E G Browne, *op. cit.*, II, p. 247

By the time Sanjar became sultan the empire built up in the west by Alp Arslan and Malikshah had fallen away. In Anatolia the Sultanate of Rum had become independent and was nudging the Byzantines westwards. The east Mediterranean coast was in the hands of the Crusaders and their massive castles guarded the approaches to the hinterland. They had captured Jerusalem from the Fatimids in 1099—eighteen years before—and no serious effort had been made to rescue the city or the Christian-occupied territories.

Sanjar turned his attention to the east and in particular to the north-east frontier where nomads in their thousands were once again pressing in from the steppes. After the Samanid kingdom had collapsed in 999, the Qara-Khanids, a Turkish tribe, had moved into Transoxiana and occupied an area to the east of the Aral Sea. They had been subjugated in 1125 by invaders from the borders of northern China, the Qara-Khitai. These formidable warriors had also displaced some Ghuzz nomads, who had crossed into Khurasan. In 1141 Sanjar marched against the Qara-Khitai and besieged Samarqand without success and he was forced to withdraw. Twelve years later his attempt to drive the Ghuzz back across the Oxus resulted in disaster. The cities of Merv, Nishapur and Tus were sacked and many Khurasanians put to the sword. Sanjar himself was taken prisoner and a grief-stricken Anwari poured the *Tears of Khorasan* into his lament to a prince of Samarqand:

> Waft, gentle gale, oh waft to Samarcand,
> When next thou visitest that blissful land,
> The plaint of Khorassania plunged in woe:
> Bear to Turania's King our piteous scroll,
> Whose opening breathes forth all the anguished soul,
> And close denotes what all the tortur'd know'.
>
> E G Browne, *op. cit.*, II, p. 386,
> tr. W. Kirkpatrick and E H Palmer.

Sanjar escaped back to Merv after four years only to find his beloved city in ruins. He died a few months later.

With his passing in 1157 effective Saljuq rule in Iran came to an end. Once again the plateau was divided. In Fars and Azarbaijan the *atabegs*, who were generally military commanders as well as guardians of the young princes, seized power and in the east a new wave of Khwarazm Turks from their capital of that name (later Khiva) took over. In Baghdad the 'Abbasids lingered on, caliphs in name only. Their days too were numbered.

The Saljuqs strengthened the hold of orthodox Islam on south-west Asia and extended it westwards into Asia Minor. But they did not succeed in destroying the Assassins nor did they challenge the heretic Fatimids, and Shi'ism survived to come into its own in a later age.

In the visual arts the Saljuqs' most notable contribution was architecture. By the 11th century, when they arrived on the plateau, the building materials of previous ages, mainly mud-brick and undressed stone, were giving place to baked brick. They were quick to exploit the new medium that was more durable than the first,

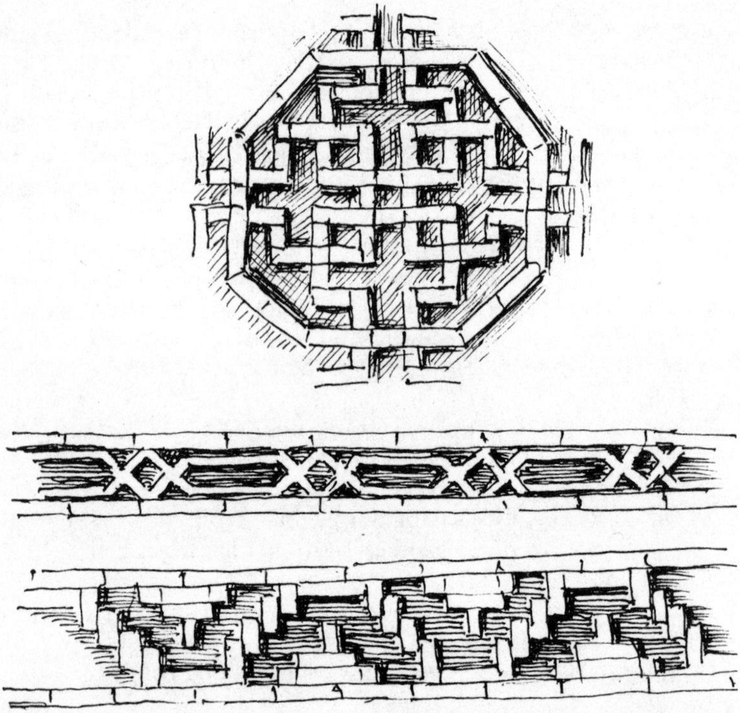

Fig. xvi. Details of Saljuq brickwork from the Jami' Mosque at Sava (after Antony Hutt and Leonard Harrow, *Iran 1*, London, 1977)

more versatile than the second and were soon employing it for construction purposes as well as decoration. The Jami' mosque in Isfahan, where some of the interior domes and walls are in brick, has already been mentioned (see pp. 162-163).

On the exteriors of their monuments, many of which were circular towers, the bricks were arranged in a wide variety of bands or geometric patterns and courses were sometimes recessed to achieve the maximum effect from moving shadow. In their inscriptions they would occasionally alternate the natural monochrome with a blue glaze to considerable effect.

The Saljuqs studded the face of Persia with their insignia of tomb towers and inland lighthouses to guide the traveller. Others, in the form of minarets, were incorporated into their mosques, where they stood sentinel beside the great dome chambers and the massive *ivans*—all testimonies to the self-confidence of their builders and to the strength of their faith.

THE MONGOLS

Genghis Khan

Transoxiana, that quadrilateral country beyond the Oxus, bounded on the west by the Aral Sea, on the east by the Tien Shan mountains, and to the north and south by the Jaxartes and the Oxus (the Syr Darya and Abu Darya) rivers, had long been the main invasion route into southern Asia. To Scythians, Saka, Massagetai, Hephthalites, Turks and others—whoever the invaders of the time were—Transoxiana was the passageway. The Persians called it 'Turan', the land of the barbarians—though this was a misnomer for a country which had its Alexandria (Khojend, now Leninabad), which lay in the path of the Silk Road, which was the birthplace of Avicenna and which the Samanids themselves had ruled from Bukhara.

Following the demise of Saljuq power after the death of Sanjar in 1157, the Khwarazmians had won control of Transoxiana. They had conquered both the Qara-Khitai and the Qara-Khanid Turks and by 1212 had staked out an imposing empire, which extended from the Jaxartes through eastern Persia to the borders of Ghaznavid India.

This was the situation when one day in the year 1218 a caravan from the Great Khan of the Mongols, Genghis Khan, arrived at the gates of the Khwarazm frontier town of Utrar. The governor suspected the merchants were spies and (having appropriated their goods) cast them into prison where they were later killed. Genghis Khan on hearing this sent a mission to Muhammad II, the Khwarazm-Shah, demanding reparation; that envoy too was killed and his two companions, having been deprived of their beards, were sent back.

Two thousand miles of steppeland separated the Khwarazm kingdom from the Mongol capital and Muhammad had no doubt thought that he was safe from attack from that quarter, especially as he had amassed a large army. Had his governor observed the civilities normally accorded to strangers at the gate instead of robbing, killing and insulting them, the history of thirteenth century Asia could conceivably have taken a different course. It could hardly have been worse. Genghis Khan, who had risen to power from obscurity, who had formed the Mongol nomads into a highly organized mobile military state and had conquered north China, was not one to tolerate insults or to ignore provocation. He had been served with a challenge—if he needed one. The caliph too evidently played into his hands. Alarmed at Muhammad's growing power he is said to have entered into correspondence with the infidel khan encouraging him to attack the Khwarazm territory of his co-religionist.

Within a year of the beardless envoys' return, the Mongol cavalry armies were advancing on the Khwarazm frontier and Utrar was under siege. The campaign was carefully planned and brilliantly directed by a man of genius. Genghis Khan has been ranked with Alexander and Napoleon. His wars in China had introduced him to mechanical warfare and to the siege equipment requisite for attacks on civilization's townships. Like other northern nomads his men, each of whom had several horses, could live in the saddle. Their diet was dried meat, their arms the bow and arrow, sword and spear; they numbered 150,000 and possibly more.

Utrar fell after five months and the offending governor suffered death by having molten silver poured into his eyes and ears. Rather than risk open battle Muhammad had dispersed his armies to defend the towns individually. Nevertheless Bukhara and Samarqand surrendered in rapid succession. Only Khwarazm, the capital, held out for some seven months.

Muhammad meanwhile had fled south to Balkh with detachments of Mongol cavalry in pursuit. He turned westward along the Khurasan Highway, which Darius Codomannus had followed to his death some 1,500 years before. After several narrow escapes, and harried to the last with arrows as his boat drew away from the shore, he reached the safety of an island in the Caspian Sea where he died shortly after.

In the spring of 1221 Genghis Khan himself crossed the Oxus into Persia. The elegant cities of Khurasan and other provinces in the south with their village communities, where people lived by growing crops and raising cattle on permanent or semi-permanent pasture were anathema to the barbarian nomad. Much of the steppeland of central Asia and China was already within his realm. It was his mission to carry on with his task and conquer the world. '[I am] the scourge of God sent to men as a punishment for their sins,' he is said to have told the terrified citizens of Bukhara (P K Hitti, *op. cit.*, p. 483) and punishment was due to all peoples who acknowledged another's sovereignty. Tus, Merv, Nishapur, Rayy, Qazvin, Hamadan, Qum, Kashan—the famous cities of the north—all in their turn were destroyed. Tabriz alone succeeded in buying the enemy off. People were slain by the thousand, some being subject to torture before death brought release. In Merv, which had been rebuilt and which was once again a cultural centre, only a handful of craftsmen were spared to slave for their Mongol masters. The city itself was wrecked and never recovered its former glory:

> The people of infidelity and impiety roamed through those abodes; that erring and contumacious race (the Mongols) dominated over the inhabitants, so that those palaces were effaced from off the earth as lines of writing are effaced from paper, and those abodes became a dwelling for the owl and the raven; in those places the screech-owls answer each other's cries, and in those halls the winds moan responsive to the simoom.
>
> E G Browne, *op. cit.*, II, p.432,
> quoting Yaqut al-Hamawi.

Muhammad's empire collapsed behind him like a pack of cards. Only in the Afghan mountains did the invader suffer a set-back when Jalal al-Din, brave successor of an unworthy father, rallied his supporters and defeated a Mongol army in the Parwan valley of the Hindu Kush. But some of the victors quarrelled among themselves, he failed to capitalise on his success and was forced to retreat. On the banks of the Indus he made a last stand and when the day was lost he threw his armour away and plunged into the river. Genghis Khan's admiration for the bravery of his enemy for once got the better of him. He ordered his men to hold their arrows and Jalal al-Din's horse carried his master to safety.

The lava-flow of destruction did not extend into southern Persia nor did it penetrate far into India—the climate in those latitudes was too hot—and in 1223 Genghis Khan began the journey back to the north. Herat, which lay in his path, was razed to the ground; Balkh, and Bamiyan, a former centre of Buddhism, had already been sacked. He died four years later on his way to China.

The indefatigable Jalal al-Din resumed the war in western Persia where for some years he fought sporadic battles with roaming units of Mongol cavalry. He met his death at the hands of an itinerant Kurd.

The Eclipse of the Caliphate

Genghis Khan had divided the empire among his sons, who were charged to complete his mission and conquer the world. Southern

China, the Russian steppelands and the east Mediterranean seaboard had yet to be mastered. Towards this objective some thirty years after the Great Khan's death, his grandson, Hulagu, crossed the Oxus into Persia en route for Syria. But first the Assassins and the caliphate had to be eliminated as divided authority, even where it was more symbolic than real, could not be tolerated.

Hulagu (as we have seen) invaded the Alamut valley in 1256. He soon had the measure of the youthful grand master, Rukn al-Din, who was easily cowed and persuaded to order his followers to surrender. Most of them responded to the call. As they came down from their castles the Mongols moved in and set them on fire. (One or two fortresses held out for some months before they were overcome). Rukn al-Din, who with reason had been well treated by Hulagu, was sent at his own request to the Mongol camp-capital at Karakorum. But the Great Khan refused to see him. He had served his purpose and on his way back he was murdered.

General relief among the orthodox Muslims at the destruction of the Assassins and their lairs turned to anxiety when Hulagu took the road to Baghdad. Caliph Mu'tasim, fearing that his own armies could not stave off the impending attack, called on Divine Providence to protect his person and endeavoured to play on pagan superstitions by calling down the forces of the supernatural on the invader who was informed:

> If the caliph is killed the whole universe is disorganized, the sun hides its face, rain ceases and plants grow no more.
>
> P K Hitti, *op. cit.*, p. 487

But in vain. Hulagu was not impressed: he had consulted his own astrologers.

Siege engines battered the walls of the beleagured city, cavalry showered arrows over the battlements and after a week of continuous bombardment a breach was made by the Khurasan gate.

As the enemy swarmed up the ramparts the caliph and his entourage came out and surrendered and as the firing ceased the slaughter began. In a few days the stench of death was so strong that even the Mongols were temporarily driven out. Tens of thousands were killed.

> There took place . . . such wholesale slaughter and unrestrained looting and excessive torture and

> mutilation as it is hard to hear spoken of even generally . . . There happened what happened of things I like not to mention; therefore imagine what you will, but ask me not of the matter!'
>
> E G Browne, *op. cit.*, II p. 463, quoting from *Kitab al-Fakhri*.

The treasures of the 'Abbasid house—the accumulation of five centuries—were carted out and piled up round Hulagu's tent. The Great Mosque and the Golden Palace,—it almost goes without saying—were desecrated or destroyed. The caliph was taken away, rolled up in a carpet and trampled to death by horses, as Mongol superstition forbade the shedding of royal blood at the hands of their own people. Only the Christian community which had gathered in a church was spared, thanks to the intervention of Hulagu's chief wife who was a Christian.

Two years later Hulagu invaded Syria. Aleppo had fallen, he was pressing south and Egypt was already in his sights, when he heard that the Great Khan, his eldest brother Mönke, had died. Leaving an army to continue the onward march, he returned to Persia to await events in the far north.

In Cairo a Mongol envoy called on the city to surrender. Egypt at this time was in the hands of the Mamluks. They were tough fighters, mainly of Turkish origin and they were not intimidated. General Baybars led their forces across the Sinai desert into Palestine and at 'Ayn Jalut north of Jerusalem he won a decisive victory. The enemy were routed, their commander taken captive and killed. The 3 September 1260 proved to be a turning point in the tide of Mongol aggression, their record of invincibility had at last been broken, Egypt and the holy cities had been saved from destruction.

The Mamluks became the leaders of a disjointed Arab world. In Syria, which they occupied, they destroyed the last of the Crusader strongholds. In Cairo they restored the caliphate by enthroning vestigial 'Abbasids and investing them in the trappings of office. But these scions carried no authority, their duties were purely ceremonial, they made little impact and Cairo never achieved the eminence of Baghdad. In 1517, when Egypt fell to the Ottoman Turks, the caliphate was transferred to Constantinople and it passed to the Ottoman sultans.

In dismantling the caliphate the Mongols had disposed of an instrument that had outlived its usefulness. At the same time the destruction of Baghdad brought the classical age of Islam to an end.

The Arabic language, which had played such an important part in the dissemination of the faith, had been steadily losing ground to non-Semitic languages—to Persian and Turkish. Everywhere outside Arabia the Islamic scene was changing.

Among those who welcomed the downfall of the 'Abbasids were the Shi'ites and the Christians, some of whom attempted to check the spread of Islam by winning the Mongols over to their faith. Several papal embassies made the long journey to Karakorum but without success. Yet despite the sufferings of the Muslim world, Islam was ultimately the victor in south-west Asia and it would not be long before Hulagu's successors embraced the faith themselves.

The Il-Khans

Hulagu never returned to the north. His elder brother, Kubilai,[2] conqueror of China, became Great Khan. He abandoned the Mongolian capital, Karakorum, in favour of Peking. Technically he ruled the empire on the family's behalf but in practice the several khanates over which individual members presided assumed separate indentities and Hulagu, though he remained loyal to Kubilai, founded his own dynasty—the Il-Khans of Persia.

Neither Hulagu nor his heirs succeeded in wresting Syria from the Mamluks. Hulagu spent most of his remaining five years in Azarbaijan. He died there after a heavy drinking bout and was buried on an island in Lake Urmia. There he had taken his share of the 'Abbasid treasure (the rest had gone to Mönke) and there, according to custom, a supply of Mongol maidens accompanied him into his tomb.

Abaqa, son of Hulagu, whose appointment as Il-Khan was confirmed by Kubilai, was faced with threats to his northern boundaries from rival khanates. Dissension had broken out in the family after Mönke's death which Kubilai, preoccupied with his vast programme of conquests in China and Japan, was unable to control. From now on the Il-Khans had to fight off incursions from cousin khans of the Golden Horde in the Russian steppelands and the Chagatai Khanate in Transoxiana, who tried to push through the Caucasus and across the Oxus. In the west the Sultanate of Rum on the fringes of the Mongol empire remained tributary to the Il-Khans.

In Persia itself the areas which had not lain in the invaders' path—the southern states and Gilan on the Caspian Sea—retained their emirs and submitted to Mongol overlordship. In the despoiled and depopulated Khurasan and the lands straddling the Khurasan trunk road, recovery was hampered by the inadequacies of Hulagu's immediate successors. Tabriz served as the capital and an administration was formed under a Persian vizier. Ministers and others, who failed to please or were the victims of intrigue, were put to death and execution became an overworked tool of Il-Khan rule; government was unstable; law and order was only partially restored and bands of redundant horsemen ravaged the countryside harrassing the peasants who attempted to bring their lands back into cultivation. The tax burden, already heavy, was exacerbated by extortionate collectors.

Yet in spite of these discouragements caravans from China crossed the Oxus and passed through Tabriz on their way to Trebizond where the goods were shipped to Europe. Marco Polo, who stayed in Tabriz on his way to Kubilai's court at Peking, thought the new capital was a splendid city. He described it as a trading centre for merchandise from Baghdad, southern Persia and India, where silk and cloth of gold were woven and where precious stones were found in the vicinity.

Though in Mesopotamia and elsewhere the armies of Islam had been defeated in the invasions and many thousands had been killed, the spiritual armour of the surviving believers had remained resolutely intact. Under the Il-Khans, as the passage of time loosened the links with their homeland and the pagan practices of their northern kinsmen, they were gradually drawn towards Islam until they began to identify with the very civilization which Genghis Khan had sought to demolish. Islam was triumphant when thirty years after Hulagu's death a ruler emerged who was in sympathy with the interests—and the faith—of the subject peoples.

Ghazan Khan, great-grandson of Hulagu, became a Muslim within days of his accession. Whether he became a Sunni or a Shi'ah is not clear but with the fervour of the new believer he set about destroying the churches, temples, monasteries and synagogues of the other faiths. He was a ruthless man with a convert's zeal and a determination to introduce a programme of reforms. Aided by his worthy vizier, the historian, Rashid al-Din, he set out to regularize the tax system, check the abuses of officialdom and reduce banditry in rural areas. He revalued the coinage, introduced a legal code, encouraged farmers to bring their lands back into production, improved irrigation systems and built caravanserais and bridges along the main routes. But he failed to drive the Mamluks out of Syria and he suffered heavy losses in making the attempt. Ghazan

Khan died in 1304 after a brief nine year reign and before his reforms could be fully realised. He was succeeded by his brother Öljeitü. He too favoured reforms but he lacked the drive to sustain them. Öljeitü invaded Gilan, a land of swamps and impenetrable primeval forest sandwiched between the Alburz mountains and the Caspian Sea, whose humid climate and difficult terrain had saved it from aggressors in the past.

The Il-Khans had by now adopted the Muslim faith. Their conversion had severed any lingering allegiance to the Great Khan and had led to certain changes in their mode of life. They spoke Persian and Turkish (their soldiers were mostly Turks), they wore the turban and they sponsored public building programmes but they did not give up the nomadic way of life and the government came with them when they moved their tents to summer pastures.

Ghazan Khan was a builder and patron of the arts. In Tabriz he built a mosque, two madrasas, a library, a hospital and an observatory. Öljeitü is remembered for his mausoleum in the centre of his new capital at Sultaniyyah, west of Qazvin. The city was shortlived but the tomb with its egg-shaped dome, regarded by Arthur Upham Pope as 'one of Persia's supreme architectural achievements',[3] survives. Native craftsmen at this period delighted in tiling buildings inside and out in all the kingfisher hues ranging from green through turqoise to deep blue.

Rashid al-Din was commissioned by Ghazan Khan to write the history of the Mongols and their conquests. He later incorporated it into his *Jami' al-Tawarikh*, a history of the world of Eurasia. Others took to writing histories at this time but Rashid's 'vast encyclopedia' was the first of its kind.

Though many scholars and writers fell victim to the invaders, the thirteenth century produced some famous Persian poets. Jalal al-Din Rumi, the Sufi mystic, has been mentioned. His contemporary, Sa'di was another. Forced to flee from his home in Shiraz in 1226, he wrote of the traumas of the real world:

> O knowest thou not why, an outcast and exile,
> In lands of the stranger a refuge I sought?
> Disarranged was the world like the hair of a negro
> When I fled from the Turks and the terror they
> brought.
>
> E G Browne, *op. cit.*, II, p. 528

Hafiz, the great poet of the fourteenth century, also came from

Shiraz. He too lived in troubled times and, as will be seen, it was perhaps thanks to his own native wit that he survived. Hafiz beguiles his readers with his love poems, his delight in wine and his descriptions of nature: bird song, roses, trees, the wind. These lines from an ode in more serious vein are inscribed on his tomb which lies in a garden in Shiraz:

> Where are the tidings of union? that I may arise—
> Forth from the dust I will rise up to welcome thee!
> My soul, like a homing bird, yearning for Paradise
> Shall arise and soar, from the snares of the world set
> free.
> When the voice of thy love shall call me to be thy
> slave,
> I shall rise to a greater far than the mastery
> Of life and the living, time and the mortal span:
> Pour down, oh Lord! from the clouds of thy
> guiding grace,
> The rain of a mercy that quickeneth on my grave,
> Before, like dust that the wind bears from place to
> place,
> I arise and flee beyond the knowledge of man. . .
>
> *Poems from the Divan of Hafiz*,
> tr. Gertrude Bell, London 1897, p. 118

By the second decade of the fourteenth century the days of Mongol domination were coming to an end. Whether their people were absorbed by local communities, whether they intermarried with the nomads or whether they became susceptible to some disease, such as bubonic plague, is not clear. But for one reason or another their numbers declined. The Il-Khans, who had sizeable harems of wives and concubines, reared relatively few children and infant mortality generally must have been unusually high.

After Öljeitü's death in 1316 a boy of twelve was placed on the throne. Courtiers and ministers hovering in its shadow intrigued with one another and Rashid al-Din, now in his seventies, like others before him became the victim of a plot. He was ousted from office and executed. Disturbances at court were followed by scrambles for power in the provinces where military chiefs and others founded break-away dynasties: the Jalayirids in Baghdad and Azarbaijan, the Muzaffarids in Fars and the Kurts in Herat.

In 1336, eighty years after Hulagu had crossed the Oxus, Il-Khan rule in Persia came to an end. The central government collapsed and the country fell into a state of anarchy. In that same year a son was born to a chieftan far away in Transoxiana who became known in the west as Tamerlane.

THE TIMURIDS

Tamerlane 'Lord of Asia'

I hold the Fates bound fast in iron chains,
And with my hand turn Fortune's wheel about,
And sooner shall the sun fall from his sphere
Than Tamburlaine be slain or overcome.

Tamburlaine the Great, I, ii

Marlowe wrote the drama about him, Handel composed an opera, Gibbon devoted nearly a chapter. His military campaigns, his indefatigable energy, his phenomenal conquests and his specialist atrocities have won him a place in the rogue popularity polls, just as Samarqand, his fabulous capital city, has drawn the sightseers.

Yet, set against those of Genghis Khan, his achievements and character compare less favourably. The Great Khan founded an empire which endured for over a century: Tamerlane's disintegrated after his death. Genghis Khan was a steppeland nomad: Tamerlane was brought up in a civilized environment a day's ride from Samarqand. Mongol crimes against humanity were hideous enough: those of Tamerlane were even less pardonable—his caligulisms included building pyramids of skulls, burying prisoners alive and throwing people over cliffs. Genghis Khan held a brief from his god to punish men for their sins: not so Tamerlane; he was a Muslim, though whether his victims were of his own faith or infidel it mattered not. It has been truly said that Tamerlane 'one of the greatest warriors, was one of the worst of monarchs' (Sir John Malcolm, *History of Persia*, 1815, pp. 482-3).

Yet on occasion even Tamerlane showed traces of humanity. When he demanded an indemnity from the people of Shiraz, it is said that Hafiz pleaded bankruptcy. He was brought before Tamerlane who rebuked him for writing the lines:

If that unkindly Turk would take my heart within her hand,
I'd give Bukhara for the mole on her cheek, or Samarqand.

> 'With the blows of my . . . sword have I subjugated most of the habitable globe, and laid waste thousands of towns and countries to embellish Samarqand and Bukhara . . . and you, miserable wretch that you are, would sell them both for the black mole of a Turk of Shiraz!'
>
> E G Browne, *op. cit.,* III, p. 188-9

Hafiz pleaded that it was because of such profligacy that he was in such a sorry state. Tamerlane laughed at his reply, Hafiz was reprieved and allowed to go on his way.

Timur the Lame, as he was known after a youthful skirmish had left him lame for life (Tamerlane in Western parlance), was not a Mongol, though he had Mongol ancestry. He is said to have claimed descent from Genghis Khan and he saw himself as his successor. Born in 1336, he was the son of a minor Turkish chieftain from Kish who came to power on the backs of the weakening Chagatai Khans. By the age of 44, having seized control of all Transoxiana and Khwarazm, he set out on the first part of his self-appointed mission and led his armies south across the Oxus.

To the people of Persia it was as if the Mongols had returned. As crops were fired, cities destroyed and populations massacred, it was the same sorry story over again. Only this time hardly a province escaped. Starting in Khurasan the Timurid armies rode westwards overthrowing the petty dynasties—Kurts, Muzaffarids and others—that lay in their path. Like the hosts of Genghis Khan 'they came, they supped, they burnt, they slew, they plundered, and departed.' And sometimes they came back. The Jalayirid prince escaped from Baghdad before it fell in 1393 but when he dared to return eight years later the city was singled out for special punishment and, within fifty years of being sacked by Hulagu, Baghdad was razed to the ground.

Nevertheless it took Tamerlane the best part of seven years to subdue Persia. His Tartar armies, like the Mongol hordes, were well trained but they were smaller and he suffered reverses. Also his position at home had to be safeguarded and in the winter months he usually returned to Samarqand. Once brought to heel Persia became the springboard for other conquests. As well as Iraq he invaded, Syria, Armenia and Georgia, he traversed the empty quarter of the Russian steppelands to Moscow in the far west, he penetrated the Indian subcontinent to Delhi, he conquered Asia Minor, where he checked the rising power of the Ottoman Turks and took their sultan prisoner.

By 1405 Tamerlane had the greater part of central southern and western Asia and the lands adjoining Persia and Transoxiana in his grip. All that is save one. He was now an old man of 70 and partially blind. Undaunted he set out to conquer China, but he died at the old Khwarazm border. And so it was that two centuries of barbarian invasions, the darkest in the history of western Asia, ended where they began—on the banks of the Jaxartes river at Utrar.

The Black and White Sheep

The ravaged countries of Asia soon freed themselves from the Timurid yoke. In India and Asia Minor the old regimes resumed power while in Persia only Khurasan remained firmly linked to Transoxiana. The rest of the country floated helplessly through the fifteenth century like a storm-battered ship adrift on the high seas with boarding parties gaining a foothold from time to time but never retaining the prize for long.

Western Persia during these years became the scene of a power struggle between two rival groups of Turcoman tribes, the Qara-Qoyunlu and the Aq-Qoyunlu. The Black and White Sheep, as they were known from the emblems on their banners, had been among the early Turkish immigrants. The Black Sheep appeared to be the more formidable: they controlled Azarbaijan and the Euphrates-Tigris valley (where they had supplanted the Jalayirids, the petty dynasty that came in after the Il-Khans). The power base of the White Sheep lay further west in the region of Diyar Bakr (formerly Amida).

In the east, after some wrangling among the members of Tamerlane's family, his fourth son, Shah Rukh, emerged in 1407 as the Timurid's successor. Leaving his son, the astronomer Ulugh Beg, to govern Transoxiana, he moved to Khurasan and established his capital at Herat. Unlike Tamerlane Shah Rukh was more interested in the pursuits of peace than the profession of arms. He made good some of the damage of the previous two decades and he built up a brilliant court which attracted the leading scholars and artists of the time.

Shah Rukh claimed to be ruler of all Persia. He attempted to disperse the hostile elements in the west but, though he three times went to war with the Black Sheep, by the time he died, after a reign of forty years, he had not succeeded in dislodging them. Nor did the next three Timurid rulers fare any better. Power struggles and assassinations within the royal house had weakened their hold on the kingdom. Not until fifteen years after Abu Sa'id, a great-grandson of Tamerlane, had fought his way to the throne was the war in the west resumed.

Abu · Sa'id marched into Azarbaijan in 1467. But he had miscalculated. Pre-occupied with establishing his position in north-east Persia and Transoxiana, he had underrated the strength of the White Sheep and the skill of their leader, the fearsome Uzun Hasan (the 'Tall'). Fresh from a resounding victory over the Black Sheep he advanced against the Timurids. At Tabriz in 1469 Abu Sa'id was out-manoeuvred, defeated, taken captive and summarily killed.

Weakened by rivalries at home and by losses on their western front, the Timurids were by now in disarray. The White Sheep had triumphed, Khurasan and indeed all Persia appeared to be within their grasp.

Yet even more powerful forces were building up in the wings. In 1472 the Ottoman Turks took the field and attacked Hasan the Tall in the rear. He suffered several crushing defeats at their hands and finally withdrew from the contest altogether.

The Timurid dynasty struggled on long enough to see the century out and under Husayn Bayqara the court at Herat enjoyed a brief revival. But within a year of his death in 1506 the central Asian cauldron boiled over again. Another wave of Turks—Uzbegs from the foothills of the Ural mountains—had invaded Tansoxiana and, as they crossed into Khurasan, they swept the last Timurids out of Herat.

Once again Persia was threatened with a huge influx of nomads from beyond the Oxus. But this time salvation was at hand. The White Sheep in their turn had been routed by a nationalist revolutionary movement of Safavid origin whose leader, Isma'il, had been proclaimed Shah in Tabriz. The provinces in the north and west had declared for him and in 1510 Isma'il marched against the Uzbegs. In a battle near Merv they were defeated, their leader Muhammad Shaybani was killed and Isma'il could justly claim to be the Shah of Persia.

With the Safavid flag nailed firmly to the masthead, its new master had taken the drifting Persian vessel in tow and brought it back to port.

The Court at Herat

If the military record of Tamerlane's successors was unimpressive, their cultural legacy was a splendid one. Persian architects and craftsmen who had been put to work in Samarqand and Bukhara, the old Samanid capital, returned home under Shah Rukh to help with renewed vigour in the task of renovation and construction. Mosques, mausolea and madrasas rose up on a monumental scale. *Ivans* were heightened, domes were lifted on to drums and at Yazd and Mashhad minarets pierced the sky in pairs.

Gawhar Shad, wife of Shah Rukh—a woman of great piety and a patron of the arts—built the famous mosque at Mashhad adjoining the shrine of the Eighth Imam. Only the faithful enter but it is said that somewhere within its precincts an inscription reads 'to appreciate its full height and glory, the Heavens use the Sun and Moon as binoculars'. (W Blunt, *A Persian Spring*, London, 1957, p. 87)

In the course of time the call to prayer ceased to be intoned from the encircling balconies of the minarets and the muezzin was more conveniently accommodated on the roof of the mosque. Like the drum below the dome, the minaret presented yet another surface for embellishment and calligraphers circumscribed them with texts from the Qur'an.

Men of exceptional and varied talents frequented the Herat court and its environs: poets and painters, musicians and astronomers, historians, bibliophiles and men of letters, book illustrators, calligraphers and bookbinders. The son of Shah Rukh, Ulugh Beg, should also be mentioned, not for his short and unsuccessful reign after the death of his father, but for his work as an astronomer. His observations and calculations were so accurate that they were published two centuries later (about 1650) by the professor of astronomy at Oxford. Of the painters, no name is more illustrious than that of Bihzad, head of the Herat school of miniature painting. The figures he depicted, whether they are engaged in battle, building a palace or just standing around are refreshingly free from the formalism that characterises some oriental art.

Jami, the last of the great classical poets, lived near Herat. Such was his acclaim that no frontier was barred to him and he either visited or corresponded with the leaders of the Black Sheep, the White Sheep and with the Ottoman Sultan, Bayazid II. Jami died a few years before Isma'il won the throne but he was revered by the early Safavid kings who were fanatically devout. He, like their forbears, was a Sufi:

> O Thou whose sacred precincts none may see,
> Unseen Thou makest all things seen to be;

Thou and we are not separate, yet still
Thou hast no need of us, but we of Thee
tr. A J Arberry, *Classical Persian Literature*,
London, 1967, p. 429

Of all the invasions that Persia has suffered through the 3,000 years of her history, none was more devastating than those of Genghis Khan and Tamerlane. Yet, viewed from the armchair comfort of retrospect, even the Mongols served some purpose. They wiped out the Assassins, which the Saljuqs never succeeded in doing. And, though their methods were hideous, in disposing of the 'Abbasid Caliphate they relieved the Muslim world of an institution that no longer served a worth-while purpose.

The inadequacies of Timurid rule, that followed the collapse of Il-Khan government and the eruption of Tamerlane's armies on to the plateau, left the country vulnerable to a take-over once again. Persia could so easily have been subjected to another dose of central Asian rule but the critical battle near Merv in 1510 determined otherwise.

At some stage after the Mongol invasions the work of restoration had to begin. That it started under the Il-khans only thirty years after Hulagu's death, is a pointer to the civilizing influence the Persians exercised over their conquerors. Ghazan Khan's rebuilding programme and his encouragement of agriculture represented a remarkable change of attitude. Perhaps by the time he came to the throne some integration with the population had already begun. If so Ghazan's conversion to Islam would certainly have assisted the process.

Altogether the legacy of these four and a half centuries is a rich one. In architecture, though their names may not be known, some of the works of the masters and their craftsmen survive. In other fields eminent names come to mind: in mathematics and astronomy 'Umar Khayyam and Ulugh Beg, in theology al-Ghazali, in painting the miniature school associated with Bihzad, in history the work of Rashid al-Din. Lastly medieval Persia was the age of the classical poets. And here tribute is due to those translators who have laboured to bring the work of Persian writers to the west. The quality of the poetry in the 13th and 14th centuries in particular suggests that if there was a golden age of Persian literature it was in the time of the northern hordes.

Notes

1 The name was probably derived from *suf* (arabic for wool) and was associated with the woollen robe customarily worn by members of mystical religious orders.
2 Coleridge's Kubla Khan.
3 *Persian Architecture*, London, 1965, p. 172.

CHAPTER 8
The Royal Road
1500-1794

THE CHANGING WORLD OF THE SIXTEENTH CENTURY

As the world rotated in its sixteenth century orbit, the expanse of its oceans and the extent of its land surfaces were becoming more clearly defined: navigators were sailing into hitherto uncharted seas and travellers were venturing into the interiors of unknown lands. Bartolomeu Diaz had rounded the Cape of Good Hope, Vasco da Gama, following in his wake, had reached the Indian subcontinent, and Christopher Colombus had crossed the Atlantic to the New World.

Then in 1522 a leaking Spanish galleon of 85 tons sailed up the Guadalquivir River and cast anchor. The *Victoria* was one of five ships which had set off three years before towards the south Atlantic under the command of the Portuguese navigator, Ferdinand Magellan. Hugging the south American coast they had sailed southwards, they had negotiated the passage between Patagonia and the windswept desolation of the Tierra del Fuego (since named Magellan strait) to emerge into a vast open sea beyond. Three months and many hardships later they had crossed the Pacific and reached Guam in the Mariana Islands. Eighteen survivors of a crew of 270, who had set out from Spain, had cirumnavigated the globe and proved that the oceans of the world were interlinked. Magellan himself was not among them—he had been killed in the Philippines—but as he had sailed to Malacca in 1511 he is regarded as the first circumnavigator.

While the merchant adventurers of Spain and Portugal were unrolling the map of the far west, other European countries, long dormant under the heavy blanket of medievalism, were waking to the dawn of a more modern age. Just as developments in the field of space science, nuclear energy and computer technology are making an impact on our lives today, so in the 16th century a variety of new scientific discoveries, new technologies, new inventions brought about far-reaching changes in human life and thought. Among these, for example, was the revelation, by Copernicus, the Polish astronomer, that the earth revolved round the sun, and the devising of a formula for the manufacture of gunpowder on a scale large enough to add a new dimension to warfare. But the invention which more than any other brought Europe into modern times was the brain-child of a diamond polisher in Mainz. In the 1450s Johannes Gutenberg had set up the first printing press. Within fifty years the Bible alone had run into as many editions and the numbers of books produced in the West could be counted in millions.

Even so the Westerners were not the first in the field with these and other finds. The process of civilizing this 'rude unpolish'd world' as Addison termed it, had begun long before in China. In the days of the great imperial dynasties of the Tang and the Sung (c. 600–1200) while Europe slept, the Chinese themselves had manufactured gunpowder (and used it in their wars with the Mongols), they had invented paper and moveable type. They had also explored the mysteries of magnetic science and their compass with its 'south pointer' had found its way into the hands of Iberian sailors and facilitated their navigations.

Nor would the more deductive approach to scientific method, which Renaissance scholars of the sixteenth century so eagerly began to pursue, have been possible without the pioneering work of their Asian predecessors. In the field of astronomy, in mathematics and medicine, Persia had already made a contribution while the so-called 'Arabic' numerals that were replacing the Roman had their origins in India.

In Florence, the heart of Renaissance Italy, Brunelleschi rejected the gothic style of the middle ages and returned to the principles of classicism. His architectural vision found a response in the sculptures of Ghiberti and Verrocchio, some of whose works were on public display. But the writings of Dante, Machiavelli and the classical authors, the paintings of Michelangelo, Botticelli and Veronese were mainly in private collections. They graced the libraries, adorned the Vatican chapels or the walls of the Medici and Doge palaces. Now, thanks to the arrival of the printed book and the art of engraving, the works of these and other masters could be reproduced in the mass for transmission to the wider public. This revival of interest in learning, in science and the arts, which echoed back to classical antiquity, funnelled up through the Italian peninsula into Europe to a world that was getting smaller.

A widening demand for foreign products—especially luxury goods—during the sixteenth century brought east and west into closer touch. Venetian merchants, for instance, following in the footsteps of Marco Polo, established trading houses in Tabriz and Persian metalwork came on sale in Venice. But it was the opening of the sea-lane round the Cape of Good Hope to India and the Far East that was to create a whole new perspective for international trade. First in the field were the Portuguese who in 1557 founded a settlement at Macao in China; a century later English and Dutch trading stations were operating on the coast of the Indian subcontinent.

With the exception of the Portuguese the Europeans did not as yet harbour colonial ambitions. Indeed, the great empire builder of the time came from Transoxiana. Babur, a Timurid prince, carried the Muslim faith from northern India to Bihar in the east. After his death in 1530 he was followed by a long line of Mughal emperors. Along with Turkey and Persia the empire he founded became one of the most important Islamic powers. The early Mughals were enlightened rulers. They tolerated other faiths.

Through his court Babur handed on a tradition of Persian art. The school of miniature painting, deriving from the Herat school that came into being in the time of his grandson, shows that Persian culture was continuing to exert its influence on the work of Mughal artists. In the 1630s Akbar's grandson, Shah Jahan, built the Taj Mahal at Agra. Most of the petty states of the subcontinent were eventually incorporated and at its height Mughal rule extended from Bombay to Calcutta, from Kabul to the borders of the Deccan. It was the collapse of their empire in the latter part of the 18th century which drew the major trading nations into conflict and resulted ultimately in India becoming part of the British empire.

The most formidable of the Islamic powers, the most agressive and perhaps the most widely feared was Ottoman Turkey. In 1453 Constantinople, last stronghold of the former Byzantine empire, had fallen to the janissaries of Mehmet II. He had authorised three days of unrestrained pillaging. Countless treasures—the accumulations of centuries—were lost and from that time on, the hallowed precincts of Hagia Sophia, crowning glory of Byzantine architecture and Justinian's affirmation of the sovereignty of Christ on earth, responded to the sound of Muslim prayers.

'There should be only one Empire', he reportedly said, 'only one faith and only one sovereign in the whole world'.

Cambridge History of Islam, 1970, IA, p. 296

The Ottomans came nearest to realising these aspirations during the 16th century in the time of Sulayman the Magnificent. With Constantinople at the centre the tentacles of the Ottoman octopus spread out from its Anatolian body: the Balkans had been among the first victims; Hungary and the lands round the Black Sea to the Crimea followed; to the south the old Mamluk empire, the Levant, Egypt, the Hijaz—Iraq too—all were caught up. Only in the east did the Ottomans fail to make a lasting penetration and the Persian homeland survived.

Like the Mughals the Ottomans benefited from Persian cultural traditions, especially in painting and literature. Persian had been the language used at the court of the Sultanate of Rum and the famous

Fig. xviii. Brass ewer with a tulip spout, late 16th century (Victoria and Albert Museum)

Persian Sufi poet, Jalal al-Din Rumi, had lived and been buried at Konya.

By the end of the sixteenth century most of the countries that fanned out round the Persian border were coming sufficiently into focus to be identifiable through twentieth century lenses. Though Afghanistan did not appear on the map until after the collapse of the Mughal empire, the principality of Muscovy—at first a cloud no bigger than a man's hand—had expanded in the 1550s when Russian armies reached the Caspian Sea and overran the old Mongol Khanate of the Golden Horde. Later they advanced into Transoxiana and the Caucasus. The Turkish empire meanwhile had passed its peak but Iraq (after a brief return to Persian rule) remained in Ottoman hands. As for China, under the Ming she lived on in an introspective world of her own until 1644, when the Manchus overran the country and installed their own dynasty, the Ching, on the throne.

But these moves on the international chessboard of Asia lay in the future. In the changing world of the sixteenth century the remarkable feature of the Persian scene was that the country survived intact. The ever-present menaces to her land frontiers in the west and the east, supplemented by another along her coastline with the arrival of a Portuguese fleet in the Gulf, were compounded by threats to her unity from within. Yet, despite these challenges, she emerged into the brief but glorious heyday of the reign of Shah 'Abbas as a national sovereign state.

THE SAFAVIDS

The Shi'ite route to power

The Safavid kings took their name from their ancestor, Shaykh Safi al-Din, who lived in the time of the Il-Khans. He was a saintly man and a devout Sufi, who moved from Ardabil to Gilan on the shores of the Caspian where he became head of the local Sufi order. People locally came to consult him; his reputation spread and, after their conversion, he is said to have acquired a following among the Mongols.

Shaykh Safi's descendants inherited the headship of the order but the contemplative life did not satisfy later generations. They sought power of a more temporal nature and it led them to Shi'ism on an increasingly militant scale. They became a revolutionary movement.

From their power-base centred on Ardabil and the north-west they drew support from seven tribes spread over eastern Turkey, Armenia and Azarbaijan, who were in revolt against the Ottomans. These lean hill-country nomads were excellent fighters and under Shaykh Haydar (great-great-great-grandson of Safi and the father of Shah Isma'il) they formed the movement's military wing. The *Qizilbash*, as they were called, wore the red turban with twelve pleats signifying their allegiance to the Twelve Imams.

During the disturbances under the Timurids the Safavids sided with the White Sheep but after 1467, when the Black Sheep had been eliminated from the contest, relations between the allies deteriorated. Haydar was killed in a skirmish, his elder son, 'Ali, was murdered and his second son, Isma'il, while still a boy, found himself at the head of the movement.

Sufi agents and party activists had been busy enlisting support among the Persians. The peasantry, no doubt beguiled by promises of a better life in the next world if they failed to realise it in this, were urged to make their way to paradise through Shi'ism and declare for Isma'il.

Isma'il was thirteen when in 1500 he left his refuge in Gilan and began the campaign which took him to the throne. In the mountains of eastern Turkey he assembled an army of 7,000 and the following year at Sharur in Azarbaijan he decisively defeated the White Sheep. That autumn he entered Tabriz in triumph and proclaimed himself shah.

There were no forces now in western Persia that could challenge him. From Tabriz he marched into Gilan, Mazandaran and Gurgan, then west to attack Diyar Bakr, the White Sheep headquarters, and south into Iraq, which brought the all-important Shi'ite shrines of Kerbela and Najaf into his possession. Fars followed and by 1510 he felt himself strong enough to tackle the Uzbegs. As we have seen, in a major battle near Merv, Muhammad Shaybani was killed and Khurasan was freed from the Uzbeg menace for the time being.

Thus within a decade Isma'il had brought the country under his control and his rule extended from the Oxus to the Euphrates. At intervals over 800 years, since the downfall of Yazdigird III, the last Sasanian king, Iran had been invaded, partitioned, fragmented; she had languished under the rule of foreigners, military governors, petty princes or simply been left to founder in anarchy. Arabs, Saljuqs, Mongols, Il-Khans, Turks and Timurids had successively overrun the plateau. Yet following each onslaught the older civilization had in time reasserted itself. Iran had persianised her conquerors by assimilating their descendants into her own society; she had incorporated certain of their cultures or fused hers with theirs.

Of all the invaders who occupied the country through those centuries, none had left deeper, more indelible imprints in their wake than the Muslims. Not only had the Persians adopted some forms of their calligraphic script, but they had embraced their religion. This too, under the national monarchy was to take on a Persian complexion. For, as disciples of the Twelve Imams, the Safavids associated themselves with the hereditary aspect of the faith. When Isma'il proclaimed himself shah and declared Shi'ism to be the state religion he confidently asserted he could trace his ancestry back to the Seventh Imam and through him to 'Ali and the Prophet himself. The claim was probably no more valid than the earlier one that 'Ali's son, Husayn, had married the daughter of Yazdigird, the last Sasanian king. But it served to link the faith with the state under one hereditary overlord. Such filaments of continuity, however thinly drawn, were useful aids in establishing the new dynasty. For in the eyes of the believers, when Isma'il started on his royal progress along the road which the kings of antiquity had travelled before, he—like them—must have been divinely guided.

Contemporary accounts describe Isma'il as good looking, brave and generous. He was a man of considerable charm who inspired an almost fanatical devotion among his followers. But he was also narrow, intolerant, impulsive and cruel. To him there was no middle way and those who did not renounce the Sunni doctrine had to be punished.

> God and the Immaculate Imams are with me, and I fear no one; by God's help, if the people utter one word of protest, I will draw the sword and leave not one of them alive'.
>
> E G Browne, *op. cit.*, IV, p. 53

This was the message to the mullahs of Tabriz on the eve of his coronation and when he swept through the country with his *Qizilbash* armies many who refused to renounce their Sunnism risked torture and execution. Nor were the dead left in peace: the first three of the 'Rightly Guided Caliphs', Abu Bakr, 'Umar and 'Uthman, were publicly cursed. 'Ali alone was acclaimed the Friend of God.

But whatever his defects the people now had a king whose

paternal ancestors had been living in Persia for six generations, a king in whom both spiritual and temporal power was vested once again, whose strong leadership at the outset offered the prospect of welding the country into a national sovereign state.

And indeed during the first decade of Isma'il's rule a new spirit of nationalism was becoming discernable. It was not the emotional patriotic nationalism that we are familiar with today but rather a sense of national identity in which the faith (the main unifying factor), the language and the culture came together under a Persian sky. History too, always a feature of the landscape, played a part as people recalled the great days of old. Whilst scholars perused accounts of Persia's imperial past, history for the common folk came in the form of legend, in the poetry of the *Shahnama* and other stories which were handed down. And if the boundaries between fact and fiction, which their hero kings crossed with such facility, were ill-defined, did it matter?

What did matter was that Isma'il, in restoring the monarchy and introducing Shi'ism as the established faith, had united the country so that it was strong enough to fend off a century of attacks from without and to withstand the unedifying spectacle of rival groups competing for high offices of state at the centre. These challenges manifested themselves before his reign ended.

From the outset Isma'il had to contend with invasions on two fronts: the Ottomans in the west, the Uzbegs pressing in on Khurasan. The forceful Turkish sultan, Selim the Grim, unable to tolerate Shi'ite non-conformity within his borders and troubled by the emerging power of Persia, called off his campaigns against the Christian countries of central Europe and sent his janissary armies against the Shi'ites. They massacred tens of thousands, they retook Diyar Bakr, they invaded Azarbaijan and at Chaldiran in 1514 near Lake Van they won a decisive victory. Isma'il had failed to modernise and mechanise his army and his cavalry were mown down by the Turkish guns. The *Qizilbash* suffered heavy casualties, Isma'il himslf was badly wounded and Tabriz was only saved from occupation by the onset of winter.

The repercussions of Chaldiran were as serious for the army as they were for the king himself. *Qizilbash* confidence in his divine guidance was shaken: he had failed to stem the slaughter and he had surrendered territory. Isma'il himself was a broken man. It was said that he never smiled again. He became morose and alcoholic, he no longer led his armies into battle and—more seriously—he lost interest in state affairs.

Traditionally the *Qizilbash* were cattle breeders or shepherds who migrated between summer and winter pastures. They had strong tribal loyalties and they did not mix with other ethnic groups. After helping Isma'il to power their chiefs had been rewarded with important posts at the expense of the Persians. Now, as the king's grip relaxed, they fell out among themselves and they quarrelled with the Persians. And when in 1524 Isma'il's ten year old son, Tahmasp, succeeded, the dissident parties each sought to gain control over the young king.

The Ottoman threat and the Qizilbash *factor*

Tahmasp comes over as a mean, treacherous, intolerant, melancholy man who sold off his old clothes in the bazaar, who surrendered a refugee prince—originally welcomed as a guest—to the sultan's executioner for pieces of gold, and who in his last years turned reclusive and never left his palace.

Against these less endearing traits must be set the achievements of a long and difficult reign. As he grew to manhood Tahmasp displayed a strength of character sufficient to gain a measure of control over the *Qizilbash*. For twenty years (1533-1553), while keeping the Uzbegs at arms length in the east, he masterminded a succession of defensive campaigns against the Ottomans. And though (as will be seen) he was hostile to infidels, that did not deter him from trying to persuade the Holy Roman Emperor, Charles V, to open a second front against the Turks in Europe.

The Ottomans were his most serious threat. The Janissaries under Sultan Sulayman the Magnificent were better armed, better disciplined, totally loyal and vastly superior in numbers and Tahmasp was in no position to engage in open battle. Instead he resorted to guerilla warfare and whenever the enemy invaded Azarbaijan and occupied Tabriz, as they did on several occasions, he laid waste the countryside. These tactics paid off as, with the approach of winter, the snow would cut the enemy supply lines and force them back across the frontier.

But Tahmasp was unable to defend Iraq against such a powerful adversary and the Ottoman invasion of the Euphrates-Tigris valley was the first in a chain of events that led to its permanent separation from the mother country. In 1534, as winter set in in Azarbaijan, the Turks, instead of falling back across their own frontier, wheeled round to the south, they crossed the Zagros mountains and marched on Baghdad. There was little resistance. Leading Sunnis came out to greet them and Sulayman himself made a triumphal entry into the old 'Abbasid capital. When in 1555 the two powers came to the conference table and signed the Treaty of Amasya, Iraq was incorporated in the Turkish empire but Persian pilgrims were given unrestricted access to the holy cities. Sulayman had made important conquests but he failed to expunge the Shi'ite monarchy and Persia had survived as an independent sovereign state.

The next thirty years were relatively peaceful along the frontiers. But at Qazvin, to which for greater safety Tahmasp had moved from Tabriz, his increasing reclusiveness enabled the *Qizilbash* to inch their way back into the forefront of affairs. And when Tahmasp died in 1576 Persian influence in the royal household was not strong enough to prevent his son by a Turcoman woman from gaining the throne.

Isma'il II had been incarcerated in a castle far to the north for over twenty years. Long term confinement is no preparation for sovereignty and the new king, when he exchanged his prison for the throne, revealed himself as dissolute, unbalanced, insecure and altogether unfit to govern. He liquidated many *Qizilbash*, including those who had brought him to power, and he murdered or blinded all the male members of the royal family whom he could lay hands on. 'Royal tents' he is said to have explained 'cannot be held up by old ropes.'

When after eighteen months Isma'il was poisoned, one of Tahmasp's sons still remained alive. Muhammad Khudabanda's name had lain well down on Isma'il's execution list as he was partially blind and thought to be out of the running. As there was no other eligible candidate he was given the crown but he proved to be ineffective and easily led. He came increasingly under *Qizilbash* domination and was eventually induced to abdicate in favour of his son. He too had been on the dreaded list but had managed to elude the executioner. And so it was in these somewhat unpropitious circumstances that Shah 'Abbas, 'the Great Sophy', ascended the throne of Persia.

Shah 'Abbas 'the Great Sophy'

'Abbas was 17 when he replaced his father in 1587. He had inherited a crown which carried only limited authority and a kingdom that was in disarray. *Qizilbash* rivalries had brought the southern provinces to the verge of civil war, in the north and east Turks and Uzbegs had penetrated deep into Persian territory, while at Qazvin, the capital, tribal chiefs were scheming again to reduce the new king to the status of a puppet.

But 'Abbas, unlike the hapless Khudabanda, was not going to be a tool in the hands of his advisers. He saw clearly that if he was to restore the standing of the monarchy he must diminish his dependence on the *Qizilbash*. Where better to start than with his chief minister?

Murshid Quli Khan of the Ustajlu tribe had been the young prince's protector and counsellor, he had plotted his path to the throne and outwitted the supporters of his two brothers. He was ruler in all but name. Nine months after his coronation 'Abbas decided he had served his purpose and Murshid Quli Khan was seized and executed. In the circumstances it was a wise move. From that time on the king was his own chief minister and he could start to filter more Persians back into the administration.

To reduce the *Qizilbash* imbalance in the army was a more problematical but no less urgent task. It was customary for tribal leaders to supply the king with soldiers in return for grants of estates (the system of land allocation known as *iqta'*, which had been widely practised in Saljuq times). It had worked well enough with the *Qizilbash* so long as they and the king were in accord but in the unsettled climate of the late sixteenth century the monarchy could not count on the undivided support of the tribesmen or their leaders. 'Abbas's solution was to form a separate standing militia from among the victims of the Ottoman invasions. Armenian and Georgian converts to Islam were enlisted and went into training. These were the *ghulams*. They had no tribal loyalties and they served the king alone. He paid them out of income from crown lands.

In 1590 'Abbas signed a peace treaty with the sultan. The terms were humiliating—territory in the west and north, including the former capital, Tabriz, was surrendered—but he was in no position to bargain and he needed to hold the Turks in check while he tackled the Uzbegs. Even so it took him eight years to liberate Khurasan and another four passed before he was in a position to challenge the arch-enemy.

The *ghulams* had by then become a highly proficient fighting force, the Uzbeg wars having served as a dress rehearsal for the final confrontation and in 1605 'Abbas retook Tabriz. A major victory in the region of Lake Urmia resulted in the recovery of the northern territories, as well as eastern Armenia and Tiflis in Georgia. With the recapture of Baghdad in 1623 'Abbas could rightly claim that after eight-and-a-half centuries and 120 years of Safavid rule Persia was 'a nation once again'. Moreover, having defeated the Turks in the field, he had demonstrated that the power of Persia was of no less account than that of the mighty Ottoman empire.

There remained one intrusion which 'Abbas chose to regard as a lurking threat to his sovereignty. This was the presence of the Portuguese on the island of Hormuz at the entrance to the Persian Gulf. Without suitable ships the Persians could not besiege the garrison. But in 1622 'Abbas pressed into his service some ships of the East India Company that were trading in those waters. The combined operation was successful and the Portuguese surrendered.

In his desire to free Hormuz from foreign control 'Abbas was not solely motivated by considerations of prestige. The pattern of world trade was changing and he wanted to place his country on a firm commercial footing. In the Far East the old Silk Road was in decline. Goods which for centuries had lumbered overland along the latitudinous caravan routes of Asia were finding their way to ports in the south-east from which they sailed across the Indian Ocean and round the Cape of Good Hope. In the west the supply lines through Turkey and eastern Europe were controlled by the Ottomans and were better avoided. Thus Persia was in danger of becoming a backwater. The long Cape sea route was the outlet he needed and he encouraged the English and Dutch East India Companies to extend their shipping routes from India up to Bandar 'Abbas and other Gulf ports. From there cargoes of silk bales could be carried direct to Europe. Silk from Gilan was the main source of state revenue. Its cultivation, which had begun in Sasanian times, had developed into a major industry and there was a steady demand to be satisfied in western markets. 'Abbas rewarded the English East India Company for their involuntary services with free port facilities at Bandar 'Abbas. It was a promising start to a trading relationship which survived a challenge from the Dutch after his death and continued into the twentieth century.

English contacts with the Safavids had begun in the time of Tahmasp when Anthony Jenkinson, a merchant travelling through Russia, had reached Qazvin. He carried a letter from Queen Elizabeth and had been received politely by the shah. But when he enquired about his religion and Jenkinson had admitted to being a Christian, he quickly learnt that his presence was unwelcome and the audience was summarily concluded: 'Oh thou vnbeleeuer,' expostulated the king, 'we haue no neede to haue friendship with the vnbeleeuers.' (Laurence Lockhart, *Famous Cities of Iran*, 1939, p. 38) Jenkinson was bundled out of the palace and sand was scattered in the wake of his infidel footsteps.

'Abbas had no inhibitions about receiving foreigners from countries of other faiths. He welcomed them and entered into diplomatic and commercial relations with their governments,[1] especially those that were hostile to the Turks.

> I do esteem more of the sole of a Christian's shoe,
> than I do of the best Turk in Turkey
>
> E Denison Ross, *Sir Anthony Sherley and his Persian Adventure*, London, 1933, p. 208

he told a member of the retinue which accompanied the brothers, Robert and Anthony Sherley. They were a couple of English adventurers whose arrival in Qazvin had coincided with the shah's return from his wars with the Uzbegs in 1598 and they were invited to join the triumphal procession into the city. The king was:

> . . . accompanied with all his nobles and great men in diverse troops, that we could not see anything all the way but men and horses, with such thundering of trumpets, kettle-drums carried upon camels, and suchlike instruments of war, that a man would have thought heaven and earth were tilting together.
>
> E Denison Ross, *op. cit.*, p. 117

The celebrations went on for eight days. The brothers walked with the king in the city, they admired the bright lights, enjoyed the singing and dancing, attended banquets and watched the king playing polo.

One of the Sherleys' companions described 'Abbas as 'small in stature but handsome and well-proportioned . . . His complexion is rather dark . . . he has a strong and active mind and an extremely agile body' (Ross p. 158). He was called 'the Great Sophy', perhaps on account of his Sufi or Safi ancestor. But he was not deeply religious in the way that Shaykh Safi al-Din was nor was he narrow or bigotted like his grandfather, Tahmasp. Not only did he allow missionaries in from other countries but, when he moved 3,000 Armenian families to Julfa to assist in the construction of Isfahan, he allowed them to build their own cathedral.

In freeing his kingdom from the invaders and his government from *Qizilbash* domination, 'Abbas restored the equilibrium of the state and the standing of the monarchy. He re-organized the administration, laid out new roads, built bazaars and caravanserais, constructed irrigation systems and vastly improved the economy. Well might some contemporary observer—one of the foreign envoys perhaps—in the closing years of his reign have thought the country and the people were on course for the continued peace and prosperity which they assuredly needed. But he would have been wrong for he would be overlooking the one fatal flaw in an otherwise brightly jewelled crown, a flaw that must have exercised the minds of ministers. As a father Shah 'Abbas had been a lamentable failure. His treatment of his family had left those who survived unfit for public office, not least among them his grandson, whom he nominated his successor.

The insecurity of his youth combined with an innate suspicious disposition had induced in 'Abbas a fear of assassination, which haunted him throughout his reign and which in his later years amounted to an obsession. Early on he had blinded his uncles and his father. Now, as his sons in their turn grew to manhood, he feared a similar fate at their hands and he kept them under increasingly close surveillance allowing them only eunuchs and tutors for company. He was also a prey to informers and when he decided to put his eldest son to death he was probably the victim of a plot. Muhammad Baqir was a brave and spirited prince and if he had succeeded, the Safavid dynasty might have served the nation better. Two other royal princes survived childhood but each of these had been blinded so that when 'Abbas himself died in 1629 there was no son to take his place on the throne.

'Isfahan is half the world'

Shah 'Abbas was a great patron of the arts, particularly of architecture. He moved the capital from Qazvin to Isfahan where he laid out a new city between the old town and the River Zayanda.

The Allahvardi Khan bridge gave on to the Chahar Bagh, a tree-lined promenade with fountains down the centre, which led past the palace gardens towards the old town and the famous old Friday mosque. Nearby was the commercial quarter with its bazaars and caravanserais, where the English and Dutch East India Companies had their warehouses.

Fig. xviii. Turquoise glazed ewer with brass handle and dragon's head spout, early 17th century (Victoria and Albert Museum)

The Maydan or great square located at the southern end of the old town is actually rectangular in shape; its axis runs from north to south. The surrounding buildings and linking arcades survive and are well preserved. On the west side stands the 'Ali Qapu Palace with its loggia from which members of the royal household watched the ceremonies, the processions and the polo matches. (The Chihil Sutun, the charming pavilion built by 'Abbas II whose frontal columns are reflected in a pool, lies in the gardens behind). Opposite the palace is the Shah's private chapel, the Lutfallah Mosque, with its coffee coloured dome, simple in design yet 'flawless and serene' (Pope). On the north side of the square a gateway leads into the bazaars and the old town, while dominating the southern end is the imposing Royal Mosque; its portals flanked by two pairs of minarets lead the eye on towards a second pair of minarets and the solitary grandeur of the massive blue tiled dome beyond. They, along with the rest of the main structure, are set at an angle so that the *qiblah* is aligned on Makkah.

The Khaju bridge with its terraces, from which the Isfahanis sit and watch the waters, and the Madar-i Shah Madrasa, were added later. Small wonder that as he marvelled at the splendour of the city a traveller was moved to exclaim, 'Isfahan is half the World' (Laurence Lockhart, *op. cit.*, 1939, p. 14).

Tahmasp, 'Abbas's grandfather, was also a patron of the arts. He encouraged carpet weaving and the 'Ardabil' carpet, one of the largest and oldest in the world (now in the Victoria & Albert Museum in London) was woven in his reign. The design of its medallions and cartouches appeared in other textiles, in brocades, velvets and tapestries.

The school of miniature painters which had been moved from Herat to Tabriz by Isma'il followed the court to Isfahan. They illuminated Qur'anic texts with a profusion of foliate and floral patterns and illustrated the lives of the kings and heroes of antiquity with birds, animals of the chase and Chinese dragons, which had been coursing along the Silk Road to join the monsters of Persian legend in the pages of the *Shahnama* and other works of literature. The pages themselves were preserved in elegant leather and lacquer bindings.

In response to demand there was also a large and varied output of pottery, porcelain, metalwork and jewellery. Gifts were exchanged with envoys and other visitors to the capital from the Mughal and Turkish courts and from Europe where oriental *objets d'art* also found a ready market.

For those then in court circles at Isfahan there were many attractions to delight the eye but rather fewer to please the ear or stimulate the intellect. There was a dearth of literary talent and those poets who had any claim to distinction received more encouragement in the Mughal capital than in their home country. As one of them explained:

> There exist not in Persia the means of acquiring perfection:
> Henna does not develop its colour until it comes to India.
>
> E G Browne, *op. cit.*, IV, p. 166

Likewise in scientific thought and learning the epicentre of activity had moved away—to the West—where it remained until the establishment of modern universities and other institutions facilitated the exchange of information between scientists and scholars the world over.

The Inept Shahs

It was customary for the royal princes to serve their apprenticeship for high office either in the army or in provincial government. But as there were no eligible sons remaining, 'Abbas on his deathbed named his grandson, Safi, to inherit the throne. A youth who has been kept within the confines of the women's quarters is not a good prospect for high office. Small wonder then that the new shah's first action, as he emerged into open daylight from the harem, was to follow precedent and secure his own position by disposing of his relations.

But Safi exceeded all limits. Every member of his immediate family whom he could lay hands on was either deprived of his sight or his life. Nor were the women spared, not even his mother, who is believed to have pleaded for moderation. He went further: nobles, ministers, counsellors, high-ranking generals who had served his grandfather and some of their families—they too suffered a similar fate.

Persia now entered one of the darkest periods of her history. Outwardly the decline was slow to manifest itself. Through four reigns frontier disturbances (except in Iraq) were not unduly serious, trade flourished and the administration, thanks to the sound framework set up by 'Abbas, continued to function. The cause of the degeneration was the shahs themselves. By abusing their powers by neglecting their duty to govern, they were setting the country up as a target for the invader and putting their dynasty at risk in the process. Safi, 'Abbas II, Sulayman and Sultan Husayn, all of them, with the partial exception of 'Abbas II, were unworthy of their office. Ceremonial extravaganzas, alcoholism, gluttony, a whole range of indulgencies, monopolised their time and attention. Sulayman, like Safi, kept his exectutioner busy and, as one of his nobles put it, whenever he left the king's presence he always felt to see if his head was still attached to his shoulders. 'Abbas II (1642-66) took more interest in state affairs, he treated successfully with the Uzbegs, but the quality of his mercy was never strained. Sultan Husayn on the other hand avoided bloodshed; he was pious, weak and superstitious; he turned his back on any unpleasantness and on the enemy with fatal consequences for himself, his family and his dynasty. Like Safi they had all been plucked from the harem and were generally content to leave the government in the hands of court eunuchs and mullahs, who were liable to advance their own personal or sectional interests.

Under Safi in December 1638 Iraq was finally lost to the Turks and the holy cities of Najaf and Kerbela came under Sunni government. Following the course of the Tigris, Sultan Murad IV led the Ottoman armies into the siege of Baghdad. On the fortieth day the city fell. The Turks gave no quarter: 'they killed all they met.' At the Treaty of Qasr-i Shirin, which followed the conclusion of hostilites, another page of the historical atlas of the world was turned as Persia's western frontier was moved eastwards towards a line that has become familiar in modern times. But on the credit side, the long-standing disputes that had dogged the two powers since the latter days of the Timurids were settled when the sultan renounced Turkish claims on Azarbaijan.

Nineveh, Babylon, Susa, Seleucia, Hatra, Ctesiphon, Najaf, Kerbela, Baghdad. As some of the famous place names which had linked the two countries pass in review, they call to mind the leading role which the ancient river civilization had played in the history of Persia: since the time 2,000 years before when Cyaxeres effaced the Assyrian empire from the map and Cyrus, riding through the streets of Babylon, was welcomed as a deliverer and since al-Mansur built the round city of Baghdad.

For two centuries, as part of the Ottoman empire, the Land of the Twin Rivers ceased to be of much account until a day in March 1843, when the French Consul at Mosul, intrigued by the mounds that dotted the dunes roundabout, made a discovery that set the antiquarian world alight. At Khorsabad, ten miles north-east of Mosul, Emile Botta, though he did not know it, had located the summer palace of the great Assyrian king, Sargon II, the father of Sennacherib (see above, p. 18).

AFGHANS, AFSHARIDS AND ZANDS

The Afghan interlude

> When you're wounded and left on Afghanistan's
>   plains,
> An' the women come out to cut up what remains,
> Jest roll to your rifle an' blow out your brains
> An' go to your Gawd like a soldier.
>
> Rudyard Kipling, *The Young British Soldier*

The wild mountain tribesmen of Afghanistan are a fine people—lean, hard and fearless—but they could be treacherous friends and cruel enemies. They had no organized government, they offered no security to the traveller and the caravans from Khurasan and Samarqand, making their way to Kabul or Qandahar or negotiating the passes leading to the relative safety of the Indian plain, risked attack from the unseen watchers in the hills above.

This inhospitable land had been a gateway to the Indian subcontinent for the trader and the invader from central Asia and the west. But since the arrival of the Mughals it had served as a buffer between the two great Islamic powers. From time to time the Mughals and the Persians had occupied the Afghan no-man's-land round Qandahar and it was in this area in the time of Shah Sultan Husayn (1694-1722), when the province was under Persian rule, that the final chapter in the story of the degenerating Safavid dynasty opened.

In Qandahar city the Ghilzai, a Sunni tribe, had overpowered the Persian governor and thrown out the garrison. The revolt spread to Herat, Khurasan was invaded and Mashhad besieged. The shah's armies failed to suppress the rebels and by 1715 the Ghilzai were in control of the eastern border.

Shah Sultan Husayn had by then given himself up to a life of debauchery. He had surrendered the control of state affairs to those around him, notably the court eunuchs. His pliant and feeble nature made him an easy tool in their hands. In the army the ranks of the *Qizilbash* and the *ghulams* had been depleted—sacrificed no doubt—to help defray the expenses of a court given over to luxury and a steadily expanding royal harem, which imposed a burden on the economy.

Clearly the Persian state was at its most vulnerable. There was wealth and power to be won and Mahmud, the leader of the Ghilzai, seeing his opportunity, went over to the offensive. He crossed the desert, seized Kerman and early in 1722 he was marching on Isfahan.

At Gulnabad outside the city the hastily assembled Persian forces fled before the tribesmen and the capital itself came under attack. The siege lasted six months. Failure to raise help from outside, divided counsels and treachery within the city, the onset first of famine, then of plague as the bodies piled up in the streets, finally forced Husayn to capitulate to the invaders.

On 12 October 1722, riding through the streets for the last time as king, Husayn went to meet his conqueror. At the Afghan camp across the river he was kept waiting while Mahmud 'slept'.

Apparently unruffled by the insult, when he finally came before Mahmud, Husayn addressed him with calm and simple dignity:

> Son, since the great sovereign of the world is no longer pleased that I should reign, and the moment has come which he has pointed out for thee to ascend the throne of PERSIA, I resign the empire to thee with all my heart: I wish that thou mayst rule it in all prosperity.
>
> Jonas Hanway, *The Revolutions of Persia* ..., London, 1753, III, p. 145.

In the three years that followed Mahmud's invasion made little headway. He was always short of men: many drifted back home with their loot and few came out to replace them. Shiraz he starved into submission, Qazvin he held briefly before being thrown out with heavy losses.

Fearing that the fighting spirit of the Qazvinis might provoke a rising in Isfahan, Mahmud invited its leading citizens to a feast and massacred them, then he turned on the rest of the population. When the slaughter had gone on for fifteen days, the Afghans had had enough and their leader had lost his reason. Mahmud was assassinated by his own supporters and his cousin Ashraf took over.

While the Safavid dynasty was sinking into its inglorious grave, the Ottomans were looking for easy conquests in the east to offset reverses they had suffered in their European wars. Georgia in the Caucasus, Armenia and western Persia were once again in their sights but this time they had a new rival.

The Russian Tsars had been pushing out their frontiers into the borderlands of Eurasia towards the Caucasus. Muscovy, which in the early days of the Safavids was no more than a principality, was now at the centre of a major power. In 1547 Ivan the Terrible from his throne in the Kremlin had proclaimed himself 'Tsar of all the Russias'. His armies had penetrated eastwards across the Urals into Siberia and south down the Volga to its mouth on the Caspian Sea.

Now Peter the Great (from his new capital at St Petersburg) was directing his prodigous energy and driving ambition towards further colonization and the Caspian provinces were among the 'Russias' he had earmarked for conquest. For him too Persia's weakness was his opportunity and in 1722 he shipped an army down the Volga into the Caspian, landed on the west coast and captured the fortress of Darband at the same time that the Ottomans were invading Georgia.

Happily for the Russians and the Turks there was no call for confrontation between them on this occasion. Finding that their respective claims could be resolved at the expense of the third interested party, the Tsar's representatives reached an amicable settlement with the Porte round the conference table at Constantinople. A treaty signed in 1724 envisaged the partition of Persia with Russia taking her Caspian provinces and the Ottomans having a free hand in the north and west. The shah (they conceded) should be supported in his claim to the rest of Persia.

Tahmasp II, a son of Husayn, had escaped from Isfahan during the siege and fled north. Like his father he was a feeble character who was inclined to wait on events. He had failed to rally an army large enough to challenge the Afghans and he weakly agreed to surrender the Caspian territories (including the silk-producing provinces of Gilan and Mazandaran) to the Tsar in return for his help in restoring him to the throne. But Peter's death in 1725 put an end to Russian activities in the south for the time being and their forces were later withdrawn.

It was Ashraf who stemmed the Turkish advance in the west. Though his brutalities were on a par with Mahmud's, he was a more devious character than his cousin and he had some appreciation of the arts of subterfuge. While his envoys at the Porte were criticising the Turks for treating with a Christian power his agents were infiltrating the ranks of the invading armies persuading them that it was wrong for Sunni to fight against Sunni. Eventually hostilities were halted and in 1727 a settlement was reached: the Ottomans retained their conquests but they recognized Ashraf as shah.

Meanwhile a member of one of the seven Turcoman (*Qizilbash*) tribes had arrived at Tahmasp's court in Mazandaran at the head of an army and offered his services which had been accepted. Nadir Quli Afshar was a Sunni, a man of humble origin, a camel driver turned soldier who had climbed to command in the service of the governor of Khurasan, where he gained a reputation as a ruthless but brave and brilliant general.

In a hard-fought campaign Nadir drove the Afghans out of Khurasan. Encouraged by his successes men rallied to his standard, Tahmasp promoted him to commander-in-chief and by the autumn of 1729 he was ready to attack their main army. In a matter of months the Afghans sustained two major defeats, first at Damghan and again at Murchakhar near Isfahan, where they suffered heavy losses. Before making this last stand they had gathered their women and children into the citadel at Isfahan and, as a precaution against a rising, Ashraf had massacred another 3,000 Isfahanis. Husayn and other members of the royal family had already been executed.

As the Afghans fled from the battlefield they paused only to collect their families and baggage before retreating to Shiraz. Few saw their homeland again. Harried by Nadir's men, burdened with their womenfolk (and in the early stages with the inevitable loot), from Shiraz they fled eastwards. Those who were not overtaken and killed died of cold or hunger in the desert. Ashraf himself was hunted down by Baluchi tribesmen and murdered.

So ended the Afghan invasion which had lasted seven years, in which perhaps a million Persian lives were lost from famine, disease, killing or death in battle, in which the Safavid dynasty sank to new depths and much of the beautiful city of Isfahan was reduced to ruin.

> 'One might suppose', said a visitor some 80 years later, as he viewed the still clinging wreckage, 'that God's curse had extended over parts of this city… Houses, bazars, mosques, palaces, whole streets, are to be seen in total abandonment; and I have rode for miles among its ruins, without meeting with any living creature, except perhaps a jackal peeping over a wall, or a fox running to his hole.'
>
> James Morier, *A Second Journey through Persia, Armenia and Asia Minor*, London 1818, p. 134.

Nadir Shah Afshar

In 1729 Tahmasp had returned to Isfahan and amid the shambles of the ruined city he had duly been crowned. As the only surviving son of Sultan Husayn he was the undisputed ruler and the Safavid dynasty had to outward appearances been restored. In reality he was little more than a figurehead. For Nadir, in his meteoric rise to the military summit, had determined to win the throne for himself. He had already undermined the king's authority by declining to drive the Afghans from Shiraz until Tahmasp had granted him the right to levy taxes.

The young king soon played further into Nadir's hands. In 1731 he joined in a war with the Ottomans in which he lost the western territories that his commander-in-chief had recently won back. Nadir, who had left the front to quell a revolt in Khurasan, loudly denounced the resulting settlement as being 'contrary to the will of heaven' and on his return to Isfahan he forced Tahmasp to abdicate. He was too astute to seize the crown straight away. Instead he proclaimed Tahmasp's infant son as Shah 'Abbas III and himself as regent. Four years later in 1736, when the young 'Abbas died, Nadir ascended the throne and the Afsharids were acknowledged as the ruling house.

The way was now clear for the country to lick its wounds and settle down to a period of stable government. During the regency the disputed territories in the north and west had been reclaimed and the neighbouring great powers had retreated. But Nadir had no intention of settling down to a period of peaceful rule.

Instead he embarked on a remarkable series of conquests. In Afghanistan he captured Kabul and Qandahar; in India he defeated the Mughal armies of Muhammad Shah and entered Delhi; he invaded the Uzbeg territories where he subdued the khanates of Bukhara and Khiva. Only in his wars with the Turks, in which he engaged on his return, did he sometimes fail to emerge the victor.

While in Delhi he had plundered the accumulated treasure of the Mughal emperors—more than enough to finance his campaigns and restore the mutilated city of Isfahan—but he locked up the spoil (which included the Peacock Throne[2] and the Koh-i Nur diamond) in the fortress of Qal'at-i Nadiri,[3] a natural stronghold in the mountains of Khurasan.

Nadir's avarice, his bigotted and intolerant nature became more pronounced. His attempts to impose the Sunni doctrine, the constant drain on manpower to maintain his armies, the heavy taxation and the appropriation of lands to pay for his wars—these demands on the long-suffering people, coupled with his failure to restore a proper system of government in the aftermath of the Afghan invasion, combined to make Nadir Shah a hated man. In his last years he blinded his son. His guilt served only to warp his judgment and to exacerbate his parsimony. He sought relief in punishing others, by executing the nobles who had witnessed his son's blinding and by planning to murder some of his officers. But the plot leaked out and they decided, as the saying went, 'to breakfast off him ere he should sup off them'. In 1747 Nadir Shah was assassinated by his own commanders.

So ended the career of the camel driver who rose to become Shah of Persia. He has been variously described as the second Alexander and the Napoleon of Iran. He saved Persia from the Afghans, he drove out the Turks, he freed the Caspian provinces from Russian encroachments. But when he won supreme power he used it to indulge his love of battle.

His failure to concern himself with the administration, his insatiable demands on the country's resources, his increasing tyranny and avarice—these defects in his last years served to mask his undisputed right to be known as Persia's most gifted commander, perhaps even as a military genius.

Karim Khan Zand

In a century when Persia was invaded from three directions, from Afghanistan, Turkey and Russia, a century in which the follies, the greed and the rapacity of her rulers exceeded even that of those who had gone before, it is heartening to record that in the midst of this there was a twenty year interval when peace prevailed and Persia was ruled by a man disposed to consider the needs of the people.

Three years of turmoil followed the disintegration of Nadir's armies as various contenders fought each other for the throne. When the fighting had finished and the dust had settled new patterns of authority were discernable across the country.

In the east Shah Rukh, a grandson of both Sultan Husayn and of Nadir, was ruling the state of Khurasan from Mashhad. He had been blinded, imprisoned and twice deposed but when his supporters restored him a third time he stayed on. He was ineffective as a ruler but he maintained the status quo for nearly fifty years. Further afield Ahmad Durrani, one of Nadir's Afghan generals, had occupied Qandahar where he later founded the kingdom of Afghanistan.

In the west, Karim Khan, leader of the Zand, a minor nomadic tribe, had by 1750 emerged the winner. He had driven his most dangerous rival, Muhammad Husayn Khan, back beyond the Alburz mountains to his headquarters in Gurgan. Muhammad Khan was leader of the Qajars, the most powerful of the seven Turcoman tribes, and as an insurance against further trouble Karim Khan had taken his son, Aqa Muhammad, hostage.

Karim Khan never attempted to displace Shah Rukh, nor did he take the title of shah; he ruled as *vakil* or regent for a distant Safavid prince, Isma'il III. He was a humane man, magnanimous to his enemies and tolerant of other faiths. He improved internal security, curbed tax abuse, encouraged agriculture and concerned himself with the welfare of the peasants. As trade improved and foreign merchant ships resumed their sailings up the Gulf he sponsored the establishment of trading stations at Bushire and Basra.

After Karim Khan's death in 1779 the country lapsed back into a decade of anarchy as members of his family fought among themselves and toppled each other from the throne in rapid succession. Luft 'Ali Khan, 'the last chivalrous figure amongst the kings of Persia' and the last Zand to rule, held on for five years. But in the end the Qajars triumphed.

While Karim Khan lay dying his hostage, Aqa Muhammad, had escaped back to his northern homeland in Gurgan. There he soon established Qajar supremacy over the Turcoman tribes which had spread into the neighbouring provinces of Gilan and Mazandaran. Then crossing the Alburz he gradually gained control of the central provinces. In 1794 he besieged Luft 'Ali Khan in Kerman. He escaped but was betrayed, captured and tortured to death. So ended the Zand interlude.

Shiraz the Garden City

Fars, once the home of the Achaemenid kings, had always been regarded as the true heart of Iran. Here in this most Persian of all provinces, in the beautiful city of Shiraz, once the home of Sa'di and the incomparable Hafiz, amid the vineyards that terrace the surrounding hills Karim Khan built his capital.

> Right through Shiraz the path goes
> Of perfection;
> Anyone in Shiraz knows
> Its direction.

The pathways frequented by Hafiz had disappeared down the intervening centuries but Karim Khan restored the city. His additions included the Vakil mosque and bazaar, baths, caravanserais and a palace round which he laid out garden parks or paradises.[4] In contrast to the prestige capitals of other dynasties the Zand capital was modest in scale. Earthquakes have since taken their toll but the Vakil mosque and the bazaar survive.

Today the city's inimical charm lies not so much in its architecture, much of which is undistinguished, but in the gardens which embroider it. It resides too in the facades of the merchants' houses of the Qajar period from whose painted tiles we glimpse a detail or two of the scene within: a cornucopia of pink peonies and irises, a servant girl carrying a bowl of pears, another bringing wine.

But it is their gardens that the people of Shiraz delight in: the sentinel cypresses, the umbrella pines, the luxury of running water, the scent of jasmine and roses. The visitor from the west who arrives by plane (I will not call him a traveller) is sometimes disappointed by his first sight of some famous Persian garden: the walls maybe are crumbling, the layout to him is unimaginative, the rosebushes are overgrown and there is an air of neglect about the place. But to the overland traveller who comes on it from the dust, the glare, the heat and the discomfort of the desert, this to him is akin to paradise.

> All that he demands, this denizen of a high, rocky plateau, is coolness at the end of the day's journey; coolness and greenness; the sound of trickling water after the silent desert, after the miles of shadowless plain.
>
> V. Sackville-West on Persian gardens in *The Legacy of Persia*, Oxford, 1953, ed. A J Arberry, p. 260

And it will surely be just such a garden which the traveller will see in his mind's eye when he continues on his journey.

Notes

1 The first British mission led by Sir Dodmore Cotton reached Persia, c. 1628. There were no positive results and he died shortly after his arrival.

2 The Mughal peacock throne no longer exists; it was broken up after Nadir Shah's death. Parts of it were retrieved by the Qajar Shah, Aqa Muhammad, and incorporated in the so-called peacock throne which (when I saw it in 1976) was standing in the Gulistan Palace in Tehran.

3 Lord Curzon, who visited Qal'at-i Nadiri (but failed to gain an entrance) gives a description of it in his *Persia and the Persian Question*, London, 1892. It is also described in the abridged edition ed. Peter King, *Curzon's Persia*, London, 1986.

4 The English word is derived via Greek from the old Persian *pairidaeza*, a park.

CHAPTER 9

From Medieval to Modern Times 1794-1925

AN AGE OF REVOLUTION AND REFORM

The Qajars presided over a decadent phase in Persia's history. They had the authority to order the country's internal affairs but, with the exception of Aqa Muhammad, they were incompetent. Theirs was a despotism without direction. Aqa Muhammad's successors were not unduly cruel, they were not aggressive, nor on the other hand did they concern themselves with the efficient working of the administration. Over the years as government degenerated into a state of *laisser-faire* bureaucracy, intrigue and corruption spread abroad unchecked; provincial governorships were sold to the highest bidder and the people were exploited by the officials who were meant to serve them. Foreign aid was diverted to top up depleted royal coffers. The impressive displays of pomp and power, which the monarchy indulged in to bolster their prestige, the cost of their inordinately large families and the extravagance of their courts added to the strain on an economy that was already overburdened. It has been said of the Qajars that 'they ruled the country as though it were an enemy land to be exploited for the benefit of the royal family' (P K Hitti, *The Near East in History*, Princeton, 1961, p. 393).

It was their misfortune to be ruling at a time of social and political upheaval in the West, when in the aftermath of the French Revolution the crowned heads of Europe were being called to account, and reverberations from reformist movements were being felt as far away as western Asia. The Qajars responded to the calls for change in their own country by turning their backs and refusing to listen. And when the voice of the people could no longer be ignored they were carried kicking towards the realities of the twentieth century.

But if the old-style despotism was to yield to some form of constitutional monarchy on western lines, would this be compatible with the king's role as the Shadow of God on Earth (which it was convenient to perpetuate) or would the concept fade away with the Qajar dynasty itself? In Turkey, seat of the caliph, whose Ottoman régime was no less reactionary than that of the Qajars, the reform movement begun by the Young Turks led to the creation of a secular state with Kemal Atatürk as its first president. But for Persia the search for a solution would prove to be more disruptive, more complex and would take longer to find. Ultimately for her too it would mean deviating from the royal road, perhaps never to return.

THE QAJARS

Anglo-Russian rivalries

It could be said there were six typical Qajars and there was Aqa Muhammad for, apart from an avaricious streak that he shared with other members of his house, his successors in no way resembled him. He extended Persia's frontiers—they surrendered territory; he closely supervised the administration and kept the army in good fighting order—they did neither and after his death the army's pay was frequently in arrears.

Aqa Muhammad established his capital at Tehran. He did not take the crown until 1796—two years after the death of Luft Ali Khan—and he wore it for only fifteen months before he fell to his assassins. But to ensure the continuity of the Qajar monarchy (and in an effort to avoid the anarchy that had dogged the path of Karim Khan and others who had gone before) he named his heir. The dynasty he founded gave Persia internally a century of comparative peace and, according to Sir John Malcolm, a British envoy at the Qajar court, he was 'one of the most able monarchs that ever sat upon the throne of Persia' (*History of Persia*, London 1815, II, p. 300). Yet the barbarities he perpetrated exceeded even those of his predecessors. He wreaked vengeance on the Zands and their supporters. Not only did he condemn Luft Ali Khan to a slow and painful death, but he removed 70,000 eyes (which he personally counted) from survivors of the siege of Kerman. 'Had one been wanting', he told the man charged with the operation, 'yours would have been taken' (Percy M Sykes, *Ten Thousand Miles in Persia*, London 1902, p. 69). Such was the nature of the founder of the Qajar dynasty.

Aqa Muhammad's tragedy was that he had been castrated at the age of five; his eunuchism and his long years in captivity had warped his character:

> His beardless and shrivelled face resembled that of an aged and wrinkled woman; and the expression of his countenance, at no time pleasant, was horrible when clouded, as it very often was . . . his future conduct seems to have taken its strongest bias from the keen recollection of his misery, and his wrongs. The first passion of his mind was the love of power; the second, avarice; and the third, revenge. In all these he indulged to excess; and they administered to each other: but the two latter, strong as they were, gave way to the first, whenever they came in collision.
>
> Malcolm, *op. cit.*, II, p. 300-1.

Having eliminated the Zands and secured his position in the centre and the south, Aqa Muhammad in 1795 moved against Georgia, a small Christian country sandwiched between Russia and Turkey. In response to an appeal from the ruling prince for protection, Catherine the Great had promised him military aid but failed to provide it. Aqa Muhammad ravaged the country, sacked the capital, Tiflis (Tbilisi), and on his return captured Erevan, capital of eastern Armenia. After his coronation, he invaded Khurasan. He entered Mashhad without opposition and subjected the sightless old Shah Rukh to a programme of daily torture until he had revealed the hiding places of all the Mughal treasures that remained in his possession. Shah Rukh died from the effects of his ordeal and Aqa Muhammad met his end shortly after, in 1797. He was killed by two servants who, inexplicably, while under sentence of death for some trivial offence, had been allowed to go free.

Fath 'Ali Shah, the nephew nominated by Aqa Muhammad, succeeded though not without opposition from within the family. His reign during the first three decades of the nineteenth century witnessed the start of changes in the conduct of foreign affairs. Closer communications with the West through diplomatic contacts led to the arrival of specialist missions, the setting up of boundary commissions and (later) to trading concessions. Turkey ceased to be a major threat; only Russia in her push through the Caucasus indulged in all-out war.

Persia was becoming a focus of interest to the great powers of Europe. To Russia she could provide both the outlet she wanted to the warm waters of the Persian Gulf and a passageway to the Indian subcontinent; for her a subservient Persia would be an advantage. While Britain saw a friendly independent Persia strengthened by internal reform as the best means of countering Russian designs on her empire in the east.

Persia's dilemma therefore was how to respond to the blandishments of these and other powers, who were promoting their own national interests; how to accept the financial, military and technological aid they proffered without sacrificing her own independence.

Fath 'Ali Shah's arrival on the throne coincided with the rise of Napoleon in France. Having triumphed in Europe, the Corsican general had conceived a grandiose scheme to build himself an empire in the east by following in the footsteps of Alexander the Great. But the defeat of the French fleet by Lord Nelson at the battle of the Nile in 1798 cut his communications with France and destroyed any lingering chance he had of advancing on India from Egypt.

Nevertheless the Indian Government were not reassured. They sent Sir John Malcolm, then a young officer in the army, to Tehran with instructions to treat with the shah and forestall any renewed French activities in that area. Travelling overland from Bushire to Tehran—a distance of over 700 miles—Malcolm reached the capital in 1800 and concluded a satisfactory treaty under which Britain agreed to render military aid in the event of a French attack.

However, it was not the French who started hostilities some five years later but the Russians. Fath 'Ali had ordered the prince of Georgia to send his son to the Qajar court as a hostage. Rather than submit, the prince had sought Russian protection and this time Tsarist armies had occupied the country. According to the terms of Malcolm's treaty, Britain was justified in remaining aloof from the long war that followed in the Caucasus. But Fath 'Ali felt he had been let down and retaliated by inviting a French military mission to Tehran. This time Sir Harford Jones took the road from Bushire to the capital. His offer of an annual subsidy was accepted with alacrity, the French retired from the scene and a friendship agreement was signed which formed the basis of the Anglo-Persian Treaty of 1814.[1]

Hostilities in the Caucasus, which first began about 1805, dragged on intermittently over twenty-three years until the tide finally turned in favour of Russia. At the Treaty of Turkmanchai of 1828 the Russians moved their border down to the Araxes river. And eastern

Armenia, so long a battleground between Persia and her rivals in the West, passed into the possession of the Tsars. Georgia and Armenia later became republics of the USSR.

Despite the temporary rift in Anglo-Persian relations, Fath ‘Ali was well disposed towards Britain and the Harford Jones mission was the start of permanent diplomatic relations with the British Government.

Fath ‘Ali, who died in 1834, is remembered for his avarice, for his magnificent court, for the jewelled splendour of his public appearances, for his inordinate personal vanity and for the size of his family. A conservative estimate credits him with having 150 wives, 57 sons and 46 daughters; enough to create a social problem or, as one commentator put it (especially when grandchildren were added to the total), enough to support the Persian saying, ‘camels, lice and princes are to be found everywhere.’

In her book, *The Sabres of Paradise*, Lesley Blanch cites an exchange between Fath ‘Ali and Malcolm, when wives were a subject of their conversation:

> ‘I have heard a report which I can scarcely believe,’ the Shah said. ‘It seems that your King has but one wife.’
> ‘No Christian prince may have more,’ replied the Ambassador.
> ‘O, I am well aware of that,’ said the Shah, ‘but he may have a little lady I believe?’
> ‘Our gracious King George III is an example to his subjects in both morality and restraint, in this respect, as in every other’, was Sir John’s lofty response.
> To which the Shah rejoined that such a state might be very right, but he certainly would not want to be king of such a country.
> When the Shah asked if the French were not a very powerful people, Sir John replied: ‘Certainly: otherwise they would not deserve to be mentioned as enemies of England’.
>
> Lesley Blanch, *op. cit.*, London, 1978, p. 32-3

Muhammad Mirza inherited the throne on the death of Fath ‘Ali in 1834. Like his grandfather and his son, Shah Nasir al-Din, Muhammad Mirza’s right to succeed was disputed by other Qajar princes, one of whom threatened to march against him. But Fath 'Ali had named him as his heir and the British and Russian envoys, who had no wish to see the country torn apart, escorted him to the capital where he was quickly crowned. Civil war was averted but the crisis had shown that the smooth transition of power could not be guaranteed.

Following the humiliating losses that Persia sustained in the Caucasus war, Muhammad Shah sought compensation by acquiring territory in the east. But, whereas at the turn of the century the Indian government had not objected to Persian raiding parties entering Afghanistan, by the 1830s suspicion of Russian intentions in the region had brought about a change of attitude. The area in question centred round the old Timurid capital of Herat, which the Qajars had always maintained was Persian territory. Britain now was unwilling to allow Persia to extend her Khurasan frontier further: the Qajar armies were poorly led, ill-equipped and irregularly paid. And Herat, lying as it did along the likely route to India from the north, was thought to be safer in Afghan hands.

For nearly twenty-five years as Muhammad Shah and Nasir al-Din with Russian encouragement tried to regain the city, the Herat question clouded Anglo-Persian relations. At the last attempt by Nasir al-Din in 1856, the Indian government brought the matter to a head by declaring war on Persia and sending troops to occupy Kharg Island in the Persian Gulf. If the action was drastic it was also effective. Within six months the war was over and by an agreement signed in Paris the following year, at the conclusion of the Crimean War, Persia recognized the independence of Afghanistan.

After her defeat in the Crimea, Russia expanded into central Asia, where her armies were free from the attentions of Turkey and her European allies. Rounding the northern shores of the Caspian Sea between 1865 and 1884, she occupied the Uzbeg khanates of Khokand, Bukhara, and Khiva south of the river Oxus. The lands north of the Atrek river, which included the city of Merv, were annexed and before the century was out the Russian frontier was marching with the northern border of Afghanistan.

When the Treaty of Turkmanchai was being negotiated in 1828 Fath 'Ali had asked Britain to assist in defining the frontiers with Russia and Turkey. The boundary commission that was formed then was the first of many that laboured for over seventy years to demarcate Persia's frontiers. In the west the Persian, British and Russian commissioners were joined by Turkey; in the east by Afghanistan. As the only power with no territorial ambitions

Britain's role was that of mediator, although on the eastern side her concern to protect India's borderland made her an interested party. Here the line to be determined lay southwards through Afghanistan, Sistan, Baluchistan and Makran on the coast.

The frontier west of Herat was settled at the 1857 Treaty of Paris. Sistan was partitioned between Persia and Afghanistan while further south, where there were competing claims to Baluchistan and Makran, five boundary commissions were convened before the dividing lines were finally agreed. Few of the parties with overlapping claims could have been satisfied with the compromises that inevitably had to be made. But, apart from some minor modifications, the decisions stood the test of time.

Altogether the survey teams mapped over a thousand miles of territory. They endured bitter winters, searing hot summers and primitive living conditions. And in the more remote areas—those inhabited for instance by the Lurs, the Kurds and the Baluchis—their task was rendered more difficult by local people who viewed their activities with profound suspicion.

No boundary commission met to discuss Persia's north-east frontier along a line from the Caspian Sea to the Afghan border as the Russians refused to countenance British participation.

Nasir al-Din (1848-96), overcoming opposition from his elders succeeded his father, Muhammad Shah, at the age of sixteen. More than any other member of his house he recognized the need to modernize. His father had made a start by attempting to prohibit the import of slaves and the use of torture. But above all the young shah wanted to preserve his country's independence. He had no wish to be subject to further Russian intimidation or to be used by the British to serve the interests of their empire in the east. He saw that his best insurance against foreign interference would be to create a new standing army trained on European lines, to improve internal communications and to facilitate trade and redevelopment.

To finance any development programmes Nasir al-Din had to attract foreign capital by means of loans or the sale of concessions. As Britain and Russia were the only countries who were prepared to invest on a large scale (France having withdrawn from the field), he hoped the benefits of modernization would offset the cost of the undertakings.

Thus it was that towards the end of the century the face of Persia began to change. The British installed a telegraph service and opened up the Karun river to shipping; Russian Cossacks trained a cavalry brigade and both countries introduced banking facilities. Some road construction was begun (there were practically no highways that could take wheeled traffic). One of the more successful enterprises was the reorganization of the customs administration undertaken by the Belgians which produced some revenue.

Nevertheless the melancholy fact was that the administration—an essential interface to ordering the country's new look—was not equal to the task. Government ministers were either unable or unwilling to respond to the demands of their office. The expected benefits to the economy did not materialise, loans were misappropriated, corruption was widespread and by the end of Nasir al-Din's reign Persia, instead of having restored her own self-esteem, had become a tool in the hands of foreign governments. Worse still, as the toll of debts mounted the shah became increasingly initimidated by Russia. Already in 1869 he had signed away his right to sovereignty over the land beyond the Atrek river and in 1887 he yielded to secret demands that no railways or waterways were to be built without the prior consent of his Tsarist masters.

In the last years of his reign, amid increasing dissatisfaction and unrest at home, the call for a more liberal regime finally broke the surface and in 1896 Nasir al-Din was assassinated by a member of a revolutionary group led by Jamal al-Din al-Afghani (see p. 224).

The century-old rivalry between the two great powers was halted in 1907 by the announcement of the signing of the Anglo-Russian Convention. Under the agreement each of the two parties awarded themselves a sphere of influence—the one in the north, the other in the south of the country—leaving a no-man's land in between. The news was received with shocked surprise which articulated into nation-wide resentment. It was felt that Persia had been relegated by the imperialist powers to something akin to colonial status. And the British government, which had repeatedly expressed a desire to see a strong indpendent Persia, was seen to have betrayed a trust. The timing too was unfortunate as the agreement had been negotiated at a time when the people had taken the first step towards setting their house in order (a step in which Britain had played a part). Only eight months before, Muzaffar al-Din Shah, reluctantly yielding to demands from all classes, had granted a constitution.

The initial move in the call for change had come from a lone voice that had sounded across the wilderness of authoritarianism back in the time of Muhammad Shah. It was a voice that argued the case for a more tolerant and just society and it had come not from a poltical revolutionary but from a preacher.

The Bahai 'manifestation of the will of God'

Sayyid 'Ali Muhammad was the son of a cloth merchant in Shiraz who had studied theology under the Shi'ite elders at Kerbela. In 1844 he proclaimed himself 'the *Bab* or Gate through which men might gain access to the sacred mysteries and spiritual truths.' He advocated equality of the sexes, the abolition of circumcision and of the veiling of women.

Though he soon gained adherents, when he returned to his own city he was a prophet without honour and was thrown into prison. Babis were remorselessly hunted down and tortured and inevitably 'Ali Muhammad was condemned to death. On the day of his execution he was dragged before a firing squad in Tabriz and shot. When the smoke cleared the Bab had disappeared. The shot had cut the ropes and freed him. But the poor man was found and made to face the volley a second time.

The persecutions proved to be counter productive. The Bab's miraculous escape, his death and the bravery of his converts increased his following. Some years later when E G Browne was in Isfahan he visited a cemetery where the grave digger, himself a convert, showed him the unmarked graves of two of the martyrs:

> 'Some time after their death', he said, 'I saw in a dream vast crowds of people visiting a certain spot in the cemetery. I asked in my dream "Whose are these graves?" An answer came, "Those of the 'King of Martyrs' and the 'Beloved of Martyrs'" Then I believed in that faith for which they had witnessed with their blood, seeing that it was accepted of God.'
>
> E G Browne, *A Year Amongst the Persians*, Cambridge, 1927, p. 234

In 1863 the Bab's disciple Baha' Allah declared himself to be 'the manifestation of the will of God'. Exiled in Acre, where he died in 1892, he rejected the militancy of Islam and moved towards the more humanitarian tenets of the Christian faith. Unlike the Manichaean and the Mazdakite movements (see pp. 100 and 107 above) of Sasanian times, which were addressed specifically to the malcontents among the peasantry, the Bahais attracted adherents from all walks of life.

Under the Qajars Bahaism was necessarily an underground

movement and Browne describes the secret meetings and philosophical discussions he had with its members. Their numbers were not known but their influence could not be ignored and they supported the call for reform which followed the proclamation of their faith and which surfaced in the last decade of the century.

From despotism towards democracy

Being of tribal origin themselves, the Qajars in the early stages of their rule appointed local chiefs as provincial governors, particularly in tribal areas. The main tribes—Turcomans in the north, Kurds, Bakhtiyaris and Qashqais in the mountains to the west and Baluchis in the remote east—accounted for about a quarter of the total population. Elsewhere these posts provided convenient sinecures for the proliferating numbers of royal princes. As miniature despots they levied their own taxes; they were required to send a proportion of their revenues to Tehran but they were free to finance themselves out of the balances.

By the end of Muhammad Shah's reign the country was in a state of unrest and the government was deeply in debt. Corruption had permeated all levels of the administration, provincial revenues were in arrears, governorships were being auctioned and army pay was three years or more overdue.

This was the situation in 1848 when Nasir al-Din succeeded in establishing his claim to the throne. The longest to reign and the most energetic of the Qajars, he started well by appointing Mirza Taqi Khan, the Amir Nizam, as his vizier. A man of humble origin, hardworking, able and incorruptible, he checked abuses, regularized the collection of revenues and ensured that the army was paid. But a chief minister of this calibre was out of tune in Qajar Persia. He made enemies; they won the ear of the shah and three years after he had taken office Amir Nizam was dismissed. With his departure and subsequent assassination all hope of better financial management and greater efficiency in government was lost.

As the redevelopment schemes got under way in the latter part of Nasir al-Din's reign, the presence of foreigners—engineers, bankers, military missions, telegraph officers, as well as Christian missionaries who took it upon themselves to run schools and hospitals—induced feelings of inadequacy. There was a growing realisation that Persia lagged behind other nations, that she was still wrapped in a mantle of medievalism, that so long as government continued in its present form there could be little prospect of improvement. Some sort of fundamental reform was needed.

Most of the foreign capital, instead of being used to shore up the crumbling infrastructure by improving internal communications, was misdirected. Some of it found its way into the personal coffers of the Qajars for Nasir al-Din and Muzaffar al-Din in the customary manner of oriental monarchy indulged in expensive pleasures. One of them was foreign travel. In 1873 Nasir al-Din toured Europe. His entourage, which numbered nearly a hundred, included members of the royal family, court officials, ministers, secretaries, coffee servers, a barber, a water bearer, grooms for the five horses and a host of personal servants. His diary records his meeting with the heads of state of eight countries. In England he was received by Queen Victoria, who bestowed on him the Order of the Garter. Neither this visit nor his two subsequent tours brought much tangible benefit to Persia but they were a heavy drain on the country's drifting economy.

In 1896 Nasir al-Din was assassinated by a revolutionary (see p. 221). He was one of the better Qajars, he had generally striven to maintain peace with his neighbours. But he had sought solutions to his country's problems in material terms and had failed to respond adequately to the voice of the people. His attempts to industrialise the country had not been matched by any move towards constitutional reform and the legislative, executive and judicial control over the lives of its ten million people had remained in his hands.

Muzaffar al-Din, Nasir al-Din's son, whose accession was not disputed, was the archetypal Qajar—vain, self-indulgent, dissimulating, reactionary and incompetent. He was altogether a living expression of the need for change to which he was to be such an unwilling party. Throughout his reign (1896-1907) the call for greater freedom and justice continued to be voiced, though by common consent it was recognized that whatever reform might be achieved, the faith had to be protected. There was as yet no call to diminish the king's role as guardian of the faith. Religious rule went hand in hand with temporal rule. The Qajars, following in the footsteps of the 'Abbasids, claimed to be the Shadow of God upon Earth. Their right to rule, they maintained, carried divine authority and it was the duty of the people to obey them in carrying out their mission.

Most of the religious leaders—certainly the more progressive among them—came round to supporting the call for change. The *ulama'*, as the mullahs, theologians and other learned men were collectively known, looked for a redistribution of power that would give them more say in the conduct of affairs. They had already moved a step in this direction as the Qajars, being Turcoman in origin, could not (like the Safavids) claim to be descended from 'Ali or the Imams. As a result the administration of religious law, the *shari'ah,* had passed to the mullahs. At the root of this desire for a stronger voice lurked a feeling of insecurity, a fear that their own position could ultimately be threatened. They were alarmed at the presence in increasing numbers of unbelievers, especially the Christian missionaries, and they disapproved of the founding in Tehran of the Dar al-Funun, the first college of education whose purpose was not primarily religious and which was not, like the madrasas, under their control.

The *ulama'* were an influential body of opinion. Thanks to the deep and abiding attachment to the faith that pervaded all sections of society, their spiritual authority was undisputed. In administrative affairs too their views could be made known as they had access to the king. They were generally respected by the nobility and the intelligentsia; they were in close touch with the small business communities and the bazaar merchants while the lower classes regarded them as their protectors. As 'men of the pen' they helped the unlettered in legal transactions and checked the worst excesses of over-zealous goverment officials. Thus the mullahs and their like had their ears to the ground at all levels; they were witness to the hardships and injustices experienced by the great majority and when the time came for a decision they sided publicly with the people in calling for a constitution. They wanted a government whose mantle of power would be more widely spread, in which tyranny would have no place and under which all men would be equal before the law.

The prospect of reform opened up different possibilities to the various echelons of society. To the aristocracy and the intellectuals (some of whom had travelled in the West) it offered a more liberal regime and a chance to share power; to the *ulama'* the opportunity to increase their secular authority and to purge the country of unbelievers; to the minority faiths freedom of worship; to the merchants better trading prospects; to the individual peasant the chance to ease his poverty. Those who had less to gain, but who supported the cause just the same, were the tribesmen, who already enjoyed a degree of freedom.

In sum the desire for change appeared to have widespread support and, if the *ulama'* gave the lead, the nation might respond. The call, if it came, would be not for revolution—only the extremists wanted that—but for reform. As always there was the understanding that whatever the nature of the change it would endure only until such time as the Awaited One (the Twelfth Imam) returned in person to purify the world.

During the nineties, as the agitation for reform gathered momentum, the powerhouse of the movement centred on the Dar al-Funun, which Amir Nizam had founded in Tehran in 1851. Conscious of the inadequacies of the madrasas, he had sponsored a curriculum which included the military sciences, chemistry, medicine, engineering and European languages. The college was tutored mainly by Austrians. A thousand students had passed through its doors and some of them had continued their studies in the west. As yet there were no national newspapers (only a government controlled press in Tabriz) but the Dar al-Funun had its own printing press.

In 1890 a London-based Persian news sheet began to circulate. It was banned in Persia but copies were regularly smuggled across the frontiers. *Al-Qanun* ('The Law') was published by Malkum Khan, a former ambassador to the Court of St James in London, and Jamal al-Din al-Afghani, an exiled revolutionary. (It was one of Afghani's men who assassinated Nasir al-Din). They inveighed against corruption and called for a constitution and a fixed code of laws.

It was at this time that a test of will developed between Nasir al-Din and the people. A concession granted to European merchants to help finance the shah's foreign tours had given them monopoly rights on the sale of the tobacco crop. Encouraged by the Russians, the Persian merchants protested, the mullahs supported them and *Al-Qanun* construed the deal as being a threat to Islam. Once this interpretation spread round the bazaars the protest assumed national proportions. People gave up smoking and the shah, fearing the onset of violence, cancelled the concession. His withdrawal was a landmark: the failure of the tobacco *régie* demonstrated that, given sufficient support, a popular movement could successfully challenge the royal authority.

The next public expression of discontent occurred in 1905, thirteen years after the tobacco *régie,* in Tehran. 'Ayn al-Dawla, the unpopular vizier, had ordered some bazaaris to be bastinadoed. In protest merchants gathered in a mosque where day by day their numbers grew. They demanded the dismissal of 'Ayn al-Dawla. Muzaffar al-Din eventually agreed to their demands but the hated vizier remained in office and six months later he expelled a mullah from the city. This time the reaction was more serious. Some of the elders left in protest, the bazaars closed, crowds gathered and the religious and commercial life of the capital came to a halt. The rebels sought sanctuary in the grounds of the British Legation and the great *bast* (a system of providing sanctuary) began. Twelve thousand camped in the legation grounds.

By now the shah's promise to dismiss 'Ayn al-Dawla was not enough; there were demands for a code of laws and a constitution and he was forced to negotiate. Through the offices of the British minister discussions continued for three weeks. On 5 August 1906 Muzaffar al-Din signed an imperial rescript in which he undertook to call a national consultative assembly (*majlis*). He was by then a sick man and he died five months later, a few days after he had put his signature to the new constitution.

The constitution stated that the Majlis would have an upper and a lower house: a senate, in which the religious leaders would be represented, and an elected national assembly. There was no suggestion that the shah was endowed with authority from above. Clearly the concept of the Shadow of God on Earth was receding.

Though the change from the old regime to the new had been achieved without bloodshed, Muhammad 'Ali, who was crowned in 1907, had no intention of conforming to the strictures imposed on a constitutional monarch. Neither did the introduction of a parliamentary democracy commend itself to the Russian authorities. This was the year of the signing of the Anglo-Russian Convention, which they chose to interpret as being a licence to strengthen their hold on the north. They had 12,000 troops on hand and they did not hesitate to use them to this end.

In June 1908 the shah sent the Cossack Brigade, which was under Russian command, to bombard the assembly building and disperse the Majlis. Some of the deputies were killed, others were imprisoned. Martial law was declared and for a year the capital was in the charge of a Russian military governor.

The shah's action was ill-timed (it coincided with the rebellion of 1908 by the Young Turks which resulted in the deposition of the Ottoman Sultan, 'Abd al-Hamid) and it brought the country to the verge of civil war. An uprising in Tabriz, which was suppressed by the Russians who occupied the city, was followed by outbreaks of violence elsewhere. By June 1909 supporters of the nationalist movement, among them 5,000 tribesmen, had come together and were converging on the capital. After three days of fighting the shah fled to the Russian legation from which he went into exile and the Majlis named his son, Ahmad, as his successor.

Despite difficulties the Majlis did make progress in its early years. Laws were introduced to curb the expenditure of the royal household and to prohibit foreign loans. Then in 1911 a brave attempt was made to sort out the country's finances: an American, W Morgan Shuster, was appointed Treasurer-General. But the Russians requested his expulsion and when the Majlis rejected their demands they replied by moving troops into the capital. The doors of the Majlis were locked and Shuster had to go.

The Russians now had 12,000 troops on Persian soil and they continued to tighten their grip. They bombed Imam 'Ali al-Rida's shrine at Mashhad on the trumped up charge that subversive elements were at work and Persia was only saved from further occupation by the commencement of the Great War. But if the Persians regarded Russia with hostility, their attitude towards Britain was at best one of ambivalence. Any good-will gained in promoting the constitution had been offset by the Anglo-Russian Convention and when the Great War came Persian sympathies lay with the enemies of Russia rather than with Britain.

A new factor, which was to affect commercial and political relations with Britain and to transform Persia's economy, was the discovery of oil in the south-west. In 1901 W K D'Arcy, an Englishman who had made a fortune gold-mining in Australia, had been granted drilling rights and after six years prospecting over difficult terrain his venture was rewarded. The Anglo-Persian Oil Company, in which the British government had a controlling interest, was formed in 1909 and oil began to come on stream in 1913. The Persian Government received shares and 16 percent of the profits.

On the outbreak of the Great War Persia declared her neutrality but as she had virtually no army she was powerless to prevent Turkish and Russian forces from using Azarbaijan as a battleground. Nor could she deny the British the right to protect their oil installations.

Prior to 1914 Germany, anxious to make up for lost time in acquiring an empire in the east, had started on the construction of the Berlin to Baghdad railway. Her *Drang nach Osten* paid off for, although when hostilities began the line had not been completed, German agents were sufficiently on hand to stir up trouble among the tribes round Abadan and further east, where the central powers were planning a push through Afghanistan to India.

Tehran became a centre of intrigue and in the provinces the Swedish trained gendarmerie, who were in German pay, made little attempt to maintain order. In 1916 the Government reluctantly gave permission for Major Percy Sykes[2] (as he then was) to raise a local force, the South Persia Rifles, to restore order, to protect British interests and to safeguard the overland route to India. The collapse of Russia in 1917, following the Bolshevik Revolution, left the way clear for such an attack but fortunately for the allies the German and Turkish forces were by then committed in other theatres.

The end of the war found Persia in a state of anarchy: the tribes were in revolt, the country was ravaged by famine and the treasury was empty. Lord Curzon, suspicious of Bolshevik designs on India, offered to guarantee Persian independence and to supply military advisers and financial aid. A draft treaty was approved by a compliant shah while on a visit to London but the Majlis in 1921 threw out the agreement. In rejecting it they undoubtedly had substantial support in the country. Once again the British government had misjudged the climate of opinion. The Soviet-Persian Treaty on the other hand, which was signed in the same year, was well received. Not only did the Russians cancel all treaty obligations incurred under the Tsars, but they handed over all Russian property and wrote off Persia's considerable debts.

Altogether the year 1921 was a watershed. As well as determining the pattern of post-war relations abroad, it marked the beginning of the end of the Qajar dynasty and a decisive break with the past. Only a few months before Persia had been accepted into the League of Nations as an independent sovereign state. Before the year was out the shadows of western imperialism had receded, British and Russian troops had been withdrawn and Reza Khan, an officer in the Cossack Brigade, had staged a *coup d'état* and overthrown the government.

The state of Persia in Qajar times

Seen through the eyes of Western travellers the urban landscape of Isfahan, Tehran and Mashhad, to cite three examples in the latter part of the Qajar period, was in chronic disorder. Consider first E G Browne's impression as he walked along the river bank at Isfahan with one of his Babi acquaintances in the year 1887:

> On our way we visited the deserted palace . . .

> Here was visible the same neglected splendour and ruined magnificence which was discernable elsewhere. One building . . . had just been pulled down by one of the ministers . . . to afford material for a house which he was building for himself. Another, . . . 'the Chamber of Mirrors', was nearly stripped of the ornaments which gave it its name, the remainder being for the most part broken and cracked. Everywhere it was the same—crumbling walls, heaps of rubbish, and marred works of art.
>
> *A Year Amongst the Persians*, Cambridge, 1927, p. 238

Or take the capital itself as Ella Sykes (sister of Sir Percy Sykes) saw it:

> The chief roads are broad with avenues of trees, but have big holes at intervals caused by the remarkable custom of digging up the public highway to get mud to make the sun-burnt bricks; men carrying on their respective trades take up a good deal of the street; and large convoys of donkeys, so laden with brushwood that only their legs are visible, totter along with an absolute disregard to the rest of the traffic...
>
> In [the] rainy season . . . the roads are almost impassable for pedestrians, who take to wearing galoshes as they splash through mire of the consistency of pea-soup; and it is pitiable to see the women flip-flapping along in the sea of liquid mud, their heelless slippers being small protection against the wet.
>
> *Persia and its People*, London, 1910, p. 46-7

Or Mashhad, which Lord Curzon visited:

> The main feature . . . (next to the holy shrines) which endears it to the Persian imagination and distinguishes it from other Oriental capitals, is the possession of a straight street, nearly one mile and three-quarters in length ...

> This street . . . is regarded by the Oriental as the veritable Champs-Elysées of urban splendour. Down the centre runs a canal, or, as we should prefer to call it, a dirty ditch, between brick walls, about twelve feet across, spanned by frail foot bridges and planks . . . This canal appears to unite the uses of a drinking fountain, a place of bodily ablution and washing of clothes, a depository for dead animals, and a sewer. On either side . . . comes the footway, and then the ramshackle shops of the bazaar.
>
> George N Curzon, *Persia and the Persian Question*, London, 1892, I, p. 152

In common with other visitors these travellers paint a picture of a country that has lost its way, as indeed it had. Society was class-ridden, polarised and corrupt. But in a changing world Persia could not remain isolated indefinitely. Western influences for better or worse were inevitably seeping through. In the meantime, while accepting what the industrialised West had to offer, Persia retained her own national identity and culture.

In the arts the Qajar period was not without merit. Fath 'Ali Shah had his portrait painted in life-sized oils, while at the other end of the painting scale the miniaturist tradition begun by the Herat school came into prominence once again: under the supervision of Abu 'l-Hasan Ghaffari, one of the foremost nineteenth century painters, thirty-four artists were employed to illustrate a six-volume edition of *The Arabian Nights*. Floral designs were a recurring theme. They blossomed among the pages and on the lacquered covers of books, on mirrors, on pen-boxes and other trinkets and the small *objets d'art* that were in vogue at the time.

The carpet trade became a growth industry. Baleloads of antique carpets and tribal rugs were carried in caravans to Trebizond and shipped to Western ports. To satisfy increasing demand looms were set up in the towns. Modifications to the dyeing process had to be devised to offset the harshness of the new synthetic colours but traditional local designs were maintained.

In the early years of the dynasty there was some building activity. The Royal Mosque at Qazvin, an earthquake casualty, was among those that were rebuilt or restored by Fath 'Ali Shah and his successors. They also applied gold-leaf to the shrines of Mashhad and Qum and embellished older mosques with minarets whose projecting lantern-like balconies and domed tops (in contrast to the pencil-pointed Ottoman towers) were a feature of the period. At Mahan near Kerman a pair of minarets was added to the gateway of the fifteenth century tomb of Nur al-Din Ni'matallah, a sufi saint and poet who was venerated in the Qajar period, as well as in modern times. The shrine stands in an oasis on the edge of the Dasht-i Lut. Together with its domed chambers, its courtyards and its gardens the whole complex has about it an aura of serenity that would have been a welcome solace to the pilgrim arriving at his destination.

In literature, as in the visual arts, the period was not a great one. The arrival of the printing press was slow to make itself felt. But the introduction of colleges such as the Dar al-Funun and translations of the works of Western writers may have provided some stimulus. For the subject matter in poetry and prose broadened out into more secular themes and styles became less flowery. Persians have always had a feeling for language. As one young man put it, 'Everyone in Persia is a poet—it is one of our national failings.' (Robert Payne, *Journey to Persia*, London, 1951, p. 67). Fath 'Ali Shah put his verses in writing and sent his collected works to the Prince Regent. Its lacquered covers and illustrations, which are works of art in themselves, are in the Royal Library at Windsor.

Notes

1 James Morier, the author of *The Adventures of Hajji Baba of Ispahan*, was a member of the Harford Jones delegation.

2 Sir Percy M. Sykes, Consul-General in Mashhad 1905-13; author of *The History of Persia*, 2 vols., London 1930.

CHAPTER 10
The End of the Road
1925-1979

ROYAL TRAVELLERS

Five times in 500 years men of widely different origins have won the throne of Persia: Isma'il the Safavid descended from a line of sufis, who established Shi'ism as the orthodox faith; Nadir Quli Afshar and Karim Khan Zand—the one a camel driver turned warrior, who expelled the Afghans, the other chief of a minor tribe and one of Persia's most enlightened rulers—neither of whom founded a dynasty worthy of the name; Aqa Muhammad Khan, head of the important Qajar tribe and Reza Khan soldier and 'nation builder', arguably one of Persia's most able rulers for the reformist revolution that he brought about.

Seen against the trend in the West, where monarchies were being overthrown, Reza Khan's elevation to the 'Peacock Throne' in 1925 was the more remarkable. France, Russia, Austria, Germany and more recently Turkey had opted for republics. Not so Iran. Though she had been ill-served by successive Qajars, when the decision came to be taken, the Majlis commissioned another monarch, not a president, to lead the way forward.

As the Pahlavis peeled away layers of medievalism centuries thick and replaced them with a new economic and social system, the route of the royal road, on what may prove to be the last lap of its passage through history, lies through a radically changing landscape.

THE PAHLAVIS

Reza Shah 'the Nation-builder'

Reza Shah was born in 1878 in poor circumstances at Alasht, a village near the shores of the Caspian Sea. At the age of fourteen he enlisted as a private in the Cossack Brigade and by dint of hard work he rose eventually to the rank of colonel. After the Russian Revolution the White Russian officers were expelled and the year 1921 found him at Qazvin where, having taken over command, he had reorganised the entire brigade.

Here he was visitied by Sayyid Ziya' al-Din Tabataba'i, a political writer from Tehran, who urged him to march on the capital and overthrow the government. Much of the land was in a state of anarchy and Reza Khan, a great patriot, who was fired by a genuine ambition to restore his country to its former greatness, accepted the challenge. On 20 February 1921 he led his Cossacks into Tehran and occupied the city. The next day he had an audience with Ahmad Shah who authorised him to form a government. The *coup d'état* had been accomplished peacefully with hardly a shot being fired.

What sort of man was this officer who had risen from the ranks, who founded a dynasty and who laid the foundations of a modern state? Vita Sackville-West, who was in Tehran for his coronation five years later, saw him as

> an alarming man, six foot three in height, with a sullen manner, a huge nose, grizzled hair and a brutal jowl; he looked, in fact, what he was, a Cossack trooper; but there was no denying that he had a kingly presence.
>
> *Passenger to Teheran*, London, 1926, p. 142.

He was a man of simple tastes who lived a spartan existence: he slept on the floor throughout his life. He married twice. He was first and foremost a soldier and always wore uniform. But he disliked pomp and was more at home in a barracks than a palace.

In character he was fearless, proud, decisive, short-tempered and aloof. He lacked the human touch. But he was politically astute and when patience was called for he could bide his time. A man of few words, he was intolerant of inefficiency and a hard taskmaster.

Lt-Colonel Hassan Arfa (as he then was), who later had a distinguished military career, describes the arrival of Reza Shah without warning to inspect his regimental barracks on the day in 1930 when he took over command:

> He stopped in front of the windows of one of the armouries and said angrily: 'These sons of burned

> fathers can't even keep their windows clean!' And with his cane he broke all the window panes, while I calculated rapidly the price of the Imperial anger which I would have to pay out of my 135 tomans' monthly pay (£20).
>
> After having walked in silence through the barracks, Reza Shah returned to his car. Then I gathered up my courage and said: 'I have a petition to present for Your Majesty's consideration.' With one foot on the car's step, the Shah looked at me inquiringly: 'Speak!'
>
> 'I give Your Majesty my word to train this regiment according to Your Majesty's wishes, but I beg that Your Majesty will not visit the regiment again for three months. I also respectfully report to Your Majesty that I took command of this regiment only one hour ago.'
>
> The Shah looked at me with his golden eyes as if appraising me, for what seemed to me a very long time, then entered his car, and was gone'.
>
> *Under Five Shahs*, London, 1964, p. 220-1

In 1921 Reza Khan set about forming a government and securing his own position as *de facto* head of state. Ziya' al-Din Tabataba'i became Prime Minister but he soon faded into obscurity and over the next three years premiers succeeded each other in rapid succession. But whatever the composition of the cabinet Reza Khan retained the posts of Commander-in Chief of the armed forces and Minister for War.

His first task was to reorganize the army and secure its loyalty, to check the robber bands that roamed the rural areas, to curb the powers of the tribal khans and to maintain the central government's authority. The Cossack Brigade, the gendarmeries and the South Persia Rifles were merged and conscription was introduced. His next important step was to bring in an American mission under Dr A C Millspaugh to advise on reorganizing the country's finances.

Altogether it took Reza Khan three years to achieve undisputed control of the country. Not till the autumn of 1923 had he consolidated his position sufficiently to take over the premiership himself. Shortly after Ahmad Shah left for Europe in search of better health. He never returned and the way was clear for the Majlis to decide how the country was to be governed. Reza Khan, influenced by events in Turkey, floated the idea of a republic but the proposition did not win general support and it was in any case opposed by the religious authorities. In October 1925 the Majlis formally deposed the Qajar dynasty and six weeks later a National Constituent Assembly approved the only feasible alternative. They declared Reza Khan and his successors in the male line as shah.

As the first king of a new dynasty he styled himself Reza Shah Pahlavi in recollection of the great days of the Parthian empire. The coronation ceremony took place in the elaborate mirrored room of the Gulistan Palace in Tehran. Among those who took part was his six year old son, Mohammed:

> At last there came a stir; the doors were opened, and the figure of a little boy appeared. Quite alone, dressed in uniform, he marched down the length of the room, saluting, and took his place on the lowest step of the throne, His Imperial Highness Shahpur Mohammed Reza, Crown Prince of Persia . . .
>
> Escorted by his generals and his ministers bearing jewels and regalia, the aigrette in his cap blazing with the diamond known as the Mountain of Light, wearing a blue cloak heavy with pearls, the Shah advanced towards the Peacock Throne. The European women curtsied to the ground; the men inclined themselves low on his passage; the mullahs shambled forward in a rapacious, proprietary wave; the little prince, frightened, possessed himself of a corner of his father's cloak. Only the silence seemed strange; one expected a blare of trumpets, a crashing of chords, and nothing came; only a voice droning an address, and then the voice of the Shah, reading from a paper. With his own hands he removed the cap from his head, with his own hands he raised and assumed the crown, while two ministers stood by, holding the dishonoured tiaras of the Kajar dynasty. Then from outside came a salvo of guns, making the windows rattle, proclaiming to the crowds in the streets that Reza Khan was King of Kings and Centre of the Universe.
>
> V. Sackville-West, *op. cit.*, p. 148-9.

Reza Shah's mission, as he saw it, was to modernise the state, to restore the country's self-respect in the eyes of the world and to promote her economic independence.

Such a formidable remit called for a ruler of his calibre. He did not scruple to pack the cabinet and government offices with men who would follow his lead, nor did he hesitate to 'approve' candidates for election to the Majlis. If the elections themselves were rigged such tactics he considered were justified and the Majlis invariably ratified the proposals he placed before them.

By these means he was able to prune the privileges of the large landowners, to deprive the nobility of their titles, to introduce measures to compel the tribes to settle and bring them under government control. He believed their migratory way of life was not compatible with the modernised state.

Reza Shah did not challenge the power of the religious authorities but he monitored their activities. When the Minister of the Interior reported that one Sayyid Ghazanfar, who claimed to be the reincarnated Twelfth Imam, was causing a disturbance, he exclaimed: 'During my reign I shall not permit any prophets to appear,' and the man was arrested. Nevertheless he dislodged a few stones in the Shi'ite pyramid of power. He made secular education compulsory for girls as well as boys, he founded the University of Tehran, he took steps to bring about the emancipation of women (the wearing of the veil was banned) and he transferred the administration of justice from the religious to the civil courts.

These and other measures took time to bring in but already in 1927—just two years after his coronation—Clarmont Skrine of the British Consular Service, on returning to Iran after some years' absence, was reporting that the country had 'changed radically from the picturesque medieval' society presided over by the Qajars. 'A new day had dawned for Iran, self-respect had been reborn, hope renewed.' He saw little semblance of a constitutional monarchy—Reza Shah's regime was just as despotic as his predecessors' in antiquity. But no other type of government was feasible at the time.

To help get the economy moving and to stimulate exports, Reza Shah built factories for processing tea, sugar, dried fruit, nuts, caviar, tobacco and paper. In the north, where there was an unhealthy reliance on the Soviet Union to absorb surpluses, merchants were directed to seek outlets further afield. They were well received in Germany and new markets were opened. But the move, which in itself was commercially sound, was to have unfortunate political repercussions.

The first north-south railway, from the Persian Gulf to the

Caspian Sea (financed entirely within the country from taxes on tea and sugar), was constructed and camel tracks were converted into roads suitable for lorry traffic. Under town planning schemes the alleyways and mud houses of the medieval towns gave place to wide tree-lined streets and in Tehran, to symbolise the break with the past, the old city walls were torn down. Merchants turned exporters moved out of their old quarters in the bazaars into modern offices. Bankers (another emerging national breed), were among those who exchanged their traditional dress for the European city suit.

Reza Shah had long been dissatisfied with Iran's share of the royalties from the Anglo-Persian Oil Company and in 1932 he cancelled the company's concession. In the negotiations that eventually followed it was agreed that the government would receive a portion of the royalties from a 20 percent dividend and the company was renamed the Anglo-Iranian Oil Company.

To emphasize the country's refurbished look and improved self-sufficiency, in 1935 the Shah decreed that the country should be known as Iran (the land of the Aryans). This was in recognition of the Aryan origin of the people, the *Irani*, as they called themselves.

In foreign affairs he pursued a constructive policy and entered into an agreement with his Islamic neighbours, Iraq, Turkey and Afghanistan, in which all four countries laid past hostilities to rest, by signing a five-year non-aggression treaty. The Saadabad Pact was signed at the shah's summer residence in 1937. Later that year Iran was elected to a seat on the Council of the League of Nations.

But despite her desire for peace, for the second time in a generation Iran was to be caught in the crossfire of hostilities of other nations. At the outbreak of war in 1939 she proclaimed her neutrality though, for historical reasons and in her own commercial interests, for the second time she looked forward to a German victory.

In June 1941, after Hitler's armies invaded the Soviet Union, the allies needed an overland route to Russia to relieve the pressure on the Arctic convoys. They requested a passage through Iran and the expulsion of all German residents.

Reza Shah was slow to respond and in August British and Russian troops began moving in. Contrary to popular belief, the British Government had no wish to see the shah vacate the throne.[1] But to the king himself the prospect of the occupation by foreign forces was intolerable. When he heard that Russian troops, advancing from Qazvin, were 80 miles from Tehran he took the only course that was open to him. He abdicated in favour of his son, Mohammed Reza. On 16 September he left the capital for Bandar 'Abbas and eleven days later a British ship carried him into exile. He went first to the Mauritius and later to South Africa where he died in 1944.

The circumstances of the abdication were a personal tragedy for Reza Shah. Nevertheless as the shore-line of Iran faded from his view for the last time, he could justly claim to have brought about the most constructive revolution in his country's history. As his son wrote later: 'My father . . . led us Persians into the new age.'(*Mission for my Country*, London, 1961, p. 44) Reza Shah was virtually a dictator. He ruled from behind a facade of constitutional monarchy. But he was also a patriot and a reformer and during his sixteen years on the throne he introduced sweeping changes: social, economic and judicial. In the Qajar aftermath he was the man his country needed.

The Pahlavi summit

In September 1943 Iran entered the war on the side of the allies and when, after the Japanese surrender two years later, hostilities ended, she faced a crisis in the Soviet Union's attempt to take over the northern provinces.

Under a tripartite alliance signed in 1942 the allies had undertaken to withdraw their armies within six months of the cessation of hostilities. By March 1946 American and British forces had left but the Russians dragged their feet and an estimated 30,000 troops remained in the north. In Azarbaijan a breakaway section of the Tudeh (Communist) party, who styled themselves 'the Democrats', had formed a separatist movement and declared the province an autonomous republic of the USSR.

Viewed in the light of post-war history, Iran's success in defeating the Soviet challenge was a remarkable achievement. The Iranian premier, Qavam al-Saltana, appeared to go along with the conditions under which the Russians offered to withdraw. These included an oil concession, for which he initialled a draft agreement, and Tudeh representation in the Cabinet. Meanwhile the Iranian delegate to the United Nations, Husayn Ala, took his country's case to the Security Council and the Soviet Union, not as yet discredited in the eyes of the free world, was caught in the glare of unfavourable publicity. On 9 May 1946 the Russian forces were withdrawn from Iranian soil. In the elections that were held the following year the Tudeh party won only two seats and the Majlis, when it assembled, refused by 102 to 2 Tudeh votes to ratify the draft oil agreement.

In 1941 at the age of twenty-one Mohammed Reza found himself unexpectedly elevated to the throne. His European education had imbued him with an admiration for Western democracy and he was genuinely anxious, once Iran had re-gained her independence, to continue the process of modernisation begun by Reza Shah. A more sensitive, less decisive character than his father, intelligent, hardworking but aloof and a little vain, he believed he had a divine mission to rule.

The humiliating foreign occupation during the war and its prolongation in the north afterwards had induced a mood of national awareness which, once independence had been achieved, articulated into calls for reform. The immediate economic problems of the aftermath also had to be faced: foreign armies had fuelled inflation, the treasury was depleted and American aid, which had been promised when the allied leaders, Churchill, Roosevelt and Stalin, held their conference in Tehran in 1943, was slow to materialise.

Neither the elder statesmen nor the members of the Majlis were inclined to initiate reforms. The shah himself took a step towards land reform by distributing vast acreages of crown lands among the peasants who worked on them but the prosperous landed classes were not disposed to pay more than lip service to the need for economic and social improvements for the great mass of the people.

Nevertheless with some royal encouragement a start was made in 1949 and a Seven Year Plan to develop agriculture, industry, the health and education services was launched. It made little headway: a leading cleric denounced it as a 'godless enterprise' and Dr Mohammed Mussadeq, who became prime minister in 1951, opposed it. Later plans were more successful.

Under Mussadeq the shah faced the first serious challenge to his personal authority. The seventy-year-old premier was a colourful character, a showman, who gave press conferences from his bed and delivered emotional speeches from the balcony of his house in his pyjamas. As leader of the left-wing national front he won popularity by the time-honoured method of exploiting anti-foreign sentiments. The British presence in the south presented an easy target and in calling on his followers to unite in the 'struggle against imperialism' he enjoyed country-wide support. There was a feeling that the employment policies of the Anglo-Iranian Oil Comany were high-handed, that Iranians were excluded from senior posts and that the locally employed were discriminated against. Above all the government's share of the profits was too low. Mussadeq succeeded in passing a bill through the Majlis to nationalise the company and seize the installations.

But his ultimate aim was to isolate and discredit the royal family (he was implacably opposed to the Pahlavis—perhaps on account of his Qajar connections). By 1953 he had already forced the shah's mother and his twin sister into exile. And, when the shah brought the battle of wills to a head by dismissing him, he refused to go. It was the shah who fled the country. Here he had gone too far, public opinion swung against him and the crowds thronging the streets of the capital called for the shah. Helped by loyalists and some undercover support from the American Central Intelligence Agency, within a few days the shah was welcomed home in triumph; Mussadeq was tried for treason and imprisoned.

The country was by now on the verge of bankruptcy. The virtual shut-down of the oil installations and the British blockade on tankers leaving Abadan had resulted in a loss of revenue, in unemployment and the cutting off of American aid.

Negotiations to regularize the oil situation resulted the following year (1954) in the formation of an international consortium in which eight oil companies had a share. Iran's newly formed National Iranian Oil Company was to have 50 percent of the profits and the Anglo-Iranian Oil Company (now British Petroleum) a 40 percent stake and compensation for losses. Diplomatic relations with Britain, which Mussadeq had broken off, were resumed, so too was American aid. In 1955 Iran formally aligned herself with the anti-communist block by joining the Baghdad Pact (later CENTO), a defensive alliance which linked Iran, Iraq, Turkey and Pakistan with the West. And a bilateral agreement signed with the United States four years later ensured the supply of modern military equipment for her armed forces.

Once the Mussadeq crisis had been defused the shah determined he would never again allow his sovereignty to be undermined—he would rule as well as reign. A semblance of democracy was maintained with the Majlis operating a two-party system. But parliamentary candidates were vetted and party leaders had to follow guide lines. The press was censored, the army purged of leftists and SAVAK, the new secret police, working through a network of informers, was employed to track down Mussadeq sympathisers and other subversive elements.

The shah dissolved the Majlis in 1961 and two years later announced the principles of his so-called White Revolution, six measures that were designed to change the economic and social structure of society. These were:

1 the redistribution of agricultural land in private ownership to the cultivators leaving a small holding—usually one village—with the original owner
2 the nationalisation of forest land
3 the sale of factories and other state-owned enterprises to finance the land reforms and the creation of co-operatives for rural improvements
4 profit sharing for factory employees
5 the granting of votes to women
6 the creation of a literacy corps to bring basic education to rural areas[2]

In 1963, to obtain endorsement for his proposals, the shah held a referendum and, as the vast majority of the population stood to benefit from them, they won overwhelming approval. The *ulama'* were among those who opposed the plan. As a body they had a deep-rooted resistance to change. They objected to the emancipation of women and they feared the land reforms would deprive them of their independence, as they relied on the large estates they controlled for their income and for the upkeep of the mosques.

Riots in Tehran and elsewhere fomented by communists, clergy and landowners were ruthlessly suppressed. And in Qum, one of the main centres of violence, among those arrested was the Ayatollah Khomeini.

For the rest of the sixties there were no major disruptions. The army had stamped out the serious disturbances and the benefits of the White Revolution were about to be realised. Though the shah had deprived the people of some of their freedom he had promised them material rewards. Against a background of rising oil revenues it might have seemed to the casual observer that Mohammed Reza had the future of Iran in his hand.

In reality the situation was different. Though the measures the shah proposed were progressive, the methods by which he had sought to achieve them (his manipulation of the constitution) were not. In formulating his plans he had alienated the traditionalists, in implementing them he had failed to carry the intellectuals and the liberal minded with him.

The economic problems attendant upon an upsurge of oil wealth in an emerging third world country and the social upheaval that the reforms, and the rapid switch to industrialisation, brought about did not allow a bewildered population time to adjust. In the comfortable light of hindsight it is easy to point to the shah's errors of judgment. But the fact remains: time was against the shah. Nevertheless he determined to achieve what he perceived to be right and the journey back from the hardly won weak attractions of a fragile democracy to the strong magnetic pole of despotism had begun.

In 1967, following the birth of a son to his third wife, Farah Diba, and with the continuation of the Pahlavi house in the male line more securely assured, the shah went through his long postponed coronation ceremony. The *Shahanshah* (King of Kings[3]) took a new title *Aryamehr* (Light of the Aryans), and, as his father had done before, he placed the crown on his head himself.

Four years later the carefully planned and elaborately staged celebrations to commemorate 2,500 years of Persian monarchy were held at Persepolis. The occasion was designed to centre world attention on Iran. Sixty-nine heads of state or their representatives attended. The ceremonies included a military review and a pageant of Persian history which called to mind the words of Christopher Marlowe:

> Is it not brave to be a king... and ride in triumph
> through Persepolis?

The event drew countrywide criticism for its ostentation and the fact that the Iranian public were kept away. The role of Islam in shaping the history of the last thirteen centuries was played down and Ayatollah Khomeini, from his place of exile in Najaf, was one of the clergy who denounced the whole proceedings.

'The Government of God'

> If I were a dictator rather than a constitutional monarch, then I might be tempted to sponsor a single dominant party such as Hitler organized or such as you find today in Communist countries. But as constitutional monarch I can afford to encourage large-scale party activity free from the strait-jacket of one-party rule or the one-party state.
>
> *Mission for my Country*, London, 1961, p. 173

These words were written by the shah in 1960 or 1961, twenty years after he began his reign and fourteen years before he merged the two parliamentary parties to form the one-party state he apparently deplored. Though adherence to the constitution was theoretically still the order of the day, the statutes were being dismantled one by one and by the autumn of 1963 the Majlis had been in recess for two and a half years, instead of the stipulated maximum of three months.

Maybe Mussadeq's period of power had shaken the shah's confidence in himself and it was this that was reflected in his inability to trust the people. Iran, he had come to believe, was not yet ready for responsible self-government. Until universal education had improved standards of literacy and people were able to make informed judgments for themselves, there must, he reasoned, be direction from above and restriction on individual freedom. Thus the years that followed witnessed the total erosion of parliamentary government. And having once started on the slippery slope towards dictatorship, for Mohammed Reza Shah there would be no going back.

In October 1963 the shah called a general election. The composition of the new Majlis was encouraging. It was more representative of the electorate than its predecessors: fewer seats went to the large landowners, there was a sprinkling of the professional and middle classes as well as eight women. And the appointment of Hasan Ali Mansur, a young economist, as prime minister better reflected the new look. But after nine months in office Mansur was shot by a religious fanatic and was succeeded by 'Abbas Hoveida, a loyal servant of the crown, under whose stewardship Iran was converted into a one-party state.

Meanwhile the process of implementing the land reforms went ahead slowly and by the end of 1972 nearly a fifth of the cultivators had begun to benefit. Much publicised photographs showed grateful peasants receiving the deeds of their properties from the shah.

It was through well structured ceremonies such as these and other media occasions that the shah was known to his people. Tight security kept him apart (he survived five attempts on his life) and denied him the chance to assess the mood of the country. Sir Anthony Parsons (British Ambassador from 1974 to 1979), who witnessed many royal ceremonies, described the annual military parade held to commemorate the liberation of Azarbaijan from the Soviet Union. It was, he said, a sham. The occasion called for a procession through the streets of Tehran with the shah taking the salute from a dais before the assembled people. Instead the ceremony was attended by a selected audience on a deserted roadway outside the capital. The shah landed by helicopter, mounted a horse for a 200 yard ride and took the salute from a bullet-proof glass box.

The queen on the other hand moved about more freely and Parsons noted that when she visited a village unannounced on one occasion she received a rapturous reception.

Along with the rise in oil revenues[4] the economy continued to improve. By the mid sixties Iran had attained 'developed' status—she no longer needed aid from the USA, and the march towards the much vaunted Great Civilization was beginning. This phrase was coined by the shah to project the image of the world's 'fifth industrial power'. It was also intended to recall Iran's pre-Islamic imperial past and (somewhat more tenuously) the Aryan heritage which Europeans and Iranians had in common.

In 1973, following negotiations with OPEC (the Organization of Petroleum Exporting Countries), of which Iran was a founder member, the price of oil was quadrupled. In anticipation of the new wealth that would flow into the treasury from the increased revenues the recently launched fifth Five Year Plan was revised. With the shah's backing spending on defence, on industrial expansion and the social services—health, housing and education—was stepped up. Economists counselled caution; careful planning they argued was essential if a steady balanced growth was to be maintained—but Hoveida and others followed the shah's lead:

> 'The Great Civilisation', he had confidently predicted ' . . . is not a utopia either. We will reach it much sooner than we thought. We said we will reach the gates in 12 years; but in some fields we have already crossed its frontiers.'
>
> Robert Graham, *Iran: The Illusion of Power*, New York, 1979, p. 80

But the country's infrastructure could not sustain the demands that were made. Rampant bureaucracy, inadequate road, rail and dock facilities resulted in customs and transport delays. Ships arriving in the gulf ports queued for berths, dock warehouses overflowed and goods piled up on the quays. At Bandar 'Abbas, three years after they had been delivered, a consignment of trucks parked in rows along the sands was still waiting for drivers to take them to their destinations. Shortages of personnel with management and technical skills sparked off demands for pay increases while rising land and house prices added fuel to the inflationary wage spiral. Iran in 1974, as seen by Sir Anthony Parsons:

> was a land of bewildering contrasts. I would visit a modern factory and come away feeling that I had seen something on a par with its equivalent in Western Europe—could it be that the Great Civilisation was possible? I would visit a teeming bazaar which left me with the impression that nothing had changed in this most traditional of countries. I saw the docks at Khorramshahr at the head of the Persian Gulf and left despairing that order could ever be produced out of the amorphous mountains of machinery, bags of sugar, piles of solidified cement, and assorted consumer goods.
>
> *The Pride and the Fall Iran 1974-1979*, London, 1984, p. 8.

The boom brought prosperity to the professional and middle classes but left a widening gap between them and the growing reservoir of urban and rural poor for whose services there was relatively less demand.

By mid 1975, eighteen months after the price increase, world demand for oil slackened and some of the more grandiose schemes had to be cut back. Taken as a whole the boom had proved to be a mixed blessing: the population[5] was increasing, food imports were rising, production had failed to reach the predicted levels, there was an imbalance of trade and inflation was running at over 30 percent.

In March the shah, perceiving that the arrival of the golden age had been delayed, had reacted by tightening his grip. He announced the formation of the one-party state. All were urged to fall in behind him and join the king's (the Rastakhiz) party:

> We must straighten out Iranians' ranks. To do so, we divide them into two categories: those who believe in Monarchy, the Constitution, and the Sixth Bahman [the White] Revolution and those who don't. . . . A person who does not enter the new political party . . . will have only two choices. He is either an individual who belongs to an illegal organization, or is related to the outlawed Tudeh Party, or in other words is a traitor. Such an

individual belongs in an Iranian prison.
Fred Halliday, *Iran: Dictatorship and Development*, Harmondsworth, 1979, p. 47.

Though he was continuing to pay lip service to the constitution, there could by now be no doubt that the country was being ruled by a dictator. The shah himself in a frank interview with a journalist two years before had in effect admitted his belief that absolute authority should be vested in his person:

> A monarchy is the only possible means to govern Iran. If I have been able to do something, a lot, in fact, for Iran it is owing to the detail slight as it may seem, that I'm its king. To get things done, one needs power, and to hold on to power one mustn't ask anyone's permission or advice. One mustn't discuss decisions with anyone.
>
> Fred Halliday, *op. cit.*, p. 57.

With the Majlis relegated it was necessary to emphasize the close relationship between the shah and his subjects and the White Revolution was renamed the Shah-People Revolution.

To ensure his own protection the shah had retained the post of commander-in-chief of the armed forces whose sole allegiance was to the king. They were well equipped, well paid and insulated from the affects of inflation. SAVAK and the security services, so long as they claimed to be acting out of a similar loyalty, had a free hand. They could round up anyone for failing to join the king's party. If the army and the security services remained loyal his position should be secure. Meanwhile antagonism towards the state machine was mounting. There was widespread disapproval of the corruption, which pervaded all levels of society, of the mismanagement and waste that was everywhere apparent; there was indignation that oil wealth was being channelled into the purchase of huge quantities of arms from the USA and apprehension that they would be used against the people.

Foremost among the disaffected social groups were: a) *the educated classes* who resented their lack of political muscle; they believed the shah was a tool of American foreign policy and that SAVAK officials were trained by the Central Intelligence Agency, as indeed some of them were; foreign influences ('westitis')—the cinema, night clubs and liquor stores—they felt were debasing moral standards;

b) *the student population* whose numbers had grown rapidly to meet the needs of the industrialised society (in 1977 there were 21 universities and 206 institutes of higher education); since the 1963 riots their activities had been closely watched—police were permanently posted outside their campuses and members of SAVAK spied on them within; c) *the bazaar merchants* who had been bye-passed by the new order—by the national banks with their imposing western-style frontages, the shops and supermarkets that lined the pavements of smart town areas; nevertheless in those narrow shaded alleyways with their baths, tea houses and warehouses, traditional centres of commercial and social life, trade continued and the bazaaris were an important social group who had their fingers on the pulse of the communities they served; d) *the landless labourers* thrown out of work by land reforms and the recession who migrated into the towns in search of employment where they swelled the growing numbers of urban poor. In Tehran[6], the worst affected city, they were moving in at the rate of 250,000 a year and exacerbating the overcrowded conditions in the south of the city; e) *the clergy,* the most conservative of all, who opposed change and were incensed at their relegation by the shah's secularist society. Moderates like Shariatmadari, an eminent Ayatollah in Qum, approved the constitution but the more militant traditionalist faction led by the exiled Ayatollah Khomeini proclaimed Shi'ism as an all-embracing political and moral force. He called for an end to foreign infiltration, the overthrow of the Pahlavi dynasty and the creation of a theocratic state. Until the time when the Hidden Imam returned those of the faith must shoulder government and administer the divine law.

During the riots of 1963 the armed forces had been called out. They were not trained in crowd control, the number of casualties had been excessive and a thousand or more had been killed. In Qum Ayatollah Khomeini, having been arrested, imprisoned and several times released, was finally deported. From his place of exile in Iraq he continued to attack the shah's policies. He called for an end to foreign interference in Iran's affairs, and he protested against the formation of the king's party.

During the seventies there were occasional riots and demonstrations in the large cities. Two left-wing movements, the *Mujahidin* and the more extreme *Fidayin*, began operations. Trained in Palestine Liberation Organization camps and in Libya, they killed some American officers but their main targets for assassination were SAVAK officials.

Early in 1977 there was a perceptible slackening of restrictions; political prisoners were released, press censorship became less rigid, pilgrims were allowed to visit the holy places in Iraq. And to mark the change of emphasis Hoveida, who had served as prime minister for thirteen years, was transferred to another post.[7] If by such measures the shah hoped to calm the situation he was mistaken. 'Liberalisation' lifted the lid of a boiling kettle as letters of protest (some addressed to the shah) from people in public life began to circulate.

Pilgrims returning from Najaf, where Ayatollah Khomeini was living, smuggled in tape recordings of his 'sermons' which were circulated via the bazaars to a wider audience. From the safe vantage point of his exile his harangues became increasingly anti-shah in tone. He began to out-distance the more moderate clergy, some of whom had already been silenced by imprisonment or death, and to be identified as the leader of the revolutionary movement; others believed he was the Hidden Imam himself.

In January 1978 the administration played into the hands of the opposition by publishing a defamatory article on Ayatollah Khomeini in a leading newspaper. It provoked riots in Qum. For the first time since 1963 the army was called out. Soldiers fired into the crowd and perhaps 100 were killed. Forty days later trouble flared up in Tabriz: banks, public buildings and offices of the King's Party were damaged. So began a cycle of forty-day mourning periods punctuated by funerals of martyrs as disturbances occurred first in one city and then in another.

Again the shah tried to ease the tension. This time he promised free elections and complete freedom of the press. But the course of revolution could not now be stemmed either by promises of greater freedom or by the staged counter demonstrations of his supporters.

8 September, 'Black Friday', was a landmark. In Tehran several hundred were killed when troops crushed a demonstration. Three weeks later the bazaars closed and a series of nationwide strikes began. They spread from the oil installations to the banks, post offices, water services and power supplies. Against this sort of mass civil disobedience even the military government, which had taken over, was powerless to act.

The eye of the storm was in Tehran where the mullahs staged the great protest marches. People of all classes joined in the carefully martialled processions through the streets, among them the *Mujahidin* and the *Fidayin*, who came into the open, the rich, the impoverished, the women and children. Banners portraying the bearded turbaned features, the steely eyes, the brooding visage of the Ayatollah were accompanied by the cries, 'Khomeini is our Leader' and 'Death to the butcher shah'. The processions were now being held in defiance of bans, the people had broken through the fear barrier. And when the Ayatollah called on the soldiers not to fire, they responded, many of them, by discharging their ammunition into the air.

The holy month of Muharram, in which the deaths of the Imams were commemorated, came in December and for those two holy days massive marches were planned. This time the military government wisely kept the soldiers in their barracks.

Standing at his embassy window, Sir Anthony Parsons watched the men and women as they thronged past to join the main procession. On both days throughout the morning they filled the street outside from end to end. Their numbers (totalling perhaps one or one and a half million each day), their 'orderliness and unity of purpose', he said, were 'awe-inspiring'.

On the second day a mullah read out a declaration over the loud speakers calling for the overthrow of the shah and the return of Khomeini. He, meanwhile, had moved his headquarters to Paris where he could direct operations better. There he joined Abol-Hasan Bani-Sadr, who became the Islamic Republic's first president.

There was no longer an effective government, riots continued in the provinces, strikes were bringing about a national paralysis, army loyalty was faltering—the country was drifting into anarchy. Yet when the end came there was no bloodshed and the proprieties were observed to the last.

It was announced on 31 December that the shah would leave the country. A caretaker government under Dr Shapur Bakhtiar fended off the arrival of the Ayatollah and his entourage. On 16 January 1979 the shah and the empress arrived at Tehran airport, where court officials and senior army officers had assembled. They bade them farewell, then they boarded their plane which flew them to Egypt and to exile.

Fifteen days later, on 1 February 1979, the Ayatollah Khomeini flew into the same airport and was welcomed by a multitude estimated at three million. On 1 April, after holding a constitutional referendum, he proclaimed the formation of the first 'Government of God', the Islamic Republic of Iran.

EPILOGUE

Mohammed Reza Pahlavi inherited the throne in unfavourable circumstances. He weathered the allied occupation and the Azarbaijan crisis but Mussadeq and his national front nearly dislodged him. He reacted by arrogating more power to himself; he wanted to make his position secure and to modernise his country. His mission as shah and father of the people was to bring a better life to all.

He steered an increasingly authoritarian course bringing into play the appliances of the police state to suppress those opposed to him, notably the communists and clergy, 'the reds and the blacks', as he called them. The security that surrounded him (essential tool in the kit of every dictator) isolated him and his attempt to counter this by promoting the shah-people relationship fell flat. By the mid seventies the country bore all the hallmarks of a police state.

Radical reforms might be embodied in the White Revolution and new developments envisaged in successive Five Year Plans but these measures did not compensate for the loss of personal freedom and political rights nor, as it transpired, did they bring the Great Civilisation any nearer. Peasants exchanged their rural homesteads for high-cost city slums and their labour in the fields for employment on the factory floor. But the promised Utopia eluded them. Small wonder then that disillusion set in and the mass of the people turned to the body that represented a familiar unchanging institution in an increasingly disorientated world: the mullahs.

Ayatollah Khomeini's message was simple: it could be understood by all. He called for an end to Pahlavi rule, for the elimination of foreign influences and for a return to traditional Islamic values.

In the months prior to his departure the Shah's health had been deteriorating and in January 1979, when he left the country, he was already a very sick man. He died in Egypt eighteen months later, where Egypt's president, Anwar al-Sadat, had given him refuge.

Has the royal road run into the sands of Islamic republicanism to be obliterated for all time or will it re-emerge, as it did once before after an interval of 800 years? Among the many imponderables which these questions raise one constant stands out: Iran's future is bound up with the Shi'ite faith and the men who win power will be its time servers.

The people await the coming of the Twelfth Imam, Muhammad al-Mahdi, who will return

> at the end of time . . . to fill the earth with justice
> after .. it has been filled with iniquity.
>
> Browne, *op. cit.*, II, p. 195

'Till He Come' whether they take the republican route or whether (as they did five centuries ago) they return to the monarchy—whichever road the people follow—let us hope that the landscape through which it passes will serve once again to uplift the spirit, to gladden the eye and warm the heart of the traveller who would follow its course.

Appendix

THE WOMAN'S PLACE IN ISLAMIC SOCIETIES

The role of women in Islamic societies has been the subject of debate, particularly in recent years. The traditional Muslim view is that women are:

> swayed by emotions and consequently [are] of incompetent and unstable discernment or judgement . . . even the most educated woman strays from the path of wisdom; whereas man is balanced, sagacious and self-controlled.[8]

Women, so the reasoning goes, need to be protected from their own inadequacies, their purity must be preserved and it is not desirable for them to attend social functions or to take part in public life.

Husbands then, as Ella Sykes noted during her travels in Persia in the time of the young Qajar, Ahmad Shah, are in charge 'looking upon their wives as inferior beings born to submit to their rule, a husband having the right, if he so chooses, of forbidding his wife to visit her own parents' (*op. cit.*, p. 230). Such revelations are not new. What is perhaps less well-known is how women came to be relegated in this way.

The Qur'an teaches that sexual pleasure experienced by men during their life on earth is the prelude to the delights that await the God-fearing in the paradise gardens where damsels:

> Having fine black eyes; and kept in pavilions from public view . . . Whom no man shall have deflowered, before their destined spouses . . . Therein shall they delight themselves, lying on green cushions and beautiful carpets.
> *The Koran*, Chandos Classics, 1890, *sura* 55

The sexuality of men therefore is an inducement to them to observe their religion—to pray, to give alms, to observe the fast of Ramadan, and so on. But the difficulty, according to the theologian al-Ghazali is the nature of women. They are seducers who tempt men away from their religious duties and men have no option but to succumb to their charms. If therefore men are to be free to serve God, women must be subjugated to their authority and segregated. And their own sexuality must be discouraged.[9]

Translated into the practicalities of daily life, it follows that the peasant woman is the servant of her husband. She is 'the camel to help man through the desert of existence'. In a nomadic society the woman necessarily is on more equal terms with him—they share the hardships. But in upper class society, in'the perfumed ennui of the harem', life as Isabella Bird saw it in Isfahan in 1890 was:

> petty, stilted, prurient, catty, cushioned, hopeless and unhealthy ... Their apartments were silken, gilt, tasselled, thickly carpeted, decorated with alabaster vases, glass lustres, lamp-shades, candelabra . . . Inside these padded cells, the women passed the time in banging tambourines, making bonbons and cucumber jams, gossiping, occasionally tearing each other's hair out, chalk-whitening their necks, clown-reddening their cheeks, smearing eyes and lashes with black kohl, concocting love-potions to excite the enthusiasm of their lords and watching performances of bawdy plays.
>
> Pat Barr, *A Curious Life for a Lady*,
> London, 1984, p. 244

Fortunately, along with the Qajar dynasty itself, the days of the harem were numbered. When the last inmates had been released, some of the 'padded cells' with their candelabras, alabaster vases and tambourines remained undisturbed for years until—as it were in another age—the doors were opened to admit the twentieth century tourist.

Under the Pahlavis (as in other Muslim countries) women were accorded voting rights and educational opportunities. But Islamic fundamentalism is no supporter of emancipation and the revolution of 1979 was a setback for the liberationists. Enveloped again in the black and shapeless anonymity of the *chador*, the woman's role is seen once more as being that of the dutiful wife and the devoted mother. Her proper place is in the home.

Notes

1 See Clarmont Skrine, *World War in Iran*, London, 1962, referred to p. 237. He accompanied the ex-shah to Mauritius.
2 Later measures included the formation of a health corps, a housing programme and the nationalisation of water resources.
3 A title dating from the time of the Persian Empire.
4 Income rose from $4.400 million in 1973 to $21.700 million in 1976. Hossein Amirsadeghi (ed.), *Twentieth Century Iran*, London, 1977, pp 280-1.
5 The population was growing at the rate of about 3.1 percent p.a. According to a census taken in 1966 the total population was just under 26,000,000.
6 In 1971 the population was over 3,000,000 (11 percent of the national total). In Isfahan, the next largest city it was in the region of 490,000. John Connell, *Tehran: Urbanisation and Development*, 1973.
7 The military government in the last days of the shah arrested him. He was executed early in 1979.
8 *The Islamic Review*, Woking, August 1952. A fatwa issued by the Mufti of Egypt alleged that the Islamic social system did not entitle women to be given electoral rights. The writer of the article quoted questions the validity of the pronouncement.
9 This explanation is based on a contribution to *Women in Islamic Societies: Social attitudes and historical perspectives*, ed. Bo Utas, London, Curzon Press, 1983, pp. 5-8, by Ida Nicolaisen.

Chronology

Generally, the dates given for the reigns of rulers in the early periods are approximate.

The Medes

BC	
834	Iranian plateau invaded by Shalmaneser III of Assyria
727	Daiaukku (Deioces) – headquarters established at Ecbatana
715	deported by Sargon II of Assyria
674-53	Khshathrita (Phraortes)
	Media unified under his sovereignty
652-25	period of Scythian domination
646	Elam destroyed by Ashurbanipal of Assyria
624-584	Cyaxeres
	Scythians expelled
615	alliance with Nabopolassar of neo-Babylonia (Chaldea)
612	fall of Nineveh
590	Asia Minor invaded
584-50	Astyages
	defeated by Cyrus of Anshan (later Cyrus the Great)

The Achaemenids and Alexander the Great

550-30	Cyrus the Great founds the empire of the Medes and Persians
547-46	conquest of Lydia; Croesus taken prisoner
539	capture of Babylon
530-22	Cambyses
526	invasion of Egypt
522-486	Darius
512	expedition against the Scythians across the Danube
499	Ionian revolt
490	battle of Marathon
486-65	Xerxes
480	invasion of Greece; battles of Thermopylae and Salamis
479	battles of Plataea and Mycale
465-24	Artaxerxes I

449	Peace of Callias
423-05	Darius II (Ochos)
	Pissouthenes and Tissaphernes successively satraps of Sardes
405-359	Artaxerxes II
405	Egypt achieves independence
401	battle of Cunaxa and the march of the Ten Thousand
396	invasion of Asia Minor by Spartan King Ageislaus
387	declaration of the King's Peace
362	revolt of the satraps
359-338	Artaxerxes III (Ochos)
	temporary recovery of the empire
336-30	Darius Codomannus (Darius III)
334	Alexander the Great crosses the Hellespont; battle of Granicus
333	battle of Issus
332	siege of Tyre; conquest of Egypt
331	battle of Gaugemala;
330	burning of Persepolis; death of Darius
330-23	Alexander the Great
330-25	campaigns in eastern Persia, Sogdiana, Afghanistan and northern India
323	death in Babylon

The Seleucids and the Parthians

BC	
312-280	Seleucus Nicator founds the Seleucid dynasty
301	battle of Ipsus
250/47	Arsaces founds the Arsacid dynasty
247-11	Tiridates I
211-191	Artabanus I
223-187	Antiochus the Great (Antiochus III)
	campaign against the Parthians
189	battle of Magnesia
175-64	Antiochus Epiphanes (Antiochus IV)
171-38	Mithradates I
	spread of Parthian power across the Iranian plateau
145-40	Demetrius II
140	captured by Mithradates I
139-29	Antiochus Sidetes (Antiochus VII)
	defeated and killed by the Parthians
138-27	Phraates II
	Seleucids driven out of Media
	killed fighting the Saka (Scythians)
127-23	Artabanus II
	killed fighting the Saka
123-90/87	Mithradates the Great (Mithradates II)
	expulsion of the Saka
	expansion of Parthian empire into Mesopotamia
71-58	Phraates III
66	surrender of Tigranes II (the Great) of Armenia to Pompey
58-39	Orodes II
55	his brother 'Mithradates III' executed
53	battle of Carrhae
40	invasion of Syria and Palestine by Pacorus
39-2	Phraates IV
36-33	expeditions of Mark Antony against Media

2 BC-4 AD	Phraataces (Phraates V)
2 AD	reigned jointly with his mother, Musa
AD	
8-11	Vonones I
11-38	Artabanus III
	temporarily dethroned by the pretender Tiridates
	growth of Kushan empire in the east
51-77	Vologoses I
108-127	Osroes
	invasion of Mesopotamia by Trajan
147-90	Vologoses IV
	destruction of Ctesiphon and Seleucia by the armies of Marcus Aurelius
190-207	Vologoses V
199	Ctesiphon sacked by Septimius Severus
	defeated in civil war with his brother, Artabanus V
213-24	Artabanus V
	defeat of Macrinus near Nisibis
224	killed in battle against Ardashir

The Sasanians

224-40	Ardashir
	Iranian plateau and Mesopotamia conquered
240-70	Shapur I
260	wars with Rome in north Mesopotamia.
	Emperor Valerian captured
	Growth of Manicheanism
270-71	Hurmizd I
271-74	Bahram I
	execution of Mani
274-93	Bahram II
293	Bahram III
293-302	Narseh
297	defeated by Galerius
	Tiridates III of Armenia adopts Christianity
302-09	Hurmizd II
309-79	Shapur the Great (Shapur II)
330	Constantinople founded
	wars with Romans in the north and Huns in the east
363	Emperor Julian killed retreating from Ctesiphon
383-8	Shapur III
387	Armenia partitioned ("Persarmenia")
399-420	Yazdigird I
420-38	Bahram Gur (Bahram V)
	Chief of the Ephthalite Huns is slain
459-484	Peroz
	defeated and killed by Ephthalite Huns
488-96	Kavadh I (first reign)
	Mazdakite movement
498-531	Kavadh I (second reign)
	wars with Byzantine Romans and Huns
531-79	Khusraw of the Immortal Soul (Khusraw I)
557	Huns finally expelled
532/62	peace treaties with Emperor Justinian
c. 570	birth of Muhammad
579-90	Hurmizd IV

579-90	Hurmizd IV
590-628	Khusraw Parviz (Khusraw II)
590-1	revolt of Bahram Chubin
613-19	conquest of Syria, Egypt and Asia Minor
622-27	counter offensive by Emperor Heraclius and defeat of the Persians
622	the *Hijrah*
628	murder of the king
628	Kavadh II
	peace negotiations with Heraclius
632-51	Yazdigird III
632	death of Muhammad
633	Arab invasions begin
635	capture of Damascus
636	battle of Qadisiyya
637	fall of Ctesiphon
642	battle of Nihavand and flight of the king
651	murder of the king; Arab conquest of Persia

The 'Rightly Guided' Caliphate

632-44	Abu Bakr (first Caliph)
634-44	'Umar (second Caliph)
644	murder of the Caliph
644-56	'Uthman (third Caliph)
	rebellion in Kufa
	murder of the Caliph
656-61	'Ali (fourth Caliph and first Imam)
656-61	civil war
661	murder of 'Ali

The Umayyad Caliphs

661-80	Mu'awiyah I
661	transfer of caliphate from al-Madinah to Damascus
667-79	expansion into Transoxiana and northern India
680-83	Yazid I
680	Husayn killed at Kerbela
685-705	'Abd al-Malik
	further expansion into central Asia
705-14	al-Walid
	Arabs reach Spain
744-50	Marwan II
749	revolt led by Abu 'l-Abbas
750	murder of the Caliph

The 'Abbasid Caliphs

750-54	al-Saffah (Abu 'l-Abbas)
754-75	al-Mansur
763	Baghdad founded
875-85	al-Mahdi
	Muqanna', the 'Veiled Prophet of Khurasan'
785-86	al-Hadi

786-809	Harun al-Rashid
	the Golden Age
803	fall of the Barmecides
809-13	al-Amin
813	murdered by the armies of al-Ma'mun
813-33	al-Ma'mun
	Baghdad continues in its prime
833-42	al-Mu'tasim
836	seat of the caliphate moved to Samarra
870-92	al-Mu'tamid
873	disappearance of Muhammad al-Mahdi (the Twelfth Imam)
892	caliphate returns to Baghdad
1258	murder of the last caliph

Minor dynasties

(1) Saffarids

861-79	Ya'qub b. al-Layth
861	seizure of Sistan
	westward expansion
900	defeated by the Samanids
908	reduction of the kingdom

(2) Samanids

874-892	Nasr I
900	Khurasan seized from the Saffarids
	expansion into Transoxiana and within Persia
976-97	Nuh II
	patron of Avicenna
999	dynasty overthrown by Mahmud of Ghazna

(3) Buyids (Buwayhids)

932-67	Mu'izz al-Dawlah
945	Baghdad occupied
976-83	'Adud al-Dawlah
	expansion eastwards
1055	Baghdad captured by Saljuqs and dynasty overthrown

(4) Ghaznavids

998-1030	Mahmud
1002	Samanids overthrown
1000-30	raids on northern India
1000	Firdawsi writing at this time
1030-40	Mas'ud I
1040	defeated at battle of Dandanqan

The Great Saljuqs

1038-63	Tughril Beg
1040	battle of Dandanqan – defeat of the Ghaznavids
1055	entry into Baghdad
1063-72	Alp Arslan
1071	battle of Manzikert – defeat of the Byzantines
	beginning of the viziership of Nizam al-Mulk
1072-92	Malikshah
	expansion into Transoxiana

1090	Assassins seize the stronghold of Alamut
1117-57	Sanjar
1153	defeated and taken prisoner by the Ghuzz Turks
1194	collapse of the Great Saljuqs

Khwarazm-Shahs, Mongols and Il-Khans

1200-21	rise of Muhammad II Khwarazm-Shah
1200-15	conquest of Transoxiana extending to India
1219-27	Genghis Khan
1219	invasion of Transoxiana
	Muhammad put to flight
1221-2	invasion of northern Persia
1221-31	Jalal al-Din Khwarazm-Shah
	his opposition to the Mongols
1223	Genghis Khan returns to the north
1256-65	Hulagu
1256	overthrow of the Assassins and destruction of Alamut
1258	destruction of Baghdad and murder of the last 'Abbasid caliph
1260	battle of 'Ayn Jalut; Mongol advance halted
1265-82	Il-Khan Abaqa
1271	Marco Polo passing through Persia
1259-1304	Ghazan
	Rashid al-Din vizier
1304-16	Öljeitü
1336	collapse of Il-Khan rule

Petty Dynasties

1340-1401	Jalayirids
1353-93	Muzaffarids
1300-89	Kurts

The Timurids

1380-1405	Tamerlane
1380-87	conquest of Persia
1387-1402	Timurid armies invade Russia, India, Syria and Asia Minor
1401	Baghdad sacked
1407-47	Shah Rukh
	capital at Herat
	beginning of wars with Black and White Sheep
1447-49	Ulugh Beg
1452-69	Abu Sa'id
1466-69	Black Sheep defeated by White Sheep
	Abu Sa'id killed in battle with the White Sheep
1469-1506	Husayn Bayqara
1507	Uzbeg Turks under Muhammad Shaybani overturn the Timurids

Safavids, Afghans and Afsharids

1501	Isma'il I
	proclaims himself Shah in Tabriz
1501-10	Persia brought under his control
1514	battle of Chaldiran; defeat by the Turks
1524-76	Tahmasp I
	wars with Turks and Uzbegs
1555	Iraq passed to Turkey at treaty of Amasya
1576-77	Isma'il II
1578-87	Muhammad Khudabanda
1587-1629	'Abbas I, the Great Sophy
1598	defeat of the Uzbegs
1603-23	recovery of territories lost in Iraq and Azarbaijan
1622	expulsion of Portuguese from Hormuz
1629-42	Safi
1639	Iraq finally passed to Turkey at Treaty of Qasr-i Shirin
1642-66	'Abbas II
	Afghan territory regained
1666-94	Sulayman
1694-1722	Sultan Husayn
1715	Mahmud (Afghan) wins power in the east
1722	Isfahan besieged by Mahmud
1722-25	Mahmud (Afghan)
	takes Sultan Husayn prisoner
1725-29	Ashraf (Afghan)
	overthrows Mahmud
1729	Nadir Quli (Afshar) expels Afghans
1722-32	Tahmasp II
1732	Nadir Quli deposes Tahmasp
1732-36	'Abbas III
1736-47	Nadir Quli (Afshar) proclaims himself shah
	conquests in Afghanistan, India and central Asia
1747	murder of Nadir Shah
1748-96	Shah Rukh (Afshar)
	rules in Khurasan

Zands

1750-79	Karim Khan
	rules the west and south of Persia
1779-94	Luft 'Ali Khan
1794	overthrown and killed by Aqa Muhammad Khan

The Qajars

1794-97	Aqa Muhammad
1786	capital established at Tehran
1795	conquest of Georgia; Erevan captured
1796	Mashhad occupied; death of Shah Rukh
1797	murder of the shah
1797-1834	Fath 'Ali
1805-28	wars with Russia
1828	treaty of Turkmanchai
1834-48	Muhammad (Muhammad Mirza)
1848-96	Nasir al-Din

1850	the Bab executed
1857	treaty of Paris: Herat incorporated into Afghanistan
1869-84	Russian encroachments in north-east
1890-92	the tobacco régie
1896	assassination of the shah
1896-1907	Muzaffar al-Din
1905	public demonstrations in favour of reform
1906	imperial rescript issued setting up a national consultative assembly
1907-09	Muhammad 'Ali
1907	Anglo-Russian convention
1908	Majlis closed by the shah; nationalist uprising
1909	flight of the shah
1909-25	Ahmad
1913	oil production started in south-west
1920	Persia admitted to League of Nations
1921	Reza Khan overthrows the government
1925	The shah is deposed by the Majlis

The Pahlavis

1925-41	Reza Khan proclaimed shah by the Majlis
1935	name of Persia changed to Iran
1937	Sadabad Pack signed
1941	abdication of the shah
1941-75	Mohammed Reza
1943	Iran declares war on the axis powers
1953	the Mussadeq crisis; the shah temporarily leaves the country
1955	Iran joins Baghdad Pact (later CENTO)
1963	referendum approves the White Revolution
1975	formation of the one-party state, the Rastakhiz party
1978	riots in Qum are followed by disturbances in other cities
1979	1 January the Shah and the Empress leave the country
1979	Ayatollah Ruhollah Khomeini
	formation of the Islamic Republic, the 'Government of God' on 1 April

Glossary

Anatolia Asia Minor
Aramaeans semitic nomads who settled in northern Syria in the 12th century BC
Aryans Indo-European migratory tribes from central Asia who spread south and westwards into Europe in 1st millenium BC
Atabeg guardian of a Saljuq prince
Avesta collection of writings attributed to the sayings of Zoroaster (*q.v.*), probably compiled in 5th century AD
Ayatollah 'Sign of God', title accorded to leading Shi'ite clergy
Bahaism an ethical faith founded by 'Ali Muhammad, 'the Bab', in 1844
Bast sanctuary
Caliph successor, vicar of the prophet, guardian of the faith
Cataphractarii Parthian noblemen and their chargers clad in iron mail
Cuneiform the oldest known system of writing; wedge-shaped signs pressed into soft clay with a stylus or 'pen'. In use from about 3,000 BC in Sumer
Dhimmis tolerated religious minorities – Jews, Christians and Zoroastrians – living under Muslim rule
Diadochi Alexander's successors in western Asia
Dihqan village headman; often in some periods a small landowner.
Divan central government office which controlled the administration
Fars region of south-west Persia (ancient Parsua, Persis)
Fertile Crescent grasslands between the desert and the mountains stretching from the eastern end of the Mediterranean to the northern shores of the Persian Gulf
Ghulams Muslims, Armenian and Georgian militia formed by Shah 'Abbas
Hellenization influence of Greek life and culture on Persian society after the death of Alexander
Hijrah the migration of Muhammad from Makkah to al-Madinah in 622 and the initiation of the Muslim calendar
Hoplites heavily armed Greek infantry who fought in close formation
Imam title of the first 12 leaders of the Shi'ite community; the leader of prayers in the mosque
Immortals professional body of 10,000 infantry formed by Darius. So-called because their numbers remained constant
Iqta' grant of land, or its usufruct, often to a soldier, in return for his services; the system was widely used in the Saljuq period.
Isma'ilis followers of Isma'il, son of the Sixth Imam, also known as Seveners
Ivan opening into a barrel-vaulted three-sided hall
Jihad holy war

Jizyah poll-tax levied on non-Muslims
Ka'bah holy building at Makkah which houses a black stone received by Abraham from the angel Gabriel
Kharaj land tax
Madrasa theological college
Magi priestly caste, probably of Median origin, mainly associated with the Zoroastrian faith
Manicheanism a universal faith founded by Mani in the 3rd century AD
Mawali early non-Arab converts to Islam
Mazdakites a heretical sect led by Mazdak who preached a form of communism
Mesopotamia tract of land between the Tigris and the Euphrates (modern Iraq)
Parsua Persis ancient Fars, south-west Iran
Proskynesis a form of homage paid to Achaemenid kings usually by bowing and kissing the finger tips
Qanat irrigation system which directs water sources and melted snow from the mountains into underground channels
Qiblah the direction of Makkah to which prayers should be said
Qizilbash 'Red heads', seven Turcoman tribes from the north-west borderlands; so-called in Safavid times because the 12 red pleats in their turbans signified allegiance to the Twelve Imams.
Satrap provincial governor under the Achaemenids
Senmurv dogbird; a mythical creature with the head of a dog and the tail of a bird depicted in Sasanian art
Seveners see Isma'ilis
Shari'ah the religious law of Islam
Shi'ah party of 'Ali
Sufi Muslim mystic; one who seeks a closer union with God
Sultan title originally accorded to temporal rulers from Ghaznavid times by the caliph
Sunni a member of the majority group in Islam
Tower of Silence charnel-house where the dead were exposed in the Zoroastrian tradition
Turcomans Turkish nomads from the Ghuzz tribes who entered Persia with the Saljuqs
Twelvers followers of the Twelfth (the Hidden) Imam
'Ulama' Islamic scholars; men of the pen
Ziggurat a staged or stepped temple-tower usually leading to a shrine
Zoroaster the prophet of Ahuramazda

Select Bibliography

The principal works from classical times are all available in the Loeb Classical Library or in the Penguin Classics. They include: *Ammianus Marcellinus*, Arrian *The Campaigns of Alexander*, Dio's *Roman History*, Herodotus *The Histories*, Plutarch *Fall of the Roman Republic*, Procopius *History of the Wars*, Thucydides *The Peloponnesian War*, and Xenophon *The Persian Expedition*.

Asian Affairs is the Journal of the Royal Society for Asian Affairs (JRSAA), formerly the Royal Central Asian Society (RCAS). *Iran* is the Journal of the British Institute of Persian Studies (JBIPS).

Amirsadeghi, Hossein (ed.) *Twentieth Century Iran*, London, 1977
Anderson, B W *The Living World of the Old Testament*, London, 1978
Arberry, A J (ed.) *The Legacy of Persia*, Oxford, 1953
—*The Koran Interpreted*, London, 1963
Arfa, Hassan *Under Five Shahs*, London, 1964

Barr, Pat *A Curious Life for a Lady. The Story of Isabella Bird*, London, 1984
Bevan, E R *The House of Seleucus*, London, 1902
Boyce, Mary 'The Zoroastrians of Iran', *Asian Affairs* (JRSAA), XVI, October, 1985
Boyle, J A 'Rashid al-Din: the First World Historian', *Iran* (JBIPS), IX, 1971
Breasted, J H *The Conquest of Civilization*, New York, 1954
Bridge, Antony *Suleiman the Magnificent*, London, 1983
Browne, E G *A year amongst the Persians*, Cambridge, 1927
—*A Literary History of Persia*, 4 vols., Cambridge, 1956-59
Browning, Robert *The Emperor Julian*, London, 1975
—*The Byzantine Empire*, London, 1980
Burn, A R *The Pelican History of Greece to the Death of Alexander the Great*, Harmondsworth, 1974
Burton, Richard F *Personal Narrative of a Pilgrimage to Al-Madinah and Meccah*, London, 1915 & 1919
Bury, J B and Meiggs, Russell *A History of Greece to the Death of Alexander the Great*, London, 1975
Byron, Robert *The Road to Oxiana*, London, 1981

Cambridge Ancient History, vol. III, 1925
Cambridge History of Iran, vol. 2, 1985; vol. 3(1), 1983; vol. 4, 1975; vol. 5, 1968; vol. 6, 1986

Cambridge History of Islam, vols. 1A and 1B, 1980
Chambers, James *The Devil's Horsemen—the Mongol Invasion of Europe*, London, 1979
Chiera, Edward *They Wrote on Clay*, Chicago, 1960
Christensen, Arthur *L'Iran sous les Sassanides*, Copenhagen, 1944
Colledge, M A R *The Parthians*, London, 1967
—*Parthian Art*, London, 1977
Collins, Robert *The Medes and Persians*, London, 1974
Cook, J M *The Persian Empire*, London, 1983
Culican, William *The Medes and Persians*, London, 1965
Curtis, John *Ancient Persia*, London, 1989
Curzon, G N *Persian and the Persian Question*, London, 1892 (abridged version ed. Peter King *Curzon's Persia*, London, 1986)

Debevoise, N C *A Political History of Parthia*, Chicago, 1938
De Burgh, W G *The Legacy of the Ancient World*, London, 1947
Der Nersessian, Sirarpie *The Armenians*, London, 1969

Eddy, S K *The King is Dead, Studies in Near Eastern Resistance to Hellenism*, Lincoln, Nebraska, 1961
Elwell-Sutton, L P *Modern Iran*, London, 1941

Ferdowsi *The Epic of the Kings: Shah-Nama*, tr. Reuben Levy, London, 1977
Ferrier, R W 'Persepolis', *Asian Affairs* (JRCAS), vol. 59, February, 1972
—The European Diplomacy of Shah 'Abbas I and the First Persian Embassy to England', *Iran* (JBIPS), XI, 1973
Ferrier, R W (ed.) *The Arts of Persia*, Yale, 1989
Frye, Richard N *The Heritage of Persia*, London, 1976

Ghirshman, R *Iran from the earliest Times to the Islamic Conquest*, Harmondsworth, 1978
Gibbon, Edward, *The History of the Decline and Fall of the Roman Empire*, vols. I-V, London, 1903-4
Glubb, John B *The Great Arab Conquests*, London, 1963
—*The Empire of the Arabs*, London, 1963
—*The Course of Empire, the Arabs and their Successors*, London, 1965
Graham, Robert *Iran: the Illusion of Power*, New York, 1979

Graves, Robert *Count Belisarius*, Harmondsworth, 1978
Guillaume, Alfred *Islam*, Harmondsworth, 1969

Halliday, Fred *Iran: Dictatorship and Development*, Harmondsworth, 1979
Herodotus *The Histories*, tr. Aubrey de Selincourt, Harmondsworth, 1961
Herrmann, Georgina *The Iranian Revival*, Oxford, 1977
Hinz, Walther *The Lost World of Elam*, London, 1972
Hitti, Philip K *The Near East in History*, Princeton, 1961
—*History of the Arabs*, London, 1982
Hopkirk, Peter *Foreign Devils on the Silk Road*, London, 1980
Huart, Clément *Ancient Persia and Iranian Civilization*, London, 1976
Hutt, Antony and Harrow, Leonard *Islamic Architecture: Iran*, vols 1 and 2, London, 1977 and 1978

Keall, E J 'Qal'eh-i Yazdigird: The Question of its Date', *Iran* (JBIPS), XV, 1977
Knobloch, Edgar *Beyond the Oxus, Archaeology, Art and Architecture*, London, 1972

Lambton, Ann K S *Landlord and Peasant in Persia*, London, 1953
—*Qajar Persia*, London, 1987
—*Continuity and Change in Medieval Persia*, London, 1988
Lane Fox, Robin *Alexander the Great*, London, 1975
Lang, David M *Armenia Cradle of Civilization*, London, 1980

Leach, John *Pompey the Great*, London, 1978
Le Strange, G *The Lands of the Eastern Caliphate*, London, 1966
Lewis, Bernard, *The Arabs in History*, London, 1950
—*The Assassins: a radical Sect in Islam*, London, 1985
Lloyd, Seton *Twin Rivers, a Brief History of Iraq*, Oxford, 1961
Lockhart, Laurence *Famous Cities of Iran*, Brentford, 1939
—*The Fall of the Safavi Dynasty and the Afghan Occupation of Persia*, Cambridge, 1958
Longrigg, S H and Stoakes, F *Iraq*, New York, 1958
Luckenbill, D D *Ancient Records of Assyria and Babylonia*, vol. 1, Chicago, 1926

MacMullen, Ramsay *Constantine*, London, 1970
Malcolm, John *The History of Persia*, London, 1815
The Travels of Marco Polo, tr. Ronald Latham, Harmondsworth, 1958
Matheson, Sylvia A *Persia: an Archeological Guide*, London, 1976
Morgan, David *The Mongols*, Oxford, 1986
Medieval Persia 1040-1797, London, 1988
Mortimer, Edward *Faith and Power, the Politics of Islam*, London, 1982

Nasir al-Din *The Diary of H. M. the Shah of Persia ... in 1873*, London, 1874

Oates, Joan *Babylon*, London, 1986
Olmstead, A T *History of the Persian Empire*, London, 1970

Pahlavi, Mohammed Reza *Mission for my Country*, London, 1961
—*Answer to History*, New York, 1982
Parsons, Anthony *The Pride and the Fall, Iran 1974-1979*, London 1984
Piotrovsky, Boris B *Urartu*, Geneva, 1969
Phillips, E D *The Mongols*, London, 1969
Pope, Arthur Upham *Persian Architecture*, London, 1965
Porada, Edith *Ancient Iran*; London, 1965
Postgate, Nicholas *The First Empires*, Oxford, 1977

Reade, Julian *Assyrian Sculpture*, London, 1983
Ross, E Denison *The Persians*, Oxford, 1931
—*Sir Anthony Sherley and his Persian Adventure*, London, 1933
Rogers, Michael *The Spread of Islam*, Oxford, 1976
Rogers, J M *Islamic Art & Design 1500-1700*, London, 1983

Sackville-West, V *Passenger to Teheran*, Hogarth Press, 1926
Saggs, H W F *The Greatness that was Babylon*, London, 1962
—*The Might that was Assyria*, London, 1984
Saunders, J J *History of the Mongol Conquests*, London, 1971
—*A History of Medieval Islam*, London, 1982
Schacht, J with Bosworth, C E (ed.) *The Legacy of Islam*, Oxford, 1979
Shaw, Stanford *History of the Ottoman Empire*, vol. 1, Cambridge, 1976
Skrine, Clarmont *World War in Iran*, London, 1962
Shawcross, William *The Shah's Last Ride*, London, 1989
Stark, Freya *The Valleys of the Assassins and other Persian Travels*, London, 1937
Stevens, Roger *The Land of the Great Sophy*, London, 1971
Stronach, David 'Excavations at Pasargadae, Third Preliminary Report', *Iran* (JBIPS), III, 1965
Sykes, Ella C *Persia and its People*, London, 1910
Sykes, Percy M *Ten Thousand Miles in Persia or Eight Years in Iran*, London, 1902
—*A History of Persia*, London, 1930

Talbot Rice, David *Islamic Art*, London, 1979
Titley, Norah M *Dragons in Persian, Mughal and Turkish Art*, London, 1981

Utas, Bo *Women in Islamic Societies*, London, 1983

Walker, C J 'Armenia: a Nation in Asia', *Asian Affairs* (JRSAA), XIX, February, 1988
Welch, S C *Royal Persian Manuscripts*, London, 1976
Wilber, Donald N *Iran Past and Present*, Princeton, 1958
Willey, Peter and others, 'The 1972 Assassin Expedition', *JRCAS*, V, February, 1974
Wilson, Arnold T *The Persian Gulf*, Oxford, 1928
Wright, Denis *The English amongst the Persians*, London, 1977
The Persians amongst the English, London, 1985

Zaehner, R C *The Dawn and Twilight of Zoroastrianism*, London, 1961

Index